Talk about China

用英语介绍中国
美食文化

孙成统 刘景琳 尉策 李楠楠◎编著

中国水利水电出版社
www.waterpub.com.cn
·北京·

内 容 提 要

中华饮食文化经过几千年的历史积淀，已成为我国传统文化不可或缺的组成部分，是人类饮食文化宝库中一颗璀璨的明珠。我国疆域辽阔、地大物博，各地在气候、物产、风俗习惯等方面存在差异，逐渐形成了独特的饮食文化与习俗。本书以中英双语的方式介绍了我国七大饮食文化区域各自的代表性美食，着重从地理条件、历史文化、发展演变、独特风味及制作方法等维度对各菜式进行阐释，旨在帮助读者用英语与外国友人畅谈中国的美食文化，对外讲好中国美食故事。

本书配美式外教录音，读者可扫描封底二维码在线听。本书适合想用英语介绍中国美食文化，尤其是备考大学英语四、六级或研究生的读者使用。

图书在版编目（CIP）数据

用英语介绍中国美食文化 : 英汉对照 / 孙成统等编著. -- 北京 : 中国水利水电出版社, 2023.8
ISBN 978-7-5226-1723-7

Ⅰ. ①用… Ⅱ. ①孙… Ⅲ. ①英语—汉语—对照读物②饮食—文化—中国 Ⅳ. ①H319.4: TS

中国国家版本馆CIP数据核字(2023)第136235号

策划编辑：陈艳蕊　　责任编辑：邓建梅　　封面设计：梁　燕

书　　名	用英语介绍中国美食文化 YONG YINGYU JIESHAO ZHONGGUO MEISHI WENHUA
作　　者	孙成统　刘景琳　尉策　李楠楠　编著
出版发行	中国水利水电出版社 （北京市海淀区玉渊潭南路 1 号 D 座　100038） 网址：www.waterpub.com.cn E-mail：mchannel@263.net（答疑） sales@mwr.gov.cn 电话：（010）68545888（营销中心）、82562819（组稿）
经　　售	北京科水图书销售有限公司 电话：（010）68545874、63202643 全国各地新华书店和相关出版物销售网点
排　　版	北京万水电子信息有限公司
印　　刷	三河市德贤弘印务有限公司
规　　格	170mm×240mm　16 开本　13 印张　233 千字
版　　次	2023 年 8 月第 1 版　2023 年 8 月第 1 次印刷
定　　价	49.90 元

前言

没有文化底蕴，哪来侃侃而谈？没有文化个性，哪能妙趣横生？每一个中国人，在外国人眼里，都是承载中国文化的个体。能用英语跟他们天南地北地聊中国文化，外国友人肯定为你的深厚文化特质所折服！

中华文化博大精深，是中华民族的智慧结晶，是中国人民思想观念、风俗习惯、生活方式、情感样式的集中表达。它不仅体现了中国人民对生活的美好追求和向往，更是中国人民生产生活经验的总结和积累。党的二十大报告指出，要“讲好中国故事、传播好中国声音，展现可信、可爱、可敬的中国形象。加强国际传播能力建设，全面提升国际传播效能，形成同我国综合国力和国际地位相匹配的国际话语权。深化文明交流互鉴，推动中华文化更好走向世界。”在此背景下，本书以中华美食文化为话题，中英双语介绍我国各地的传统美食以及美食背后的文化内涵，旨在帮助读者用英语与外国友人畅谈中国的美食文化，对外讲好中国美食故事。

美食文化是中华传统文化中不可或缺的组成部分，是人类饮食文化宝库中一颗璀璨的明珠。我国疆域辽阔、地大物博，各地在气候、物产、风俗习惯等方面存在差异，逐渐形成了独特的饮食文化与习俗。本书介绍了 7 个区域的饮食文化——东北地区饮食文化、京津地区饮食文化、中北及西北地区饮食文化、黄河中下游地区饮食文化、长江中下游地区饮食文化、东南地区饮食文化和西南地区饮食文化。遴选出各个区域具有代表性的美食，从特定地理条件、历史文化渊源、发展演变过程、独特风味特点以及烹饪制作方法等多个维度对菜式进行阐释，力求读者能更加了解全国各地的美食，感知丰富多彩的美食文化，尽享传统饮食文化之精髓。

中国的美食数不胜数，每个人的成长与记忆中会有不同的家乡味道。一种美食、一方风土、一种牵挂、一份祝福、一腔热爱。由于篇幅所限，本书仅选取了部分美食，挂一漏万，谨希望读者通过本书能对中华各地的美食文化有大致的了解，使读者乐于、勇于用英语介绍、推广自己家乡的美食，从而为促进中华优秀传统文化“走出去”贡献自己的一份力量。

目录

Chapter 03
The Cuisine in the Mid-North and Northwest Region

Chapter 04
The Cuisine in the Middle and Lower Reaches of the Yellow River

Chapter 07

Chapter 01

The Cuisine in the Northeast Region

东北地区饮食

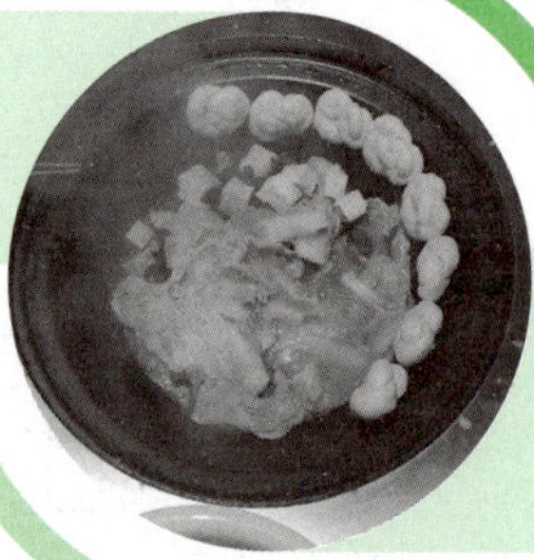

The Dietary Culture of the Northeast Region
东北地区饮食文化

The northeast of China brings to mind images of fertile land, uncontaminated pastures, and vast plains. It abounds with a variety of crops, mountain products and aquatic products. It has long rigid winters and is sparsely populated. Since ancient times, there lived a lot of ethnic groups. People there are fond of stewed dishes for high caloric intake against the rigid winters. It is their tradition to consume scallion and garlic, frozen food or preserved food. Frozen food and fruits can help boost the intake of vitamins and prevent scurvy, a disease caused by vitamin deficiency. People there are so fond of frozen food that the selling season of popsicles is the winter. Scallion and garlic are good for the treatment of indigestion and bacterial infection. Every household keeps jars for making and keeping preserved vegetables or paste as fresh vegetables are scarce in winter. Over the time, people there gradually adapt to the strong flavor as the preserved vegetables have to be heavily salted in order not to go bad. Since the middle of Qing Dynasty, increasing numbers of pioneers have immigrated to the north of the Shanhaiguan Pass to reclaim and cultivate the land. Nomadic lifestyle and gathering gave way to agriculture which became the major mode of production and the diet patterns changed accordingly.

Features: The food generally has mixed flavors in one dish that tastes distinctly salty or sweet. Thoroughly cooked and savored with a great variety of ingredients with a fresh color. Common cooking methods include: sauteed, stir-fried, braised, deep-fried, roasted, steamed, stewed, among which sauteed, deep-fried, braised, and stewed dishes are characteristic of the northeast diet.

Classic dishes: Braised Pork with Vermicelli, Fried Pork in Scoop, Mixed Stew, Hot Candied Sweet Potatoes, etc.

我国东北地区土地肥沃，草场优良，平原广阔，五谷杂粮与山货水产都很丰富，冬季寒冷漫长，人口稀少。历史上这片土地长期生活着许多少数民族。人们好食炖菜，摄取高热量的动物脂肪以御寒冬。当地人有吃葱蒜、冻食和腌菜的习惯。吃冻菜、冻水果可帮助增加维生素，避免一味吃热食导致缺乏维生素而得坏血病。吃冷冻食品已发展成人们的一大嗜好，哈尔滨一年的雪糕竟然大部分是在冬天消费的。吃葱蒜可以帮助消化杀菌。因寒冷的气候使冬季缺少新鲜蔬菜，腌菜和泡菜占了很大比重，几乎每家都有大大小小的酱缸。因而随着时间的变化，人们逐渐适应了腌菜的咸重口味。自清中叶以后，关内大量移民涌入东北开荒垦殖，农业取代游牧和采集业成为主要生产方式。东北的饮食方式亦随之发生了一些变化。

口味特点：一菜多味、咸甜分明、用料广泛、火候足、滋味浓郁、色鲜味浓、酥烂香脆，烹调方法长于熘、爆、烧、炸、烤、蒸、炖，以熘、炸、烧、炖为主要特点。

经典菜肴：猪肉炖粉条、锅包肉、乱炖、拔丝地瓜等。

Braised Pork with Vermicelli 猪肉炖粉条

必用三句

1 Before winter comes, it is common practice for every household to hoard the Chinese cabbages, the major vegetable consumed in winter days in the north. 每个冬季来临之前，家家户户都囤积一些大白菜，它们也是北方过冬的主要食材。

2 Bring everything to a boil and turn to a low heat to simmer until the vermicelli is well cooked. 开锅后改小火慢慢炖一会儿，一直等到粉条烂了即可。

3 It is a very pleasant and comforting dish to have in the cold winter days. 寒冬腊月里来上一碗，热腾腾的甚是可口。

双语赏析

Braised Pork with Vermicelli is a signature food in Northeast China, the No.1 stewed dish of the Four Famed Stewed Dishes. It is well loved by people in the northern provinces as well as people from the south. The stewed dish in the northeast often combines two ingredients and stews them together over high heat. Before winter comes, it is common practice for every household to hoard the Chinese cabbages, the major vegetable consumed in winter days in the north. It is also a custom to butcher a pig and get the meat to prepare for the New Year feast. Chunks of pork are stewed with vermicelli every time there are guests in the house. Vermicelli, made from potato starch, is an indispensable part of the daily diet of the northeast. When stewed with pork, it soaks up the flavor and tastes extremely palatable.

The dish consists pork, Chinese cabbage, vermicelli, scallion, ginger, garlic, star anise, wild pepper, fennel and etc. First add the pork in hot oil to fry out the fat. When the meat is done, first add the cabbage, then the vermicelli and water. The dish needs more than ordinary amount of water as the vermicelli tends to soak up the water. Bring everything to a boil and turn to a low heat to simmer until the vermicelli is well cooked. The dish tastes salty while the vermicelli, soaked up the broth, tastes soft and smooth. It is a very pleasant and comforting dish to have in the cold winter days.

The Northeast China is vast in territory with a large population. Different accompaniments are added according to different flavor preference. In addition to the classic version of using mainly pork and vermicelli, there are derivatives such as Braised Pork with Vermicelli and Tofu, Braised Pork with Turnip, Cabbage and Vermicelli, to name a few. With the variations, the dish can better suit the different tastes of people, as well as adding more flavor and nutrition.

猪肉炖粉条是东北菜的一道响亮的招牌，是“东北四大炖”的第一炖，深受南北方人的喜爱。东北炖菜的特色，多是两两搭配，大火炖烂。每个冬季来临之前，家家户户都囤积一些大白菜，它们也是北方过冬的主要食材。东北人过年必杀猪，大块大块地切下来，有亲友来访，便和粉条一起下锅炖。粉条在东北是人们生活中不可或缺的好吃的食物，用东北特产土豆淀粉轧制而成。用猪肉来炖粉条，把滋味儿都炖进粉条里边去了，奇香无比。

这道菜由猪肉、白菜、粉条、大葱、姜、蒜、八角、花椒、小茴香等食材做成。先用热油把五花肉炒出油脂，等到肉熟得差不多了，把切好的白菜倒进去，炒匀。之后便要加入适量的水和粉条。因为粉条是很吸水的，因此水一定要加足。开锅后改小火慢慢炖一会儿，一直等到粉条烂了即可。白菜猪肉炖粉条口味咸，粉条吸收了汤汁表面的油脂，软而光滑。寒冬腊月里来上一碗，热腾腾的甚是可口。

东北地区地域辽阔，人口众多，猪肉炖粉条这道菜由于各家口味的不同也就衍生出了无数不同的食材添加的做法，在保留猪肉炖粉条菜品优点的同时也衍生出了一些味道层次更加丰富的菜品，例如猪肉粉条炖豆腐、萝卜白菜炖猪肉粉条等。更多的食材添加也丰富了菜品的营养和色香味，也就能适应更多人的口味。

词汇笔记

- **hoard** [hɔːrd] *v.* If you hoard things such as food or money, you save or store them, often in secret, because they are valuable or important to you. 贮藏，囤

- **starch** [stɑːrtʃ] *n.* Starch is a substance that is found in foods such as bread, potatoes, pasta, and rice and gives you energy. 淀粉
- **simmer** ['sɪmər] *v.* When you simmer food or when it simmers, you cook it by keeping it at boiling point or just below boiling point. 用文火炖；煨
- **derivative** [dɪ'rɪvətɪv] *n.* A derivative is something which has been developed or obtained from something else. 衍生物

Demoli Fish Stew 得莫利炖鱼

必用三句

1 Demoli Fish Stew is a Northeast specialty, one of the Four Famed Stewed Dishes in the northeast. 得莫利炖鱼是东北特色菜，是东北四大炖菜之一。

2 Demoli is a word transliterated from Russian. It originated from the Demoli village of Fangzheng county in Harbin. “得莫利”一词是俄罗斯语的音译，这道菜的原产地是哈尔滨郊区方正县伊汉通乡得莫利村。

3 The fish is fresh and tasty, meaty and tender, not at all fishy or greasy. 鱼肉又鲜又香，又肥又嫩，不腥不腻。

双语赏析

Demoli Fish Stew is a Northeast specialty, one of the Four Famed Stewed Dishes in the northeast. Demoli is a word transliterated from Russian. It originated from the Demoli village of Fangzheng county in Harbin. It has a history of more than one hundred years. To the north of the village lies the Songhua River from which the local villagers fish for a living. In the 1980s, an old couple opened a small eatery to serve the passers by. They made a fish stew using native fish species such as carp, catfish, crucian, or yellow catfish with tofu and broad vermicelli. This delicacy became popular instantly and spread like wildfire.

There are a few essential tips for cooking the fish stew. First, the fish has to be indigenous live fish. The fish is fresh and tasty, meaty and tender, not at all fishy or greasy. It goes especially well with such accompaniments as vermicelli or pork. Second, the essential accompaniments are marinated tofu and vermicelli. The last is the secret ingredient rugosus which is a local herb commonly seen in the fields of the northern provinces. This herb is an excellent flavor enhancer that can bring out the unique taste the fish.

It is quite a simple dish to prepare. Bring the soy-bean oil to a boil. Then add shredded scallion and wild pepper and stir a bit. Scale and gut the fish and remove the gills. Then shallow fry the fish before adding water or broth in the wok and stew it. Add a piece of pork skin to thicken the broth. Wait until the broth boils before adding some tofu and vermicelli. Stew another ten minutes and it is done. It is traditionally served steaming hot in an enamel basin, enough to serve three to five people.

得莫利炖鱼是东北特色菜，是东北四大炖菜之一。“得莫利”一词是俄罗斯语的音译，这道菜的原产地是哈尔滨郊区方正县伊汉通乡得莫利村，已有一百多年的历史。由于这个村北靠松花江，在鱼多的时候，这里的村民主要靠打鱼来维持生计。在20世纪80年代初，村里的一对老夫妇在路边开了间小饭店，招待路上歇脚吃饭的过路人。他们把当地的活鲤鱼（也可以用鲇鱼、鲫鱼、嘎鱼）和豆腐、宽粉条子炖在一起，味道鲜美，后来菜的做法不胫而走。

得莫利炖鱼有几个必不可少的条件，必须选用本地产活鱼，佐以粉条、白肉等料，鱼肉又鲜又香，又肥又嫩，不腥不腻。炖鱼必不可少的辅料是卤水豆腐和粉条。据传，得莫利炖鱼的秘密武器是藿香，这种植物在北方的田间地头随处可见。炖鱼的时候折一个藿香的枝放在锅里，炖出来的鱼味道鲜美无比，十分独特。

烹调过程很简单：豆油烧开，葱花、花椒面炝锅，把去鳞并摘掉鳃和内脏的鲤鱼两面用滚油稍微煎一下，接着加水（有放少许老汤的）炖煮。加入一块生猪肉皮可使汤更浓郁。开锅马上加入粉条和豆腐。十几分钟后，出锅。炖鱼都是用搪瓷的盆盛上来，热气腾腾的，足够三五个人大吃一顿了。

词汇笔记

- **vermicelli** [ˌvɜːrmɪˈtʃeli] *n.* very fine strands of pasta, used in soups 意大利细面条，粉条
- **indigenous** [ɪnˈdɪdʒənəs] *adj.* indigenous people or things belong to the country in which they are found, rather than coming there or being brought there from another country 本土的；当地的 [正式]
- **accompaniment** [əˈkʌmpənimənt] *n.* An accompaniment is something that goes with another thing. 相配物
- **marinate** [ˈmærɪneɪt] *v.* If you marinate meat or fish, or if it marinates, you keep it in a mixture of oil, vinegar, spices, and herbs before cooking it, so that it can develop a special flavour. 使受腌汁浸泡；腌泡
- **gill** [gɪl; dʒɪl] *n.* Gills are the organs on the sides of fish and other water creatures through which they breathe. 鳃 [usu pl]

Shenyang Chicken Skeleton 沈阳鸡架

必用三句

1 It may not be fancy or big name food, but it is the indispensable part of the daily diet and brings supreme joy to the local people. 这道美食，或许不甚精致，又或者不被外人所知，但却是当地人日常饮食中不可或缺的一部分，是他们心中的顶级快乐。

2 The bones are cooked thoroughly until crispy and marinated with the spice mixture. 烹饪后的鸡骨酥酥烂烂，被各种香料调得有滋有味。

3 With its palatable taste and affordable price, it has won the heart of Shenyang people. Eating Chicken Skeleton becomes the best pastime for workers to hang around after work with friends. 这种又便宜又美味的下酒菜赢得了沈阳人的心。吃鸡架成为工人们下班后与友人小聚时的最好选择。

双语赏析

Every city has its signature food. It may not be fancy or big name food, but it is the indispensable part of the daily diet and brings supreme joy to the local people. Not as exquisite and haughty as the Peking Roast Duck nor the folksy and approachable as the Wuhan spicy crawfish, Shenyang's delicacy, the Chicken Skeleton, mirrors the history of the Northeast heavy industry.

Chicken Skeleton is the remains of the chicken when the skin, thighs, breast meat, head, neck, wings and internal organs are all removed. Most often than not, people in Shenyang, the capital city of Liaoning province, eat Chicken Skeleton not to satisfy their hunger, but to satisfy their mouth. It gives people utmost delight to drink with friends and chat over a plate of Chicken Skeleton. The best part is the bones. The bones are cooked thoroughly until crispy and marinated with the spice mixture. A bite of Shenyang Chicken Skeleton can make you chill and relax and savor the joy of simple pleasures of life.

In Shenyang, there are countless ways to cook the Chicken Skeleton. Whether grilled, fried, smoked, stewed in shallow water, or stir-fried, it delights all the Shenyang people despite their varied preference of flavor. With a total population of 7,000,000, they take up half the amount of the Chicken Skeleton consumed in China. What now becomes a favorite delicacy of the local people used to be a choice of necessity. In the 1990s, China's chicken industry developed rapidly. At the same time, tens of thousand lay-off workers lost their sources of income. Shenyang people who loved drinking and chatting lacked delicious dishes to go with liquor. They set their sights on the affordable meat scraps: the Chicken Skeleton. Chicken Skeleton is the by-product in the procession chicken and is cheap to buy while the thighs, breasts, claws, and heads sell high on market. With its palatable taste and affordable price, it has won the heart of Shenyang people. Eating Chicken Skeleton becomes the best pastime for workers to hang around after work with friends. And Shenyang becomes the centre of Chicken Skeleton consumption.

几乎每座城市，都有自己的标志性美食。这道美食，或许不甚精致，又或许不被外人所知，但却是当地人日常饮食中不可或缺的一部分，是他们心中的顶级快乐。没有北京烤鸭的精巧贵气、武汉小龙虾的江湖气息，沈阳人的鸡架充斥着满满的重工业风情。

鸡架就是去掉皮、大腿、胸脯肉、头、脖子、翅膀、内脏之后，几乎只剩下骨头的部分。大多时候，人们在沈阳，辽宁的省会，吃鸡架不是为了充饥，而是为了满足味蕾（解馋）。一盘鸡架，几瓶啤酒，三五好友，边吃边唠嗑。啃鸡架的乐趣，自然还在于鸡骨头本身。烹饪后的鸡骨酥酥烂烂，被各种香料调得有滋有味。一口鸡架能使你震颤、放松，品味到生活中的简单快乐。

在沈阳，有无数种鸡架吃法。几乎每个沈阳人，都有自己最喜欢的一种。烤鸡架，炸鸡架、熏拌鸡架、炆鸡架、辣炒鸡架。700 多万沈阳人竟然消耗掉了全国一半的鸡架。这道人人追捧的美食，当初诞生时却饱含着迫不得已。20 世纪 90 年代时，我国养鸡业快速发展，同时下岗潮也让数十万工人失去了经济来源。爱喝酒聊天的沈阳人少了可口的下酒菜，便将目光锁定在了鸡架上，因为鸡腿、鸡胸肉、鸡爪、鸡头这些部位的市场需求都很高，可以单独售卖，鸡架属于边角料，成本很低。这种又便宜又美味的下酒菜赢得了沈阳人的心。吃鸡架成为工人们下班后与友人小聚时的最好选择。就这样，沈阳成了全国最大的鸡架消耗中心。

词汇笔记

- **haughty** ['hɔːti] *adj.* You use haughty to describe someone's behaviour or appearance when you disapprove of the fact that they seem to be very proud and to think that they are better than other people. 傲慢的，上等的
- **savor** ['seɪvər] *v.* If you savour an experience, you enjoy it as much as you can. 尽情享受
- **liquor** ['lɪkər] *n.* strong alcoholic drinks such as whisky, vodka, and gin can be referred to as liquor 烈性酒
- **palatable** ['pælətəbl] *adj.* If you describe food or drink as palatable, you mean that it tastes pleasant. 美味的［正式］

Grilled Noodles 烤冷面

必用三句

1 Grilled Noodles is a ubiquitous street food in Heilongjiang province which emerged from Mishan county in Jixi City of Heilongjiang province. 烤冷面，是黑龙江省的特色小吃之一，起源于黑龙江省鸡西市密山市。

2 Different versions were developed such as grilled and deep-fried noodles as the street vendors used different cooking utensils. 由于小贩用不同的烹饪器具，于是便有了碳烤、油炸等做法。

3 A perfect paste appears reddish orange and tastes salty or sweet and sour, which is really comforting and appetizing. 一份优秀的烤冷面酱汁呈橙红色，咸口或酸甜口，吃起来既爽口又开胃。

双语赏析

Grilled Noodles is a ubiquitous street food in Heilongjiang province which emerged from Mishan county in Jixi city of Heilongjiang province. There are various ways of cooking it, including deep-frying or using a hot iron plate. The most common practice is to bake the noodles on an iron griddle. In the early twenty-fist century, it has become the most popular street delicacy to sate late-night cravings in northeastern China and went viral across the country.

The exact origin of Grilled Noodles is unknown. It is generally believed that Grilled Noodles was created by a street vendor from Mishan city of the northeastern China's Heilongjiang province in the 1990s, who fried cold noodles with savory sauce and made a hit with the hungry students filing out of class. The noodles were supposed to be stiff and crispy when fried, but opposite to common belief, they came out soft and tender. The "noodle" part comes from the fact that the roll is actually made from cold noodles pressed together, creating the grooves on its surface. The noodles were sold out in a few minutes and spread across town overnight. Different versions were developed such as grilled and deep-fried noodles as the street vendors used different cooking utensils.

A few years later, fried noodles became out of favor and the Grilled Noodles sold much better. Originally it was popular to prepare noodles on a gas-fueled griddle. The noodles would be pressed between two grids and grilled over charcoal. Oil and then paste was applied to both sides while grilling. Later they just used a hot plate to grill the noodles. Though some street vendors try to cash in by advertising their noodles as "authentically Korean", the two products are unrelated. The main ingredient is a sheet of starch. It is served hot by grilling it and an egg on an iron griddle, rolling it up with fillings like sausage, onions, and coriander, and chopping the roll into small pieces. The soul of the Grilled Noodles is definitely the paste. Changes are if the paste doesn't taste good, it will ruin the noodles. A perfect paste appears reddish orange and tastes salty or sweet and sour, which is really comforting and appetizing.

烤冷面，是黑龙江省的特色小吃之一，起源于黑龙江省鸡西市密山市。烤冷面起初有多种做法，包括油炸、高温铁板碾压等，后改良为铁板成块煎烤。21 世纪初烤冷面已经火遍全国的大江南北，是东北街头小吃届的扛把子。

烤冷面的确切来源已不可考，但一般普遍认为烤冷面是 20 世纪 90 年代黑龙江省密山市一街头小贩发明出来的。那位师傅把冷面刷上美味的酱汁油炸，受到了放学后饥肠辘辘的学生们的热烈欢迎。本以为面条油炸后会又硬又脆，结果恰恰相反，面条又软又嫩。之所以叫“面条”是因为那个面卷是面条压在一起制成的，它的表面丝丝分明。面条在极短的时间内就销售一空，并在一夜之间名贯全城。由于小贩用不同的烹饪器具，于是便有了碳烤、油炸等做法。

几年后，油炸面失宠，铁板烤冷面销量远大于油炸。最初烤冷面是明火烤的，碳火上面放两个铁帘子，两个铁帘子中间夹着原料烤，边烤边刷油，烤好后刷酱汁，后来才演变成用铁板烤的。虽然叫卖是把它称作“朝鲜”烤冷面，但两者并不相干。其原材料不是朝鲜族的冷面，而是一种经过加工改良的干制面皮，把面皮在铁板上烤软了，就打上个鸡蛋，卷上烤肠、洋葱、香菜，并把面卷切成小段。一份烤冷面的灵魂是酱汁，如果酱汁不成功，那么冷面也就毁了。一份优秀的烤冷面酱汁呈橙红色，咸口或酸甜口，吃起来既爽口又开胃。

词汇笔记

- **ubiquitous** [juːˈbɪkwɪtəs] *adj.* If you describe something or someone as ubiquitous, you mean that they seem to be everywhere. 无所不在的 [正式]
- **sate** [seɪt] *v.* to satisfy (a desire or appetite) fully 充分满足 (欲望或食欲)
- **utensil** [juːˈtens(ə)l] *n.* Utensils are tools or objects that you use in order to help you to cook, serve food, or eat. 器皿；用具
- **charcoal** [ˈtʃɑːrkoʊl] *n.* Charcoal is a black substance obtained by burning wood without much air. It can be burned as a fuel, and small sticks of it are used for drawing. 木炭
- **appetizing** [ˈæpɪtaɪzɪŋ] *adj.* Appetizing food looks and smells good, so that you want to eat it. 引起食欲的

Fried Pork in Scoop 锅包肉

必用三句

1 The dish is golden in color, sour and sweet in taste, crispy and tender, savory yet not greasy, which makes it a perfect dish for summer as it works up the appetite. 成菜色泽金黄，酸甜可口，外酥里嫩，加上爽口不油腻的特点，有开胃增食欲之功效，很适合夏天食用。

2 As it is stir-fried over a high heat and the sauce is poured all over the pork in the hot wok, hence the name Guo Baorou (meaning an explosive dish in Chinese). 由于用急火快炒，把铁锅烧热，把汁淋到锅里，浸透到肉里，所以起名叫“锅爆肉”。

3 It is well loved by people in the northeast region who prefer a rich and intense flavor. 味道浓郁，口感厚实，是广大东北人民喜爱的口味。

双语赏析

Fried Pork in Scoop is a northeast delicacy that originated in Harbin, a well-received dish with its crunchy and palatable taste. Marinate pork tenderloin slices to taste, wrap the meat in frying sauce and twice fry it. For the first time, fry it until the meat is cooked. For the second time, fry it until golden in color. Then stir fry and thicken with paste. The dish is golden in color, sour and sweet in taste, crispy and tender, savory yet not greasy, which makes it a perfect dish for summer as it works up the appetite.

It is a dish invented by Zheng Xingwen, a private cook for Du Xueying, the mayor of Daotai, in Harbin in Qing Dynasty. In 1907, he began to work as an apprentice in the kitchen of the mayor. Banquets were often held to entertain foreign guests, especially those from Russia. They all fancied sweet and sour food, so the mayor ordered the cook to modify the taste of the dish. Thus Zheng changed the dish from salty fried pork to sweet and sour taste. The Russian guests liked the dish so much and ordered the dish every time. As it is stir-fried over a high heat and the sauce is poured all over the pork in the hot wok, hence the name Guo Baorou. As the Russians always pronounced Bao (with a falling tone) as Bao (with a level tone), after a while the dish got its present name Guo Baorou with the level tone.

Years later, Liaoning people improved the taste of the Fried Pork in Scoop by adding ketchup or tomato paste before it is out of the wok. It looks very much like Cherry Pork, only less golden and more reddish orange. The crunchy meat coated with tomato paste tastes marvellous. It is well loved by people in the northeast region who prefer a rich and intense flavor.

锅包肉是一道东北风味菜，起源于哈尔滨。它香酥甜脆的口味令人拍案叫绝。锅包肉用猪里脊肉切片腌入味，裹上炸浆，经两遍油炸而成。第一遍将肉炸熟，第二遍将肉炸至金黄色。下锅拌炒时勾芡即成。成菜色泽金黄，酸甜可口，外酥里嫩，加上爽口不油腻的特点，有开胃增食欲之功效，很适合夏天食用。

锅包肉于光绪年间始创自哈尔滨道台府府尹杜学瀛厨师郑兴文之手。郑兴文于1907年在府尹的厨房里当学徒。道台府里经常会宴请国外宾客，尤其是俄罗斯客人。由于外国人喜欢吃甜酸口味。杜学瀛就命府内厨师变换菜肴口味。郑兴文就把原来咸鲜口味的“焦烧肉条”改成了酸甜口味的菜肴。这道菜让俄罗斯客人非常喜欢，每次吃饭都要点这道菜。由于用急火快炒，把铁锅烧热，把汁淋到锅里，浸透到肉里，所以起名叫“锅爆肉”。俄罗斯人发“爆”音为“包”，时间一长，“锅爆肉”就演变成为“锅包肉”。

后来辽宁人对锅包肉进行了改造，最后一步改用番茄酱或者番茄沙司，外观像极了哈尔滨的“樱桃肉”，减少了锅包肉原有的香酥金黄。炸得酥脆的里脊肉裹在浓厚的番茄酱里形成了无比奇妙的口感。味道浓郁，口感厚实，是广大东北人民喜爱的口味。

词汇笔记

- **apprentice** [ə'prentɪs] *n.* An apprentice is a young person who works for someone in order to learn their skill. 学徒
- **fancy** ['fænsi] *v.* If you fancy something, you want to have it or to do it. 想要，喜欢
- **ketchup** ['ketʃəp] *n.* Ketchup is a thick, cold sauce, usually made from tomatoes, that is sold in bottles. 番茄酱

Pancake with Salted Fish 咸鱼饼子

必用三句

1 Pancake with Salted Fish is a traditional delicacy in the northern coastal provinces of China. It belongs to the Dalian dish from the Jiaodong branch of Lu cuisine. 咸鱼饼子是北方沿海省份的特色传统名小吃，属于鲁菜系胶东帮中的大连菜。

2 To preserve the authentic taste of old Dalian style, local people use palm-sized autumn marine fish, washed in sea water before dried. 为保持“咸鱼饼子”中老大连的“原汁原味”，当地人选用的鱼是秋天巴掌大小的海鱼，用海水洗完后进行晾晒。

3 Slice the pancakes and serve them with the salted fish and you will have an authentic taste of the sea. 用刀将饼子切成块，咸鱼与饼子同食，是正宗的沿海风味。

双语赏析

Pancake with Salted Fish is a traditional delicacy in the northern coastal provinces of China. It belongs to the Dalian dish from the Jiaodong branch of Lu cuisine.

As a quick and easy food for fishermen, Pancake with Salted Fish originated in eastern Liaoning province and eastern Shandong province. Fishermen would leave early for the sea in order to come back early to sell their catch and they ate one meal at sea. Pancake with Salted Fish, as it was easy to carry and quick to eat, became a popular choice of food. It was also favored by the housewives since there was limited choice of fresh vegetables during the winter in the northern areas except Chinese cabbage and turnips. In order to spice up the daily diet, it is common practice in every household to preserve and dry some fish to sustain the cold long winter. The popular combination is the salted fish with corn pancake, which is a must-have for home cooking and for eating out. This dish gained its popularity in the coastal villages before being introduced to the city. Now you can order the dish at eateries and restaurants in Dalian.

The dish is easy to prepare. To preserve the authentic taste of old Dalian style, local people use palm-sized autumn marine fish, washed in sea water before dried. Repeat the process three times and then fry the fish until crispy. Pancakes are made from fermented dough using fresh corn flour. Divide the dough into small balls, flatten them and stick them to the inside wall of the wok.

Add firewood to heat up the wok and remove the firewood when steam starts to come out of the wok. Allow the cakes to cook through and form the crust. Slice the pancakes and serve them with the salted fish and you will have an authentic taste of the sea.

咸鱼饼子是北方沿海省份的特色传统名小吃，属于鲁菜系胶东帮中的大连菜。

咸鱼饼子早期是辽东和胶东渔民的便捷食品。为了早点靠岸卖出海货，渔民必须早出海，有一顿饭是一定要在海上吃的，吃咸鱼饼子省事、方便。对一般市民来说，以前冬季新鲜蔬菜少，只有白菜萝卜，调剂菜肴时，经济实惠又随处可买的小鱼儿就成为家庭主妇的首选，家家户户每年都要盐渍和晾晒一些咸鱼。咸鱼和苞米面饼子成为最佳组合，家中吃饭、外出带饭都少不了。这道小吃首先在沿海村庄获得了名声，随后传入城市。现在无论大连的大小餐馆都有这道菜。

这道菜的做法比较简单，为保持“咸鱼饼子”中老大连的“原汁原味”，当地人选用的鱼是秋天巴掌大小的海鱼，用海水洗完后进行晾晒，风干后用海水再洗一遍继续晾晒，反复三次，把鱼晒成咸鱼，稍炸一下用油煎得外焦里嫩、酥香可口。饼子是当年的新玉米面，用农家大铁锅添水烧开，把玉米面团一个个拍成饼子贴在锅边，盖锅加柴草大烧，锅边冒大气并溢出饼子香气即迅速撤掉灶内柴草，用其余热烘出饼子底面嘎巴儿，用刀将饼子切成块。咸鱼与饼子同食，是正宗的沿海风味。

词汇笔记

- **sustain** [sə'steɪn] *v.* If you sustain something, you continue it or maintain it for a period of time. 保持，维持
- **preserve** [prɪ'zɜːrv] *v.* If you preserve food, you treat it in order to prevent it from decaying so that you can store it for a long time. 保藏
- **fermented** [fɜːr'ment] *v.* If food, drink, or other natural substance ferments, or if it is fermented, a chemical change takes place in it so that alcohol is produced. This process forms part of the production of alcoholic drinks such as wine and beer. 使发酵；发酵
- **crust** [krʌst] *n.* A crust is a hard layer of something, especially on top of a softer or wetter substance. 硬外壳

Chapter 02

The Cuisine in Beijing-Tianjin Region

京津地区饮食

The Dietary Culture of Beijing-Tianjin Region
京津地区饮食文化

Beijing is not only of political and culture significance but also boasts of it rich history. It has been established as the capital city by three successive dynasties, namely the Yuan Dynasty (1206–1368), the Ming Dynasty (1368–1644), and the Qing Dynasty (1616–1911). Tianjin has been the center of canal transportation, salt administration and commercial trade since ancient times. As the integration of economy and culture of the capital city and its environs, this region has become a merging pot of people from walks of life and levels of society including high-rank officials, military troops, and professionals. The regional diet is highly diverse and vastly varied.

From the banquets of the imperial court and aristocratic mansions to street food of the market place, the diet presents a unique diversity. Economic and political impact surpasses that of the natural environment.

Features: food source comes from local produce mainly, supplemented by high quality specialties from all over the country. The taste is salty and savory, diversified yet compatible.

Classic dishes: Beijing Roast Duck, Sauteed Shredded Pork in Sweet Bean Sauce, Goubuli Baozi, Jianbing Guozi.

北京不仅是中国的政治、文化中心，还因为其悠久的历史而闻名遐迩。它是元（1206—1368）、明（1368—1644）、清（1616—1911）三朝古都。天津自古以来就是漕运、盐务和商业发达的都会，与北京共构经济一体和京畿文化。京津地区聚集着诸多衙属官吏、庞大驻军以及乐医百工，众多民众汇聚于此，形成了五方杂处的局面。饮食的层次性和变化性特别明显。

从皇宫御膳、贵族府宴到市井小吃，形成了全国特有的层次性饮食文化。政治经济的影响超过了自然环境对饮食风格的影响。

口味特点：食料还是以周边地区为主，辅以全国各地精华物产，咸香为主，兼容并蓄八方风味。

代表菜肴：北京烤鸭、京酱肉丝、狗不理包子、煎饼馃子等。

Luzhu Huoshao 卤煮火烧

必用三句

1 As one of the three famous traditional Beijing-style delicacies, a bite of it gives you an authentic experience of Beijing traditional diet, as well as the Hutong culture. 作为北京的“老三样儿”之一，（卤煮）不仅体现了老北京人的饮食习惯，更包含着人们对胡同文化的认同。

2 The cakes are fully soaked and softened by the broth and not cooked into nothingness, the meat stewed soft but not overdone, and the intestines rich and decadent. 火烧透而不腻，肉烂而不糟，小肠则酥软味厚。

3 “Xiao Change Chen” has the same qualities as other time-honored restaurants: select materials, excellent workmanship and generous quantities, so it soon made a name for itself. 跟所有的老字号一样，选料精致，做工认真，用料足，“小肠陈”慢慢地干出了名堂。

双语赏析

Luzhu Huoshao (Lu Zhu for short), or stewed assorted entrails with wheat cake, is a traditional snack of Beijing. As one of the three famous traditional Beijing-style delicacies, a bite of it gives you an authentic experience of Beijing traditional diet, as well as the Hutong culture. Its main ingredients are pork intestines, pork lungs and dried Tofu. Put the dried Tofu in triangles, and chopped intestines and lungs into a supersize wok and cook them from morning to lunch time, add Huoshao, or the baked wheat cakes cut in square cubes into the broth just before it is served, and top with chili oil, smashed garlic, fermented bean curd, and smashed leek flower. The cakes are fully soaked and softened by the broth and not cooked into nothingness, the meat stewed soft but not overdone, and the intestines rich and decadent.

There two important tips to make an authentic Lu Zhu: one, the pork intestines and lungs must be clean or the broth will smell unpleasant; two, the baked wheat cake must be made of "Qiangmian"–which is a semi-fermented dough kneaded by adding some dry flour–or the baked wheat cake will be easily overdone. Just like most of other dishes in northern China, Lu Zhu features a heavy flavor, because in the cooking process, a large amount of condiments are added into the broth. Based on your own taste, you can add into it chili oil, mashed garlic, vinegar, coriander and so on.

A humble meal with lofty aspirations, Luzhu Huoshao can be traced back to the Qing Dynasty (1616–1911) when it was called "su zao rou", a dish for the royal court that was well-loved by Emperor Qianlong. As an imitation of a fabled imperial dish, the expensive ingredients such as pork are replaced by cheap ingredients that the commoner could afford such as lungs, intestines, and liver and thus created the commoners' version of "palace food".

Among the countless restaurants which serve Luzhu Houshao the century-old brand "Xiao Chang Chen" is the most famous one. The first "Xiao Chang Chen" restaurant was opened in South Hengjie outside the Xuanwu Gate. "Xiao Change Chen" has the same qualities as other time-honored restaurants: select materials, excellent workmanship and generous quantities, so it soon made a name for itself. At the present day, while inheriting traditional techniques, "Xiao Chang Chen" constantly makes innovation by introducing new ingredients and adding some Chinese herbal medicines into the broth to remove the smell of the raw meat and make the soup more aromatic.

卤煮火烧，简称卤煮，是北京的一道传统小吃。作为北京的“老三样儿”之一，不仅体现了老北京人的饮食习惯，更包含着人们对胡同文化的认同。其主要原料是猪肠、猪肺和干豆腐，豆腐切三角，小肠、肺头剁小块，用大锅卤制，一般要在清晨就开始煮，快到中午吃饭时间，加入切井字刀块的火烧。待到火烧吸饱汤汁、变软，再加点蒜泥、辣椒油、豆腐乳、韭菜花，便可以吃了。热腾腾的一碗，火烧透而不腻，肉烂而不糟，小肠则酥软味厚。

味道正宗的卤煮，关键有两点：一是猪肠猪肺一定要清洗干净，二是火烧一定要饧面（用半发酵的面团加干面粉揉成）的。做不到这两点，要么汤有异味，要么火烧很容易煮烂。和北方多数饮食一样，卤煮以味儿厚见长。在卤制过程中，加入大量的佐料。食用时可根据自己的口味加入辣椒油、蒜泥、醋，以及香菜等。

这道普通甚至被认为“低贱”的小吃却有着“高贵”的起源。据说，清朝（1616—1911）宫廷中有一道名为“苏造肉”的菜肴，深受乾隆皇帝的喜爱。作为一道仿制的宫廷菜肴，民众将菜中昂贵的五花肉换成便宜的猪下水，制成大众版的“宫廷菜”。

卤煮火烧在北京最著名的是拥有百年历史的“小肠陈”。“小肠陈”最早开在宣武门外南横街。跟所有的老字号一样，选料精致，做工认真，用料足，“小肠陈”慢慢地干出了名堂。如今的“小肠陈”在继承传统的同时，不仅大胆引入从前没有的卤品，使汤锅的“内容”更为丰富，还对卤汤进行“改革”，加入几味去腥提味的中草药，让其味道更为香浓。

词汇笔记

- **entrails** ['entreɪlz] *n.* The entrails of people or animals are their inside parts, especially their intestines. 内脏；肠
- **intestine** [ɪn'testɪn] *n.* Your intestines are the tubes in your body through which food passes when it has left your stomach. 肠子；小肠
- **knead** [ni:d] *v.* When you knead dough or other food, you press and squeeze it with your hands so that it becomes smooth and ready to bake. 揉（面团等）
- **innovation** [ˌɪnə'veɪʃn] *n.* a new thing or a new method of doing something 新事物；新方法

Zha Jiang Noodles 炸酱面

必用三句

1 Among all the variations, Zha Jiang Noodles or noodles with fried soy-bean paste are the most influential, and are hailed as one of the ten signature noodles in China. 在诸多面条种类中，炸酱面的影响最大，被誉为“中国十大面条”之一。

2 It originated from a time-honoured diner in an old Beijing Hutong that specialized in noodles and has now become a symbol of food culture in Beijing-Tianjin region with its aromatic and salty flavor. 炸酱面最初源自老北京胡同一家专门以面条为主的老字号面馆，现已成为京津地区的饮食文化符号。其特点是酱香浓郁。

3 Common choices are cucumber, cedrela sinensis, bean sprouts, green beans, soybeans, and radish, finely shredded or diced as side dishes to be topped on the noodles when served. 面码儿用的是时令蔬菜如黄瓜、香椿、豆芽、青豆、黄豆、红萝卜，切丝或切丁摆在面条上。

双语赏析

Noodles have a long history in China. They've been around since the Eastern Han Dynasty for over 1,900 years and have since become a popular food for the Chinese people. Noodles come in different versions in different parts of China. Among all the variations, Zha Jiang Noodles or noodles with fried soy-bean paste are the most influential, and are hailed as one of the ten signature noodles in China. It is the most favorite staple food in Beijing, Tianjin and Heibei region. It is also popular in southern places such as Shanghai, Guangdong, as well as in north-east China, although the cooking methods vary a bit in each place. Around the year 1882 in Qing Dynasty, Zha Jiang Noodles was introduced to South Korea by the soldiers from Shandong province who stationed in Inchon, and has been enthusiastically adopted as South Korea's most popular and ubiquitous food. However, noodles with soy bean paste Beijing style have become the accepted standard.

Zha Jiang Noodles is a traditional Beijing dish full of flavor and freshness. It originated from a time-honoured diner in an old Beijing Hutong that specialized in noodles and has now become a symbol of food culture in Beijing-Tianjin region with its aromatic and salty flavor. Old Beijingers are meticulous when it comes to the preparing and eating of Zha Jiang Noodles. In winter the noodles are served steaming hot from the wok, while in summer they are rinsed in cold water and drained before transferred to a bowl. Traditionally hand-rolled noodles are preferable to ensure the chewy taste.

The accompaniments to go with the noodles may change with the seasons. Common choices are cucumber, cedrela sinensis, bean sprouts, green beans, soybeans, and radish, finely shredded or diced as side dishes to be topped on the noodles when served. The small bowlful of paste consists cubed streaky pork that has been thoroughly fired. The soul of Beijing style is the dry yellow soybean paste from the time-honoured brand as the main seasoning. One can never be too particular about the heat and timing when frying the paste. When it's done properly, it can hold an inserted chopstick. Then it is served in a super bowl topped with the paste and sprinkled with vegetables.

面条的历史由来已久。据说在 1900 多年前的东汉时期，面条就已成为中国人民喜爱的食物。因地区的不同，面条形成了若干颇具地方特色的系列。在诸多面条种类中，炸酱面的影响最大，被誉为“中国十大面条”之一。炸酱面主要流行于京津冀地区，上海、广东、东北也有不同制法的炸酱面。大约在 1882 年，当时驻扎在韩国仁川的清军中的山东人，又将炸酱面带入韩国，很快成为了当地的主流食物。不过要说味道最正宗，那还要属老北京炸酱面。

作为一道北京传统小吃，炸酱面最初源自老北京胡同一家专门以面条为主的老字号面馆，现已成为京津地区的饮食文化符号。其特点是酱香浓郁。老北京人吃炸酱面有讲究，冷天讲究吃热的，谓之“锅儿挑”（完全不过水），热天吃“过水面”，并滗尽汤水。传统上炸酱面用的是手擀面，这样煮出的面条才会筋道有嚼劲。

面码儿用的是时令蔬菜如黄瓜、香椿、豆芽、青豆、黄豆、红萝卜，切丝或切丁摆在面条上。酱讲究的是肉丁小碗干炸，肉要肥瘦相间。老北京炸酱面的灵魂是酱要用老字号的干黄酱，最讲究的是火候，筷子插到盛酱小碗里不倒，才算有了样儿。最后用海碗盛面，浇上炸酱，并且根据季节再佐以时令小菜的菜码儿。

词汇笔记

- **paste** [peɪst] *n.* a thick, soft moist substance, usually produced by mixing ingredients with a liquid 糊，糊状物
- **ubiquitous** [juːˈbɪkwɪtəs] *adj.* seeming to be everywhere or in several places at the

same time; very common 似乎无所不在的；十分普遍的

- **aromatic** [ˌærə'mætɪk] *adj.* having a pleasant and distinctive smell; fragrance 芳香的；香味的
- **shred** ['ʃred] *v.* to cut or tear something into small pieces 切碎；撕碎

Beijing Roast Duck 北京烤鸭

必用三句

1 Beijing Roast Duck, or Peking Duck, is one of the most celebrated dishes of Beijing cuisine with a long historical standing. 北京烤鸭是历史悠久的京菜最著名的代表之一。

2 The accompaniments are wrapped in a thin wheat-flour pancake, which is slathered with any of several savory sauces. 烤鸭最适合佐以黄瓜和大葱，蘸适量甜面酱，卷在荷叶饼里吃。

3 As a royal dish in the imperial age of ancient China, Beijing Roast Duck now finds its way to the dining-tables of ordinary people and has made trek westward. 随着社会的发展，北京烤鸭逐步由皇宫传到寻常百姓家，名扬海外。

双语赏析

Beijing Roast Duck, or Peking Duck, is one of the most celebrated dishes of Beijing cuisine with a long historical standing. The earliest written record of roast duck was found in *Shizhenlu* (A Collection of Delicacies) in the Northern and Southern Dynasties (420–589). The first Peking duck was roasted some time during the early 15th century, when it was a popular dish on imperial court menus of the Ming Dynasty (1368–1644). There are several restaurants devoted exclusively to the dish–Quanjude (since 1864) and Bianyifang (since 1416) being prime examples, both of which are time-honoured brands with several hundred years of history.

The authentic Beijing Roast Duck takes several days to prepare. It calls for a fatty bird called Peking duck bred specifically for the dish. After the bird is killed and dressed, air is forced between the skin and flesh to separate the skin from the meat. This insures that the skin is very crispy and the meat succulent. After the procedures such as removing the entrails, filling the belly up with water, and sugar coloring the skin, the bird is hung up to dry. Then the duck is roasted suspended in an oven, or hung over fire lit by the wood of fruit trees such as date, or pear till it becomes reddish brown with rich grease perspiring outside and has a nice odor. When served, the duck is always artfully sliced. The whole duck weighing two kilos must be sliced into exact 108 pieces and every piece has to be perfect with the complete layers of the meat and trimmed of excess fat. The duck is often sliced tableside and served alongside cucumbers and scallions. The accompaniments are wrapped in a thin wheat-flour pancake, which is slathered with any of several savory sauces. The remains of the duck bones will not go to waste. To complete the duck course, a duck bone soup with celery cabbage or wax gourd is served.

As a royal dish in the imperial age of ancient China, Beijing Roast Duck now finds its way to the dining-tables of ordinary people and has made trek westward. Braise-oven duck represented by Bianyifang and hooked duck represented by Quanjude have become the two main schools of Beijing Roast Duck. In 2008, both Bianyifang Roast Duck Technique and Quanjude Roast Duck Technique are rated as National Intangible Cultural Heritage.

北京烤鸭是历史悠久的京菜最著名的代表之一。早在南北朝（420—589）的《食珍录》中就有“炙鸭”的记载。而北京烤鸭可追溯至15世纪早期的明朝（1368—1644年），那时候这道菜是十分受欢迎的宫廷食品。在众多的北京烤鸭店中最知名的是两个中华老字号：全聚德（始于1864年）和便宜坊（始于1416年），这两家烤鸭店都已经有几百年的历史了。

正宗的北京烤鸭需要花几天时间进行准备。用料为优质肉食北京鸭，宰杀后，鸭坯要经过充气处理，使皮肉分离，以确保皮酥肉嫩。再经掏膛、灌肠、打色、晾坯等诸多环节，才可以入炉，以梨木或枣木等果木炭火，采用焖炉或挂炉方式烤制。

刚出炉的烤鸭色呈枣红，油光润泽，还飘逸着果木的清香。趁热上席，当客片下。一只 2 公斤重的鸭子，能片出 108 片为合格，每一片都要带皮带肉，肥瘦均匀。烤鸭最适合佐以黄瓜和大葱，蘸适量甜面酱，卷在荷叶饼里吃。最后以片过的鸭骨架加白菜或冬瓜熬汤，这一餐才算圆满。

随着社会的发展，北京烤鸭逐步由皇宫传到寻常百姓家，名扬海外。便宜坊为代表的焖炉烤鸭和全聚德为代表的挂炉烤鸭，已成为北京烤鸭著名的两大流派。在 2008，“便宜坊烤鸭技艺”和“全聚德烤鸭技艺”均被列入国家级非物质文化遗产。

词汇笔记

- **cuisine** [kwɪ'ziːn] *n.* the food served in a restaurant (usually an expensive one)（通常指昂贵的饭店中的）饭菜，菜肴
- **dress** [dres] *v.* clean and prepare (food, especially poultry or shellfish) for cooking or eating 清洗，准备（食物，尤其是家禽或水生有壳动物等）用于烹饪或食用
- **succulent** ['sʌkjələnt] *adj.* food, especially meat or vegetables, is juicy and good to eat 多汁味美的 [表赞许]
- **accompaniment** [ə'kʌmpənimənt] *n.* something that supplements or complements something else, especially food 配套物（尤指食物的伴随物）
- **intangible** [ɪn'tændʒəbl] *adj.* (of an asset or benefit) not constituting or represented by a physical object and of a value not precisely measurable（资产，利益）无形的

Pea Flour Cake 豌豆黄儿

必用三句

1 Pea Flour Cake is a sweet dense cake made of peas, one of the Thirteen Specialties of the traditional Beijing snacks, and a ceremonial dish eaten on the third day of March according to the Chinese lunar calender. 豌豆黄儿是黄豆做成的一种甜点，是北京小吃十三绝之一。按北京习俗，农历三月三要吃豌豆黄儿。

2 It shows light golden color but tastes sweet and refreshing with a super smooth, fudge-like texture that literally melts in the mouth. 它色泽浅黄，味道香甜，细腻纯净，入口即化。

3 The process of making Pea Flour Cake is very exquisite and strict. 豌豆黄的制作工艺十分讲究。

双语赏析

Pea Flour Cake is a sweet dense cake made of peas, one of the Thirteen Specialties of the traditional Beijing snacks, and a ceremonial dish eaten on the third day of March according to the Chinese lunar calender. It is a seasonal and festive snack often served at temple fairs, particularly during springtime. Pea Flour Cake was originally a snack of the common people, but it became a favorite of empress dowager Cixi (1835–1908) of Qing Dynasty. It shows light golden color but tastes sweet and refreshing with a super smooth, fudge-like texture that literally melts in the mouth.

Legend has it that one day the empress of Cixi was attracted by the sound of hawking coming from the street when she was resting at Jingxin Zhai in the North Sea Park. The empress was told by court eunuch that it was somebody selling the Pea Flour Cake. Cixi ordered the seller to come in. After a taste, she gave unstinted praise profusely and kept him to make the cake for her exclusively. Thus, Pea Flour Cake made its way to the royal court and became famous imperial snack.

The process of making Pea Flour Cake is very exquisite and strict. Stew peas until they are tender. Closely sieve it into paste and then add sugar and sweet-scented osmanthus. After it solidifies, cut it into small cubes, then pair it with haw jelly for the most pleasing appearance and taste. Nowadays, Fangshan restaurant, a restaurant specializing in cooking the imperial dishes, is notable for the royal Pea Flour Cake which is vastly different from those sold in the street. The common Pea Flour Cake is much simpler in production process and is made from boiled pea and jujube only and of course a lot more affordable.

豌豆黄儿是黄豆做成的一种甜点，是北京小吃十三绝之一。按北京习俗，农历三月三要吃豌豆黄儿。豌豆黄儿是民间典型的春令食品，常见于春季庙会上，原为民间小吃，后传入宫廷，因慈禧喜食而出名。它色泽浅黄，味道香甜，细腻纯净，入口即化。

据说，一天慈禧正坐在北海静心斋歇凉，忽听大街上传来敲打铜锣声和吆喝声，心里纳闷，忙问是干什么的，当值太监回禀是卖豌豆黄的。慈禧传令将此人叫进园来。慈禧尝罢，赞不绝口，并把此人留在宫中，专门为她做豌豆黄。从此，豌豆黄便成为宫廷名点。

豌豆黄的制作工艺十分讲究。将豌豆蒸软，捣成糊状，然后放糖和桂花。等它晾凉成型，切成菱形块，以金糕点缀，红黄相称，甚是诱人。如今，北京的豌豆黄儿有两种，一种是北海公园仿膳制作的所谓宫廷小吃，一种则是走街串巷的小贩出售的豌豆黄儿，这两种小吃有天壤之别。普通的豌豆黄儿制作工艺较简单，只用煮黄豆和枣，价格当然也更加低廉。

词汇笔记

- **ceremonial** [serɪ'moʊniəl] *adj.* Something that is ceremonial relates to a ceremony or is used in a ceremony. 仪式的；礼仪的
- **unstinted** [ʌn'stɪntɪd] *adj.* very generous 不吝惜的；没有限制的；足够的
- **osmanthus** [ɑːz'mænθəs] *n.* widely distributed genus of evergreen shrubs or trees of southern United States, Middle East, China and Japan 木樨属植物，桂花
- **jujube** ['dʒuˌdʒub] *n.* dark red edible fruits of a kind of spiny rhamnaceous trees 枣子

Jianbing Guozi 煎饼馃子

必用三句

1 In recent years, Jianbing Guozi has won its nation-wide popularity and international recognition for its complex, multi-layered flavour and texture. 近些年，煎饼馃子因为它丰富的口感，已经遍布全国各地，甚至走出了国门。

2 But locals in Tianjin stick steadfastly to the traditional mung bean version. 天津人依旧坚持用传统的绿豆面。

3 Jianbing Guozi of Tianjin style has been honored as the Municipal Intangible Cultural Heritage, which is the official recognition of its status as authentic. 天津地区的煎饼馃子已经申请成为了市级非物质文化遗产，这就相当于确定了天津煎饼馃子的正宗地位。

双语赏析

Jianbing Guozi is a famous snack in Tianjin. "Guo zi" refers to deep-fried dough sticks in some northern places in China. Jianbing Guozi is considered, by a large number of Chinese locals and international individuals, as a top choice of morning snack. It takes only several minutes to make and can be prepared on the spot at the request of the buyer. In recent years, Jianbing Guozi has won its nation-wide popularity and international recognition for its complex, multi-layered flavour and texture. Despite its national and international fame, it is difficult to find at a restaurant and only shows at a street food stall. Humble and affordable as it is, its making process is none the less meticulous.

It consists of mung bean flour crepe, an egg, deep-fried crackers (known as Bao Cui in Chinese). Spread flour paste evenly on a hot pan with one or two eggs, add sauces, finely chopped scallion, fermented bean curd, chilli sauce (optional) on the top. It tastes salty and savoury. Some places now offer fancier versions using soy bean flour or black bean flour, with a variety of stuffings. But locals in Tianjin stick steadfastly to the traditional mung bean version. The fried dough stick has be to freshly made to give a crunchy texture. For the finishing touch, always sprinkle finely chopped scallion rather than coriander.

The exact origin of Jianbing Guozi is unknown. As many believe Jianbing originated in Shandong province, it is suffice to say that Jianbing Guozi is the re-creation and modification of Jianbing by the native people in Tianjin. Jianbing Guozi of Tianjin style has been honored as the Municipal Intangible Cultural Heritage, which is the official recognition of its status as authentic. In March 2018, the Jianbing Guozi branch under the Tianjin Catering Industry Association was founded and issued the association standard of the Jianbing Guozi sector in Tianjin.

煎饼馃子（或煎饼果子）是天津人的小吃。在中国北方一些地方，"馃子"指油条。煎饼馃子在一大群中国人甚至外国人的早点里占据着不可动摇的位置。制作一套只需几分钟的时间，立等可取。近些年，煎饼馃子因为它丰富的口感，已经遍布全国各地，甚至走出了国门。煎饼馃子虽然出名，饭店酒楼里却吃不到，唯有在路边推着小车的商贩处，才能品味到。虽说平民至极，其制作过程却别有一番精致在其中。

它是由绿豆面薄饼、鸡蛋还有油条或者薄脆的"馃箅儿"组成。将面糊均匀地摊在一面热煎锅上，打上一至两个鸡蛋，配以面酱、葱末、腐乳、辣椒酱（可选）作为佐料，口感咸香。如今的煎饼馃子原料已经不仅限于绿豆面摊成的薄饼，还有黄豆面、黑豆面等多种选择，不同地区加的料也不尽相同。但是，天津人依旧坚持用传统的绿豆面。卷在煎饼里面的馃子一定是当天新炸的，香酥可口。最后，一定要撒上细细的香葱末，而不是香菜末。

煎饼馃子的起源不可考。许多人认为煎饼起源于山东，所以煎饼馃子应该是天津人民的"二次创作"。如今，天津地区的煎饼馃子已经申请成为了市级非物质文化遗产，这就相当于确定了天津煎饼馃子的正宗地位。2018 年 3 月，天津市餐饮行业协会煎饼馃子分会正式成立，为天津煎饼馃子制定了团体标准。

词汇笔记

- **meticulous** [mə'tɪkjələs] *adj.* If you describe someone as meticulous, you mean that they do things very carefully and with great attention to detail. 小心谨慎的

- **ferment** [fər'ment] *n.* If a food, drink, or other natural substance ferments, or if it is fermented, a chemical change takes place in it so that alcohol is produced. This process forms part of the production of alcoholic drinks such as wine and beer. 使发酵；发酵
- **crunchy** ['krʌntʃi] *adj.* pleasantly hard or crisp so that it makes a noise when you eat it 脆的 [表赞许]
- **coriander** [ˌkɔːri'ændər] *n.* a plant with seeds that are used as a spice and leaves that are used as an herb 芫荽（香菜）
- **authentic** [ɔː'θentɪk] *adj.* of undisputed origin 正宗的

Go Believe/Goubuli Baozi 狗不理包子

必用三句

1 The legendary Go Believe or Goubuli Baozi (steamed buns) is a Tianjin delicacy, the premier snack among the three unique special foods of Tianjin. “狗不理包子”是驰名中外的天津特产食品，为“天津三绝”之首。

2 Thin skinned but fully stuffed, it tastes rich and savoury, tender and succulent, meaty but not greasy. 薄皮大馅，口味醇香，鲜嫩适口，肥而不腻。

3 Officials, with the help of netizens, decided to give it a less canine English name – “Go Believe” – in order to appeal to foreign guests, as well as boost its international popularity and pave way for the overseas market. 热心网民给狗不理起了个好听的洋名字“Go Believe”，不但大大方便了每天接待外宾，也提高了狗不理的国际知名度，为狗不理走出国门发展奠定了坚实的基础。

双语赏析

The legendary Go Believe or Goubuli Baozi (steamed buns) is a Tianjin delicacy, the premier snack among the three unique special foods of Tianjin. It is one of China’s time-honored brands with a history of more than 150 years.

Goubuli Baozi was honored as the National Intangible Cultural Heritage in 2011.

Goubuli Baozi is a snack made of wheat flour and pork stuffing. Thin skinned but fully stuffed, it tastes rich and savoury, tender and succulent, meaty but not greasy. What makes its making special is the semi-leavened dough and stuffing that is thoroughly mixed with water. Besides the thin and chewy skin, the meat filling is finely chopped and mixed with ginger, soy sauce, sesame oil and rib broth. The bun is chrysanthemum shaped and turns out exactly 18 creases on each bun that are well proportioned. Folklore suggests that "Ju De Hao", the store that first sold Goubuli Baozi, was started in 1858 by Gao Guiyou, a young man with the nickname Gouzi, which means "little doggy" in Chinese. Because of the excellent workmanship and generous quantities, his restaurant quickly became popular and attracted many customers. Such was Gao's popularity that he was always busy making and selling his steamed buns that he did not even have time to talk to his customers. People joked that "doggy" sold buns and heeded nobody. Overtime the steamed buns acquired the name Goubuli, which means a dog that refuses to respond.

Since Goubuli Baozi is served at state banquets honoring the State leaders and visiting politicians each year, as well as the growing numbers of overseas tourists especially since the reform and opening-up, it takes quite some work as to the name-explaining. Officials, with the help of netizens, decided to give it a less canine English name – "Go Believe" – in order to appeal to foreign guests, as well as boost its international popularity and pave way for the overseas market.

"狗不理包子"是驰名中外的天津特产食品，为"天津三绝"之首，是中华老字号之一，距今已有150多年的历史。2011年，"狗不理包子传统手工制作技艺"列入国家级非物质文化遗产名录。

狗不理包子是一道由面粉、猪肉等材料制作而成的小吃，薄皮大馅，口味醇香，鲜嫩适口，肥而不腻。狗不理包子的特殊之处在于采用"半发面，水打馅"的制作工艺。皮子薄而有韧性；馅以精肉剁细，加入姜、酱油、香油、排骨汤等。做出的包子外形美观，特别是包子褶花匀称，每个包子都有18个褶，个个呈菊花状。"狗不理"包子铺原名"德聚号"，始创于公元1858年（清朝咸丰年间），店主高贵友的乳名叫“狗子”。因“狗子”卖包子精致且从不掺假，非常受远近食客欢迎，高贵友经常忙得顾不上与顾客说话，故得名“狗不理”包子。

狗不理每年都要接待很多国家领导人和外国政要，尤其是改革开放以来，接待了大量的海外游客，有时给外宾解释狗不理的名字很困难。后来，热心网民给狗不理起了个好听的洋名字“Go Believe”，不但大大方便了每天接待外宾，也提高了狗不理的国际知名度，为狗不理走出国门发展奠定了坚实的基础。

词汇笔记

- **succulent** ['sʌkjələnt] *adj.* Succulent food, especially meat or vegetables, is juicy and good to eat. 多汁味美的 [表赞许]
- **chrysanthemum** [krɪ'zænθəməm; krɪ'sænθəməm] *n.* A chrysanthemum is a large garden flower with many long, thin petals. 菊花
- **heed** [hiːd] *v.* If you heed someone's advice or warning, you pay attention to it and do what they suggest. 注意；听从 [正式]
- **canine** ['keɪnaɪn] *adj.* relating to dogs 犬的

Tianjin Mahua/Fried Dough Twists 天津大麻花

必用三句

1 Mahua or Fried Dough Twists, one of the Three Delicacies in Tianjin besides Goubuli Baozi, and Erduoyan fried rice cake, has been honored as one of the Chinese famous snacks at the first “Chinese Snack Food Assessment Conference”. 天津大麻花与狗不理包子、耳朵眼炸糕并称“津门三绝”，在全国首届名小吃认定会上被认定为“中华名小吃”。

2 Guifaxiang brand, founded in 1927, was appraised as “China's Time-honored Brand” and was included in the List of Representative Items of National Intangible Cultural Heritage, a well-deserved “tour de force” of the city. 诞生于 1927 年的桂发祥十八街麻花，既为“中华老字号”，又入选“国家级非物质文化遗产代表性项目名录”，是当之无愧的城市旅游特产名片。

3 Mahua tastes aromatic, sweet, and crunchy. It can be stored for up to three months without going stale or losing its crunchiness. 炸制出来的麻花香、甜、酥、脆，放置3个月不走味，不绵软，不变质。

双语赏析

Mahua or Fried Dough Twists, one of the Three Delicacies in Tianjin besides Goubuli Baozi, and Erduoyan fried rice cake, has been honored as one of the Chinese famous snacks at the first "Chinese Snack Food Assessment Conference". Out of the many shops that sell Mahua, Guifaxiang is the most renowned one. Guifaxiang brand, founded in 1927, was appraised as "China's Time-honored Brand" and was included in the List of Representative Items of National Intangible Cultural Heritage, a well-deserved "tour de force" of the city. Guifaxiang Mahua is also called the 18th Street Mahua as the original store was situated in the 18th Street. The museum of Mahua is located in Tianjin's Hexi district, where you can learn about the history of the fried food and get a glimpse of how it is made on the production line.

The 18th Street Mahua is the product of inheritance and innovation. It maintains the traditional craftsmanship such as leavened dough, boiled sugar syrup, hot oil blanching, cubic sugar filling. Mahua comprises the fried plain dough stripe, the sesame stripe and the crunchy filling stripe made of sesame, peach kernel, sunflower seeds, green prune, osmanthus, ginger, candied melon, shredded orange skin, and etc. It takes a dozen of procedures before it is done. Mahua tastes aromatic, sweet, and crunchy. It can be stored for up to three months without going stale or losing its crunchiness. Thus it is a perfect souvenir for tourists to bring the taste of Tianjin home to their friends and relatives.

天津大麻花与狗不理包子、耳朵眼炸糕并称“津门三绝”，在全国首届名小吃认定会上被认定为“中华名小吃”。在出售麻花的店铺里，最有名的要数诞生于1927年的桂发祥十八街麻花，既为“中华老字号”，又入选“国家级非物质文化遗产代表性项目名录”，是当之无愧的城市旅游特产名片。因最初店铺坐落于十八街，人们又习惯称其为十八街麻花。天津的河西区有一个麻花博物馆，在那里可以了解油炸食品的历史，并能亲眼见到它的生产线。

十八街麻花经过反复探索进行创新，制作技艺具有选料精细、工艺考究的传统，出色地运用面肥发面、熬糖提浆、热油烫酥、糖粒拌馅等传统工艺技能，在白条和麻条中间夹一条含有芝麻、桃仁、瓜子仁、青梅、桂花、闽姜、瓜条、青红丝等小料做的酥条，经过 20 多道关键工序精制而成。炸制出来的麻花香、甜、酥、脆，放置 3 个月不走味，不绵软，不变质。来天津旅游的宾客，临走时都要带上几盒桂发祥十八街麻花，送亲朋好友。

词汇笔记

- **tour de force** [ˌtʊr də ˈfɔrs] *n.* If you call something such as a performance, speech, or production a tour de force, you are emphasizing that it is extremely good or extremely well done or made. 杰作 [强调]
- **inheritance** [ɪnˈherɪtəns] *n.* An inheritance is money or property that you receive from someone who has died. 继承物；遗产
- **aromatic** [ˌærəˈmætɪk] *adj.* An aromatic plant or food has a strong, pleasant smell of herbs or spices. 芳香的

Chapter 03

The Cuisine in the Mid-North and Northwest Region

中北及西北地区饮食

The Dietary Culture of the Mid-North and Northwest Region

中北及西北地区饮食文化

In the vast central and northwest China, people's diet is generally based on beef and lamb, dairy products, poultry, and wheat flour as raw materials, supplemented by baking, fermentation, and other cooking techniques, resulting in a unique taste, and suitable for the young and old. Due to the full swing of the development of the western region in China, the communication among people in the central and northwestern region and other areas has been becoming more and more frequent, the mouth-watering delicacies being more popular all over China. The most representative region in the northwest is Xinjiang, which is an ethnic area. Thirteen ethnic groups have long lived here. Each ethnic group has a rich and unique food culture, which distinctly reflects the characteristics of Xinjiang's agricultural and pastoral areas and multi-ethnic groups.

Because of the drought and lack of rainfall, the temperature difference has resulted in a small variety and quantity of vegetables, making Xinjiang a food culture based on beef and mutton. Therefore, when you come to Xinjiang, don't miss the delicious beef and lamb-based cuisine and all kinds of noodles.

在我国幅员辽阔的中西北地区，人们的饮食普遍以牛羊肉、奶制品、家禽、小麦面粉为原料，辅以烤制、发酵等烹饪技巧，口味独特，老少皆宜。随着西部大开发的深入开展，中西北地区的人们与其他地区的人员流动日趋频繁，很多饮食也日趋受到全国人民的喜爱。西北地区最具代表性的是新疆，它是一个多民族聚居区。13个民族长期居住在这里。每个民族都有着丰富而又独特的饮食文化，这些饮食文化鲜明地反映了新疆农牧区和多民族的特色。

新颖因干旱少雨，温差大，蔬菜的品种少、数量少，形成了以牛、羊肉为主的饮食文化。因此来新疆一定不要错过以牛羊肉为原料的美食以及面食。

Xinjiang Roast Whole Lamb 新疆烤全羊*

必用三句

1 Roast Whole Lamb is a flavourful food for Uygur people in Hotan and Kashgar, and has the characteristics of golden color, tender meat, fat but not greasy, which can be compared with Beijing Roast Duck and Guangdong Crispy Suckling Pig. 烤全羊是和田、喀什等地维吾尔族人民的一种风味食品，具有色泽金黄、肉质鲜嫩、肥而不腻的特点，可与北京烤鸭、广东脆皮乳猪相媲美。

2 Legend has it that a long time ago, merchants in the southern region of Xinjiang went out to do business by camel in caravans loaded with goods, back and forth across the Gobi Desert and carrying food to feed their hunger. 传说在很早以前，新疆南部地区的商人带着驼队、货物外出经商，往返跋涉于戈壁瀚海，携带干粮充饥。

3 In high class banquets, it can be served as a traditional local dish in Xinjiang, which is favored by Chinese and foreign guests. 在高档筵席中，烤全羊是新疆传统地方风味名菜，备受中外客人青睐。

双语赏析

Roast Whole Lamb is a flavourful food for Uygur people in Hotan and Kashgar, and has the characteristics of golden color, tender meat, fat but not greasy, which can be compared with Beijing Roast Duck and Guangdong Crispy Suckling Pig.

There are more than 50 varieties of sheep in Xinjiang, Its unique geography, climate, pasture and other environmental conditions make the meat of sheep pure and tasty. There are three kinds of famous sheep in Xinjiang, namely the Altai sheep in north of the Tianshan Mountains, the black-headed

* 注：中国许多地方都有烤全羊，尤以新疆、内蒙的最为正宗，因篇幅有限，在此仅介绍其中的一处。

sheep in south of the Tianshan Mountains and the Aydin Lake sheep in east of the Tianshan Mountains, from which Xinjiang Roast Lamb has derived three brands and each with its own characteristics.

Legend has it that a long time ago, merchants in the southern region of Xinjiang went out to do business by camel in caravans loaded with goods, back and forth across the Gobi Desert and carrying food to feed their hunger. On the way, when they came across a flock of sheep, they bought a few from herdsmen to treat themselves. Since cooking utensils were hard to find, they slaughtered the sheep and roasted them whole to eat. Later, they found that the lamb roasted in this way had a special flavor. After reaching the town, they still roasted the whole sheep and served it to the guests in the same way they did on the way. Over the years, the roasting method has been constantly improved.

Nowadays, business is most prosperous in the south of Xinjiang where this dish is sold. Xinjiang Roast Whole Lamb is not only a popular meal, but also a delicacy for Uygurs to entertain distinguished guests. In high-class banquets, it can be served as a traditional local dish in Xinjiang, which is favored by Chinese and foreign guests.

烤全羊是和田、喀什等地维吾尔族人民的一种风味食品，具有色泽金黄、肉质鲜嫩、肥而不腻的特点，可与北京烤鸭、广东脆皮乳猪相媲美。

新疆绵羊的品种就有 50 多个，因为其独特的地理、气候、草场等环境条件使得羊肉的肉质纯、味道正、口感好。新疆有闻名遐迩的三大名羊，即天山以北的阿勒泰大尾羊、天山以南的南疆黑头羊和天山以东的艾丁湖细毛羊，这三大优质品种的羊群使得新疆烤全羊派生出三大品牌，各具特色。

传说在很早以前，新疆南部地区的商人带着驼队、货物外出经商，往返跋涉于戈壁瀚海，携带干粮充饥。中途若遇到有羊群的部落，他们就向牧民买上几只羊，改善一下旅途生活。由于炊具难找，他们就只能将羊宰杀后，整只羊烤熟了吃。后来发现，这样烤出来的羊肉别有风味。到达城镇后，他们仍按途中烤制的方法用以招待客人。长年累月，烤制方法不断得到改进。

如今，在南疆的巴扎上哪里有烤全羊出售，哪里就生意最兴隆。新疆烤全羊不仅是老百姓喜爱的风味大餐，也仍然是维吾尔族人招待贵宾的上等佳肴。在高档筵席中，烤全羊是新疆传统地方风味名菜，备受中外客人青睐。

词汇笔记

- **flavourful** ['fleɪvəfʊl] *adj.* food that has a strong, pleasant taste and is good to eat 美味的
- **characteristic** [ˌkærəktə'rɪstɪk] *v.* a typical feature or quality that sth./sb. has 特征
- **tender** ['tendə(r)] *adj.* easy to bite through and cut 嫩的
- **utensil** [juː'tensəl] *v.* a tool that is used in the house （家庭）厨房用具
- **prosperous** ['prɒspərəs] *adj.* rich and successful 繁荣的
- **distinguished** [dɪ'stɪŋgwɪʃt] *adj.* having an appearance that makes sb. look important or that makes people admire or respect them 高贵的

The Xinjiang Market Chicken 新疆大盘鸡

必用三句

1 The Xinjiang Market Chicken is named after the large tea plates used to serve it. 新疆大盘鸡因其使用较大体积的茶盘盛放而得名。

2 It is an example of the perfect combination of regional and ethnic food cultures, as it brings together the cooking styles and eating habits of many provinces in the northwest. 大盘鸡可谓是博采众长，集合西北多省的烹饪方式和饮食习惯，是多地区和多民族饮食文化完美结合的典范。

3 It is an all-encompassing dish, reflecting a picture of multi-ethnic harmony and coexistence. 大盘鸡包罗万象，体现出多民族融洽共处，和睦和谐的画面。

The Xinjiang Market Chicken is named after the large tea plates used to serve it, and the dish is a good mix of meat and vegetables and can be served as a main course or with other ingredients. The main ingredients in this dish are chicken, potatoes and onions, and the dish is colourful, spicy, coarse but delicate, with a reasonable price and palatable. The potatoes thicken the soup and the onions neutralise the greasiness of the chicken. There are two types of chicken in Xinjiang: Shawan and Chaiwobao. Shawan Chicken comes with a thick soup that can be enjoyed with belt noodles (shape of a belt); Chaiwobao Chicken is made by fried chicken pieces in oil and then dry-frying them with hot peppers for a chewy texture.

It is an example of the perfect combination of regional and ethnic food cultures, as it brings together the cooking styles and eating habits of many provinces in the northwest. The chicken is usually made from Three Yellow Chickens or drumsticks to ensure that the meat is tender and tasty, nourishing the body, warming the spleen and nourishing the blood. Onions are an essential accompaniment to remove the greasiness and the smell of the meat, and because they are full of sulphur compounds, they have an antiseptic effect.

It is an all-encompassing dish, reflecting a picture of multi-ethnic harmony and coexistence. When combined with broad noodles, it can become Big Plate Chicken Noodles, a similar dish to Lanzhou Ramen, presenting a unique taste of the northwest. And it can absorb the fresh and spicy flavours of the dish, forming a powerful echo of the side dishes, achieving a clever match between vegetarian and oily, fresh, spicy and sweet.

双语赏析

新疆大盘鸡因其使用较大体积的茶盘盛放而得名，其荤素搭配适宜，既能够作为主食，也可以与其他的食材搭配。制作大盘鸡主要的原材料有鸡肉、土豆、洋葱，成菜色泽鲜艳，辣中带香，粗中有细，并且价格实惠，令人大快朵颐。土豆可以增加汤汁的浓稠，洋葱能够中和鸡肉的油腻。新疆大盘鸡分为沙湾大盘鸡和柴窝堡大盘鸡两种，沙湾大盘鸡带有浓稠的汤汁，可以伴随着皮带面一起享受。柴窝堡大盘鸡是将鸡块用油炸透之后，用朝天椒干炒而成，口感更加有嚼劲。

大盘鸡可谓是博采众长，集合西北多省的烹饪方式和饮食习惯，是多地区和多民族饮食文化完美结合的典范。大盘鸡选取的鸡肉通常是三黄鸡或者鸡腿肉，以保障肉质鲜嫩、滋味鲜美，有滋补身体、温中补脾、益气养血之功效。洋葱是必不可少的辅料，能够解除肉的油腻，去掉肉的腥味，并且因为饱含硫化合物，能够起到杀菌的作用。

大盘鸡包罗万象，体现出多民族融洽共处，和睦和谐的画面。若和宽面结合，就能变成大盘鸡面，成为兰州拉面的姊妹花，呈现出独特的西北风土人情味。此外，大盘鸡面能够吸收菜品中的鲜辣味道，形成有力的配菜呼应，满足互补的原理，在素淡与油腻、鲜辣与甜甘之间达到巧妙的搭配。

词汇笔记

- **coarse** [kɔːs] *adj.* crude or undefined in taste （食物，饮料）粗劣的
- **reasonable** ['riːznəbl] *adj.* (of prices) not too expensive （价格）公道的
- **neutralise** ['njuːtrəlaɪz] *vt.* to make a substance neutral 中和
- **all-encompassing** [ˌɔːl ɪn'kʌmpəsɪŋ] *adj.* (formal) including everything 包罗万象的
- **vegetarian** [ˌvedʒə'teəriən] *adj.* of or relating to the exclusion of meat or other animal products from the diet 素食的，素的

Lanzhou Beef Ramen 兰州牛肉拉面

必用三句

1 Lanzhou Beef Ramen was originally a specialty for high-ranking guests of the nomads in the northwest. 兰州牛肉拉面原为西北游牧民族招待高级宾客之风味食品。

2 Lanzhou Beef Ramen has realized the unity and harmony of color, aroma, taste and shape of Chinese diet. 兰州牛肉拉面实现了中国饮食的色、香、味、形的统一与和谐。

3 In 1999, it was identified as one of the pilot promotion brands of Chinese fast food, and was hailed as “the first Chinese noodle”. 1999 年兰州牛肉拉面被确定为中式快餐试点推广品牌之一，被誉为“中华第一面”。

双语赏析

Lanzhou Beef Ramen was originally a specialty for high-ranking guests of the nomads in the northwest. The authentic Lanzhou Beef Ramen is widely believed to have originated in 1915 from Ma Baozi. He then went to great length to work out ways to make the broth light and clear, the taste strong and savory, to provide high quality service and operate on the basis of credibility and sincerity. Gradually Lanzhou Beef Ramen became famous around the city, and enjoyed the reputation of "Getting off the horse to taste, Getting the taste with no waste".

With its unique style of "clear and bright soup, tender and fragrant meat, thin and long noodles", Lanzhou Beef Ramen has featured something pure, something white, something red, and something green (i.e. clear soup, white radish, red spicy oil, green garlic seedlings). It has realized the unity and harmony of color, aroma, taste and shape of Chinese diet.

In its subsequent development for more than 100 years, Lanzhou Beef Ramen has gradually spread nationwide and even worldwide with its own refined quality and unique taste, and has been widely praised. In 1999, it was identified as one of the pilot promotion brands of Chinese fast food, and was hailed as "the first Chinese noodle".

Nowadays, new varieties of Lanzhou Beef Ramen have been developed, such as Braised Beef Ramen and Pickled Beef Ramen, to meet people's pursuit and enjoyment of material life. Lanzhou Beef Ramen has inherited the essence of traditional Beef Ramen, but also has been able to keep up with the times and optimize its development in accordance with modern fast food concepts, thus enabling this snack to flourish. Lanzhou Beef Ramen holds its own without lack of vitality, and adds a taste of happiness to people's lives.

兰州牛肉拉面原为西北游牧民族招待高级宾客之风味食品。正宗的兰州牛肉拉面普遍认为是起源于 1915 年一个叫马保子的人，他在“清”字上下工夫，在“味”字上谋发展，在“质”字上求实效，在“信”字上拓市场，直到兰州牛肉拉面名镇四方，享有“闻香下马，知味停车”的称誉。

兰州牛肉拉面以其“汤清而亮、肉烂而香、面细而长”的独特风格，创出了“一清、二白、三红、四绿”（即清汤、白萝卜、红辣油、绿蒜苗）的汤面口味。它实现了中国饮食的色、香、味、形的统一与和谐。

在其以后发展的 100 多年以来，兰州牛肉拉面凭借自身精良的品质、独特的味道逐渐在全国打开局面，甚至在全世界都有一定的影响力，得到广泛好评。1999 年兰州牛肉拉面被确定为中式快餐试点推广品牌之一，被誉为“中华第一面”。

如今兰州牛肉拉面也逐渐拓展新的品种，如红烧牛肉拉面、酸菜牛肉拉面等从而满足人们对于物质生活的追求与享受。兰州牛肉拉面既继承了传统牛肉拉面的精华，又能够与时俱进按照现代快餐理念优化发展，从而使得这一小吃发扬光大。兰州牛肉拉面沉稳而又不缺乏活力地守住了自己的一片天地，也为人们的生活增添了幸福的滋味。

词汇笔记

- **authentic** [ɔːˈθentɪk] *adj.* true and accurate 真正的
- **fragrant** [ˈfreɪgrənt] *adj.* having a pleasant smell 香的
- **subsequent** [ˈsʌbsɪkwənt] *adj.* happening or coming after sth. else 随后的
- **pilot** [ˈpaɪlət] *adj.* done on a small scale in order to see if sth. is successful enough to do on a large scale 试点的
- **inherit** [ɪnˈherɪt] *v.* to receive money, property, etc. from sb. when they die 继承（金钱、财产等）
- **optimize** [ˈɒptɪmaɪz] *v.* to make sth. as good as it can be; to use sth. in the best possible way 使最优化

Beef Jerky 牛肉干

必用三句

1 Beef Jerky is one of the specialties of the Mongolian people. 牛肉干是蒙古族特色食品之一。

2 The importance of Beef Jerky to the Mongols is self-evident, as it was used as military food in wartime and as a snack in normal times. 牛肉干对于蒙古人的重要性不言而喻，战时作军粮，平时作零食。

3 There are many different types of Beef Jerky, including spicy, air-dried ones and dressed with sauce, each of which brings out a different flavour. 牛肉干的种类繁多，常见的有麻辣的，风干的以及凉拌的，每种做法都能够激发牛肉不一样的口味。

双语赏析

Beef Jerky is one of the specialties of the Mongolian people. It is popular because of its aromatic flavour, chewy texture and well-preserved nutrition, and can also be used for entertaining guests, major festivals or weddings and funerals. Beef Jerky is usually made from dried yellow beef marinated with other seasonings.

The Mongolian people have been drying jerky since ancient times and it can date back to the time of the Mongolian Empire, founded by Genghis Khan. In those days, Mongol horsemen carried jerky on their backs as marching rations, thus ensuring that they would be brave and powerful in battles and that they would be lightly armed and thus could be invincible. Dried beef played an important role in the Mongolian expedition and was therefore known as “Genghis Khan’s food for the expedition”. The importance of Beef Jerky to the Mongols is self-evident, as it was used as military food in wartime and as a snack in normal times.

Beef is the second most popular meat in China, with a high protein content, low-fat content and a delicious flavour, providing a wide range of minerals and amino acids and sarcosine needed by the human body, which are important for muscle growth and recovery, and for strengthening the body. According to the theory of Chinese medicine, beef is also an important part of the Chinese medicinal diet, as it can nourish the spleen and benefit the stomach, relieve phlegm and stop thirst and salivation.

There are many different types of Beef Jerky, including spicy, air-dried and cold, each of which brings out a different flavour. Because it does not deteriorate over time and can be easily transported over long distances, Beef Jerky has been sold throughout the country and has become a popular souvenir for travel, as a gift to friends and relatives, and as an accompaniment to wine.

牛肉干是蒙古族特色食品之一，因其肉香四溢，嚼劲十足，营养得到充分保留等特点，深受广大群众的喜欢。牛肉干也可以用于招待贵客、重大节日或者婚丧嫁娶。牛肉干一般是用黄牛肉和其他调料一起腌制而成的肉干。

蒙古族自古以来就有晾晒牛肉干的习俗，并且牛肉干的历史可以追溯到成吉思汗建立蒙古帝国时期。那时候蒙古铁骑将牛肉干作为行军粮背在身上，从而保障自己的作战更加勇猛有力，轻装上阵，无往而不胜。风干牛肉干在远征作战中起着很重要作用，因此被誉为"成吉思汗的远征军粮"。牛肉干对于蒙古人的重要性自然不言而喻，战时作军粮，平时作零食。

牛肉是中国的第二大肉类食品，其蛋白质含量高，脂肪含量较低，味道鲜美，能够提供人身体所需要的多种矿物质和氨基酸、肌氨酸，对肌肉的增长与恢复、强健体魄有着重要的作用。按照中医的理论，牛肉还能够补中益气、化痰息风、止渴止涎等，实属中医药膳的重要组成部分。

牛肉干的种类繁多，常见的有麻辣的、风干的以及凉拌的，每种做法都能够激发牛肉不一样的口味。因为其久存不变质，便于长途运输，牛肉干已经可以销售至全国，并且成为人们旅游纪念、馈赠亲朋、下酒佐食的佳肴美味。

词汇笔记

- **jerky** ['dʒɜːki] *v.* meat that has been cut into long strips and smoked or dried 干肉条；熏肉条
- **entertain** [ˌentə'teɪn] *v.* to invite people to eat or drink with you as your guests, especially in your home 招待，请客
- **seasoning** ['siːzənɪŋ] *v.* a substance used to add flavour to food, especially salt and pepper 调味品；佐料
- **expedition** [ˌekspə'dɪʃən] *v.* an organized journey with a particular purpose,

especially to find out about a place 远征，考察

- **medicinal** [mə'dɪsɪnl] *adj.* helpful in the process of healing illness or infection 药用的，有疗效的

Milk Tofu 奶豆腐

必用三句

1 Milk Tofu is a common dairy product in Mongolian homes. 奶豆腐是蒙古族同胞家中常见的奶制品。

2 This cuisine, which has been handed down through thousands of years of history, is a conglomeration of the ages. 这种经历千百年历史传承的美食是岁月的凝结。

3 With a bite of Milk Tofu, one can't help but think of the ancient people who lived by the water and grass, galloping their horses across the grasslands, bringing endless comfort and hope as they continued to migrate. 吃上一口奶豆腐，令人不禁遐想古代人们逐水草而居，策马奔腾在草原上，不断迁徙的路上，奶豆腐给他们带来无尽的安慰和期望。

双语赏析

Milk Tofu is a common dairy product in Mongolian homes, usually made from coagulated and fermented milk of cows, goats and horses, and is named after its resemblance to ordinary tofu. It tastes either slightly sour or slightly sweet, with a rich, creamy flavour, and is loved by herders as a ready-to-eat food or as a solid food for traveling. It can quench both thirst and hunger, and can also be made into Shredded Milk Tofu, which is a popular dish at banquets.

The nutritional value of Milk Tofu, which is rich in trace elements and amino acids, is widely recognized and proven in academic circles. With the great pursuit of health and material well-being, Milk Tofu is becoming more and more well-received for its unique flavour and its healthy, all-natural characteristics. This cuisine, which has been handed down through thousands of years of history, is a conglomeration of the ages. With a bite of Milk Tofu, one can't help but think of the ancient people who lived by the water and grass, galloping their horses across the grasslands, bringing endless comfort and hope as they continued to migrate.

There are three main types of traditional handmade Milk Tofu: cooked Milk Tofu, Raw Milk Tofu and Curd Milk Tofu. The moulds used to make Milk Tofu come in different shapes, including peaches, pomegranates, mooncakes, fish, rectangles and squares, and some are decorated with delicate traditional ethnic patterns and floral designs, thus making Milk Tofu not only a food, but also imbued with a certain artistic component, showing the people's wisdom and positive and optimistic spirit. The seemingly simple Milk Tofu can be a surprise to the taste buds, a reflection and taste of the original taste of ordinary life.

奶豆腐是蒙古族同胞家中常见的奶制品，通常是由牛奶、羊奶、马奶等经过凝固、发酵而成，因其形状像普通的豆腐而得名。味道微微发酸，或者微微发甜，奶香浓郁，深得牧民喜爱，既可以作为即食食品，也可以作为出远门时的干粮。它既能够解渴又能够充饥，还可以做成拔丝奶豆腐，是人们在宴席上的一道风味名菜。

奶豆腐的营养相当丰富，富含多种微量元素以及氨基酸，其营养价值得到了人们的普遍认可，同时也在学术界得到证实。随着人们对于养生以及物质生活的极大追求，奶豆腐以其独特的风味、健康纯天然的特点，越来越受到欢迎。这种经历千百年历史传承的美食是岁月的凝结。吃上一口奶豆腐，令人不禁遐想古代人们逐水草而居，策马奔腾在草原上，不断迁徙的路上，奶豆腐给他们带来无尽的安慰和希望。

传统的手工制作的奶豆腐主要有三种：熟奶豆腐、生奶豆腐和凝乳奶豆腐。做奶豆腐的模具形状各异，有桃形、石榴形、月饼形、鱼形、长方形和正方形，有的还配有精致的民族传统图案、花纹等，从而使得奶豆腐不仅是一种食物，也被赋予了一定的艺术成分，彰显出人们的智慧和积极乐观的精神风貌。看似简单的奶豆腐能够给人们的味蕾带来冲击和惊喜，是对平凡生活原汁原味的体现和品味。

词汇笔记

- **resemblance** [rɪ'zembləns] *v.* the fact of being or looking similar to sb./sth. 相似，相像
- **quench** [kwentʃ] *v.* to drink so that you no longer feel thirsty（喝水）止（渴）
- **shred** [ʃred] *v.* to cut or tear sth. into small pieces（撕或切的）细条
- **trace** [treɪs] *v.* a very small amount of sth. 微量，少许
- **imbue** [ɪm'bjuː] *vt.* to fill sb./sth. with strong feelings, opinions or values 灌输；使感染；使渗透

Mutton Eaten with Hands 手抓羊肉

必用三句

1 Mutton Eaten with Hands is a medicinal diet made from the flank of mutton and coriander as the main ingredients. 手抓羊肉是以羊腰窝肉，香菜为主料制作的药膳。

2 It is sacred and crazy for an absolute carnivore traveler to eat Tan sheep of Ningxia, the best mutton, in various ways. 对一个纯肉食旅行者来说，在宁夏吃滩羊肉，吃最好的羊肉，以各种方式吃羊肉，是件既神圣又疯狂的事。

3 Ningxia in winter will treat the stomach and tongue of any traveler very well, just because there is the best Mutton Eaten with Hands here! 冬天的宁夏，不会亏待任何旅人的胃和舌头，只因为这里有最好的手抓羊肉。

双语赏析

With a history of nearly a thousand years, Mutton Eaten with Hands whose name comes from the way of eating with hands is a well-known dish of the Hui people. Mutton Eaten with Hands is widely spread in Ningxia, Gansu and other places, and is called "shou zhua" for short in Ningxia.

Mutton Eaten with Hands is a medicinal diet made from the flank of mutton and coriander as the main ingredients. Most parts of China have a tradition of cooking mutton, and the unique features of the local environment give special characteristics to the flavor of the mutton. Almost all Chinese foodies agree that mutton in Ningxia has the best texture. Ningxia is an autonomous region of the Hui people, where religious characteristics and eating habits make the people here very keen to eat mutton, and they are also very good at cooking mutton.

Mutton of Ningxia is famous for its fresh taste, tender meat, and no muttony odour, and this is the fundamental reason why the mutton of Ningxia tastes so good. Tan Sheep of Ningxia is recognized for its tasty meat, no muttony odour, and excellent taste, which has enhanced the requirement of the Ningxia people for eating mutton. Therefore, Mutton Eaten with Hands of Ningxia is usually picked from free-range Tan sheep and it is really enjoyable to eat together with the meat and bones. Mutton Eaten with Hands is produced all over Ningxia, and Mutton Eaten with Hands of Wuzhong and Yinchuan is the most famous, both of which are selected as "Chinese Muslim Famous Snacks". Mutton Eaten with Hands, as a special snack of Wuzhong, which appeared in the sixth episode of season two of *A Bite of China* has become well-known all over the country. In September 2018, Mutton Eaten with Hands was rated as one of the top ten classic dishes in Ningxia.

Mutton Eaten with Hands is also a boon for travel lovers. It is sacred and crazy for an absolute carnivore traveler to eat Tan sheep of Ningxia, the best mutton, in various ways.

Mutton is an indispensable nourishing food in winter, and the most suitable season to eat mutton is winter. Ningxia in winter will treat the stomach and tongue of any traveler very well, just because there is the best Mutton Eaten with Hands here!

手抓羊肉是回族食品中一道有名的美食，有近千年的历史，原以手抓食用而得名，广泛流传于宁夏、甘肃等地，而手抓羊肉在宁夏简称“手抓”。

手抓羊肉是以羊腰窝肉，香菜为主料制作的药膳。中国大部分地区都有烹饪羊肉的传统，各方水土也造就了羊肉风味上的差异。而几乎所有中国的美食家都认为，宁夏的羊肉质地最佳。宁夏是回族自治区，宗教特性和饮食习惯使得这里的人非常热衷吃羊肉，也极其擅长烹饪羊肉。

宁夏羊肉以味鲜、肉嫩、不膻而闻名，而这也是宁夏羊肉味道好的最根本原因。其中宁夏滩羊，以公认的肉质鲜美、无腥膻味和极佳的口感提升了宁夏人在吃羊肉这件事上的高度。因此宁夏的手抓羊肉通常选用散养滩羊，连肉带骨一起啃，非常过瘾。

宁夏手抓羊肉在宁夏区内各地均有制作，尤以吴忠手抓羊肉和银川手抓羊肉最为出名。两地的手抓羊肉均入选“中华清真名小吃”，尤其是吴忠特色小吃手抓羊肉曾在《舌尖上的中国》第二季第六集亮相，闻名全国。2018 年 9 月，手抓羊肉被评为宁夏十大经典名菜。

手抓羊肉也是旅行爱好者的福音。对一个纯肉食旅行者来说，在宁夏吃滩羊肉，吃最好的羊肉，以各种方式吃羊肉，是件既神圣又疯狂的事。

羊肉是冬季不可或缺的滋补食品，最适宜吃羊肉的季节便是冬天了。冬天的宁夏，不会亏待任何旅人的胃和舌头，只因为这里有最好的手抓羊肉！

词汇笔记

- **coriander** [ˌkɒriˈændər] *n.* a plant whose leaves are used in cooking as a herb and whose seeds are used in cooking as a spice 香菜
- **foodie** [ˈfuːdi] *n.* a person who is very interested in cooking and eating different kinds of food 美食家；吃货
- **texture** [ˈtekstʃər] *n.* the way food or drink tastes or feels in your mouth, for example whether it is rough, smooth, light, heavy, etc. 口感
- **odour** [ˈəʊdər] *n.* a smell, especially one that is unpleasant（尤指难闻的）气味，臭味
- **free-range** [ˌfriːˈreɪndʒ] *adj.* connected with a system of farming in which animals are kept in natural conditions and can move around freely（家禽）自由放养的
- **carnivore** [ˈkɑːnɪvɔːr] *n.* any animal that eats meat 喜欢吃肉的人，食肉动物（诙谐说法）

Qinghai Niang Pi 青海酿皮

必用三句

1 Niang Pi is a traditional snack with a strong local flavor in Qinghai. 酿皮是青海地方风味较浓的一种传统小吃。

2 Niang Pi has a lot of fans, and people of all ages love eating it. 酿皮拥趸极多，男女老少都爱吃。

3 It can be said that Niang Pi is a snack which means all ethnic groups live in harmony, integrate with each other and develop together. It is also a delicious delicacy that embodies the centripetal force. 可以说，酿皮是各民族和睦相处、相互融合、共同发展的一道小吃，是一道凝聚着向心力的美味小吃。

双语赏析

Niang Pi is a traditional snack with a strong local flavor in Qinghai.

The texture of Niang Pi is like jelly and is thick, dark brown or light white in color. Add gluten, pour over vinegar, chili oil, mustard, leeks, garlic puree and other seasoning and it tastes sour and spicy, refreshing and appetizing, supported by a soft and delicate taste and a long finish.

Niang Pi has a lot of fans, and people of all ages love eating it. In Qinghai and the surrounding areas, people from different regions who have different beliefs all like this snack, and especially for those who like drinking, Niang Pi is an indispensable food. The business selling Niang Pi is booming all year round, especially in summer. Although Niang Pi is a snack, it can be used as a staple food to stave off starvation, or as a dish, to go with the wine, which is served hot and cold, and can be eaten in all seasons.

With its unique flavor, Niang Pi has gently grabbed the hearts of diners and conquered the taste buds of them in the evolution of time. Today, Niang Pi stalls can be seen all over Qinghai, and Niang Pi shops dotted on the streets and alleys have their own flavors and unique tricks.

The local Han, Tibetan, Tu, Hui and other ethnic groups in Qinghai have traditional customs of making and eating Niang Pi. It can be said that Niang Pi is a snack which means all ethnic groups live in harmony, integrate with each other and develop together. It is also a delicious delicacy that embodies the centripetal force.

Whenever there are guests, especially those who come from far outside Qinghai province, the hospitable and forthright Qinghai people will introduce Niang Pi as a local special delicacy to them, and regard it as a pride handed down from hand to hand in Qinghai. And they will invite guests to taste Niang Pi and tell them its story.

酿皮是青海地方风味较浓的一种传统小吃。

酿皮质地像果冻，比较厚，颜色呈深褐色或浅白色，配上面筋，浇上醋、辣油、芥末、韭菜、蒜泥等佐料，吃起来酸辣可口、爽口开胃，口感柔韧细腻、回味悠长。

酿皮拥趸极多，男女老少都爱吃。青海乃至周边，不同地区、不同信仰的人们都喜欢酿皮这道小吃，尤其对喜欢喝酒的人来说，酿皮是一道必不可少的美食。酿皮生意一年四季都很红火，夏天更是旺季。酿皮虽是小吃，但可作主食充饥解饿，也可当菜肴，充当下酒冷盘，冷热均宜，四季可食。

酿皮以其独有的风味，在时间的演变中，轻轻“抓”住了食客的心，征服了食客的味蕾。今时今日，酿皮小摊在青海各地可谓举目可见，点缀在大街小巷的酿皮店更是各有各的风味，各有各的绝招。

青海本地的汉、藏、土、回等民族群众都有制作与食用酿皮的传统习俗。可以说，酿皮是各民族和睦相处、相互融合、共同发展的一道小吃，是一道凝聚着向心力的美味小吃。

每当有客人光临，尤其是从省外远道而来的客人，好客、豪爽的青海人就会把酿皮作为一道当地特色美食介绍给他们，并把它当作青海人心手相传的一种自豪，请客人品尝，并讲述着它的故事。

词汇笔记

- **puree** ['pjʊəreɪ] *n.* food in the form of a thick liquid made by crushing fruit or cooked vegetables in a small amount of water 浓汤；果泥；菜泥
- **starvation** [stɑː'veɪʃən] *n.*the state of suffering and death caused by having no food 饥饿，饿死
- **dot** [dɒt] *v.* to spread things or people over an area; to be spread over an area 加点；散布于，遍布
- **hospitable** [hɒ'spɪtəbəl] *adj.* pleased to welcome guests; generous and friendly to visitors 好客的，热情友好的

Condensed Yogurt 老酸奶

必用三句

1 Condensed Yogurt is a traditional snack in Qinghai, with a history of nearly a thousand years. 老酸奶是青海地区的传统饮食，已有近千年的饮用历史。

2 Traditional homemade Qinghai Condensed Yogurt does not contain any additives and preservatives, and is a real healthy and green food. 传统的自制青海老酸奶不含任何添加剂、防腐剂，是真正的健康食品、绿色食品。

3 A bowl of Condensed Yogurt can resolve all kinds of thoughts. 一碗老酸奶，化解千般思。

双语赏析

Condensed Yogurt is a traditional snack in Qinghai, with a history of nearly a thousand years.

In the traditional sense, Condensed Yogurt is made of fresh milk. The semi-finished products are filled into predetermined packages respectively. After being sealed, they are refrigerated and fermented for 72 hours. The production time is long and the shelf life is relatively short. You can add some sugar to taste when eating. The sweet and sour taste in your mouth can achieve the effect of relieving heat.

In Qinghai, real Qinghai people can all make their own yogurt. Qinghai Condensed Yogurt is different from foreign yogurt. Qinghai Condensed Yogurt is so concentrated that it can be condensed into a bowl and must be eaten with a spoon. Therefore, Qinghai people never said "drink yogurt", but "eat yogurt". Traditional homemade Qinghai Condensed Yogurt does not contain any additives and preservatives, and is a real healthy and green food.

When you arrive in Qinghai, you will find that the local people's preference for yogurt. As an ordinary drink in other places, Condensed Yogurt has become one of the first choices for holiday gifts here. On the local streets, you will see many people visiting relatives with yogurt packed in gift boxes. Due to the unique production process of Qinghai Condensed Yogurt, many tourists who have been to Qinghai are attracted. As a drink, yogurt in Qinghai is like Peking duck in Beijing and pita bread soaked in lamb soup in Xi'an, which has become a snack that foreigners must taste in Qinghai. It must be said that this is the unique charm of Qinghai yogurt.

Now, in response to the call of the country's agricultural industrialization and adhering to the path of sustainable development, the yogurt food industry with Qinghai Condensed Yogurt as its brand has begun to take shape, and has had a place on the plateau, stepped out of the plateau, and entered the world. Qinghai Condensed Yogurt will make a huge contribution to the economic development of Qinghai.

A bowl of Condensed Yogurt can resolve all kinds of thoughts. When you come to Qinghai, remember to taste yogurt, feel the delicacy bestowed by nature, and experience the deep feelings of plateau people.

老酸奶是青海地区的传统饮食，已有近千年的饮用历史。

传统意义上的老酸奶是以鲜奶为原料，将半成品分别灌装到预定包装里，密封后实施 72 小时的冷藏发酵，制作时间长，保质期相对较短，吃的时候可以放一些糖来调味，酸酸甜甜的，可以达到解暑的效果。

在青海，地地道道的青海人都会自制酸奶，青海老酸奶与外地酸奶不同，青海的老酸奶浓度大到可以凝结到碗里，必须用勺子舀起来吃，所以青海人不说喝酸奶，而是说“吃”酸奶。传统的自制青海老酸奶不含任何添加剂、防腐剂，是真正的健康食品、绿色食品。

到了青海，你会发现当地人对酸奶的偏爱，作为在其他地方的普通饮品，在这里却成为了节日礼品的首选之一。在当地的街头，你会看到许多人手提礼品盒包装的酸奶走亲戚。由于青海老酸奶制作工艺独特，许多到过青海的游客都被吸引。酸奶作为一种饮品对于青海就如同烤鸭于北京、泡馍于西安一样，成了外地人到青海必品尝的一道“小吃”，不能不说这是青海酸奶的独特魅力所在。

如今响应国家农业产业化号召和走可持续发展道路，以青海老酸奶为品牌的酸奶食品产业已经初见规模，并且已经立足高原，走出高原，走向世界。青海老酸奶将为青海经济发展作出巨大贡献。

一碗老酸奶，化解千般思。到青海记得品尝酸奶，感受大自然赐予的美味，体会高原人的浓浓情怀。

词汇笔记

- **seal** [siːl] *v.* to close a container tightly or fill a crack, etc., especially so that air, liquid, etc. cannot get in or out 密封 密封（容器）
- **condense** [kən'dens] *v.* If a liquid condenses or you condense it, it becomes thicker and stronger because it has lost some of its water. 浓缩，变浓
- **additive** ['ædətɪv] *n.* a substance that is added in small amounts to sth., especially food, in order to improve it, give it colour, make it last longer, etc. 添加剂，添加物
- **preservative** [prɪ'zɜːvətɪv] *n.* a substance used to prevent food or wood from decaying 防腐剂，保护剂

Chapter 04

The Cuisine in the Middle and Lower Reaches of the Yellow River

黄河中下游地区饮食

The Dietary Culture of the Middle and Lower Reaches of the Yellow River
黄河中下游地区饮食文化

The diet culture area in the middle reaches of the Yellow River generally includes most of Shaanxi and Shanxi, as well as Henan, Gansu, Qinghai, and Ningxia that share similar diet culture style, and is an important part of Chinese diet culture. This area where the agricultural development is the earliest and most perfect has a very splendid history and culture. And there are all kinds of livestock and whole grains here. However, due to the decline of land carrying capacity and various disasters and wars brought by the over-development, the diet culture in this area has maintained a frugal and simple life tradition except for the extravagant consumption of a few upper-class people.

People in the middle reaches of the Yellow River are famous for their good cooking skills and fondness for pastry and Shaanxi and Shanxi provinces are the most representative. The dishes in this area are also quite distinctive: snacks in Shaanxi such as noodles like belts, pancakes like pot lids, and bowls like basins with pita bread soaked in lamb soup all reflect the kindness and boldness of Guanzhong people. There are many kinds of noodles in Shanxi, known as "eating in various ways", with a wide range of ingredients and a variety of cooking methods. The diet of the middle reaches of the Yellow River emphasizes hot and sour taste, but it is slightly lighter than that of the northeast and north-central regions.

The lower reaches of Yellow River covers Shandong province and parts of Henan, Hebei, Anhui, and Jiangsu provinces. In ancient times, Shandong, which literally means the east of the mountain, refers to the region to the east of the Taihang mountain. It is also where the feudal states of Qi and Lu were situated during the Spring and Autumn Period (770 BC–476 BC), hence the region also goes by the name of Qilu. Qilu region, hometown to Confucianism represented by Confucius and Mencius, plays a major rule in the shaping of traditional Chinese culture, and in turn has a profound impact on the regional food culture. Under the influence of Confucianism, cooking is more of cultural product that advocates peacefulness and legitimism. It is believed that the acme of cooking is the pursuit of the supreme taste that conceals itself in the bland taste. Qilu region is also the converging point of the Bohai Sea and the Beijing-Hangzhou Canal, where the food culture shows characteristics of both the south and the north. Shandong cuisine, also called Lu cuisine, is one of the Eight Culinary Traditions of China and carries much weight in the northern part of China.

Features: it is known for its selection of exquisite materials and salty flavor. It has strict regulations on the use of salt and broth to bring out the flavor and the right amount of seasoning to highlight the original flavor of food. Since Shandong is a major of scallion producing area, scallions, ginger, and garlic are commonly used as seasoning in Shandong cuisine. It is adept at frying, stir-frying, grilling, always seasoned with scallions. The general flavor is fresh and salty, mixed with the pungent taste of scallions and garlic.

Classic dishes: Chicken Shreds with Egg White, Braised Prawns, Saute Sea Cucumber with Scallions, Braised Intestines in Brown Sauce, Dezhou Braised Chicken, Steamed Tofu Stuffed Vegetables, Moo Shu Pork.

黄河中游饮食文化区，在地域上大致包括陕、晋大部以及豫、陇、青、宁诸省区的饮食文化风格接近的地带，是中国饮食文化的重要组成部分。这一地区历史文化十分灿烂，农业开发最早，也最完善，各种牲畜和谷物都有。但由于这一地带的过度开发，土地承载力下降，加上各种灾害和战乱，使得这一地区的饮食文化除了少数上层社会的奢侈消费外，大多数黎民百姓保持着节俭朴素的生活传统。

黄河中游地区居民以善制和喜食面点小吃而著称，并以陕西、山西两省最具代表性。该区域的菜品也颇有特色：陕西的小吃反映了关中人的厚道和豪放，比如面条像腰带、烙饼像锅盖、羊肉泡馍的海碗如盆等。山西面食品种繁多，素有“一面百样吃”之誉，用料广泛，制法多样。黄河中游地区口味强调酸辣，味重，但又比东北和中北地区稍淡一点。

黄河下游饮食文化区大致包括山东以及豫、冀、皖、苏部分地区，主要依托现今的山东省。古以太行山以东地区为山东，春秋时代（公元前 770—公元前 476）这里曾为齐国、鲁国所在地，故又称齐鲁，属于齐鲁文化圈，有着丰富的历史文化积淀，以孔孟为代表的儒家思想对中国的传统文化影响至深，因而这一区域饮食的文化味较浓，讲究“平和正统”，大味必淡的至味境界，加之受海洋文化和京杭大运河的影响，这里成为南北饮食文化的交汇之地。山东菜，又称鲁菜，作为中国八大菜系之一，在北方的影响很大。

口味特点：讲究原料质地优良，以盐提鲜，以汤壮鲜，调味讲求咸鲜纯正，突出本味。大葱为山东特产，多数菜肴要要用葱姜蒜来增香提味，炒、熘、爆、扒、烧等方法都要用葱，尤其是葱烧类的菜肴。总体口味咸鲜，味正，具备葱蒜的辛辣。

经典菜肴：芙蓉鸡片，油焖大虾，葱烧海参，九转大肠，德州扒鸡，一品豆腐，木须肉。

Rougamo 肉夹馍

必用三句

1 Rougamo is one of the traditional specialties of Shaanxi province in China, which can be found all over the streets of Xi'an. 肉夹馍是中国陕西省传统特色食物之一，遍及西安大街小巷。

2 Marinated meat has a long history and is famous in China. With the baked bun, it enjoys the reputation of Chinese-style hamburgers, is well-known at home and abroad, and is deeply loved by people. 腊汁肉历史悠久，闻名中国，配上白吉馍，有着中式汉堡的美誉，扬名中外，深受人们喜爱。

3 Rougamo is a typical folk snack with a low price and people always couldn't get enough of it. After it was introduced to Beijing, it was called "the hamburger of the East". 肉夹馍价格低廉而食之不厌，是典型的民间小吃，传入北京后被称为"东方的汉堡包"。

双语赏析

Rougamo is the baked bun stuffed with marinated meat and is actually a perfect combination of marinated meat and the baked bun. Rougamo is one of the traditional specialties of Shaanxi province in China, which can be found all over the streets of Xi'an. In Xi'an, the baked bun is the most widely accepted staple food. And the marinated meat in baked bun is the most classic way to enjoy the buns. The buns Xi'an people eat are baked on fire. The meat is made with 30-plus seasonings and is stewed with gentle heat. So it tastes soft and glutinous. The plain buns can better highlight the mellow meat. Marinated meat has a long history and is famous in China. With the baked bun, it enjoys the reputation of Chinese-style hamburgers, is well-known at home and abroad, and is deeply loved by people.

Rougamo is a typical folk snack with a low price and people always couldn't get enough of it. After it was introduced to Beijing, it was called "the hamburger of the East". In January 2016, Rougamo was selected into the fifth batch of intangible cultural heritage list of Shaanxi Province.

Rougamo is full of mellow and delicious marinated meat and the tempting taste of the baked bun, which is really a joy in life. Thus, there is a saying: Living in Chang'an, you can see it everywhere, and you don't think it is valuable; when you are in a foreign land, the most enticing thing is this mouth-watering Rougamo.

The way of eating Rougamo is also very particular. The authentic posture of eating Rougamo is to hold the bun horizontally and bite from both sides. In this way, the gravy of the marinated meat can be fully immersed in the baked bun, so that it will not flow out. There is a word in Shaanxi called "Za shi", which means to strike a pose. But in the eyes of Shaanxi people, eating Rougamo is necessary to pay attention to and the particular way of eating Rougamo is not "Za shi", but to properly enjoy this delicious food. Whenever one goes to a place, if one is first involved in novel things, he should follow the customs and ask for advice. This will not only help increase experience, but also experience the local customs.

"肉夹馍"一词意为"肉馅的夹馍"，是两种食物的绝妙组合——白吉馍和腊汁肉。肉夹馍是中国陕西省传统特色食物之一，遍及西安大街小巷。在西安，馍是最被当地人接受的主食，而肉夹馍则是馍的最经典吃法。西安人吃的白吉馍用火烤制，加入三十多种调料慢火熬制而成的肉，软糯浓郁，馍的平淡更加凸显出肉的醇香。腊汁肉历史悠久，闻名中国，配上白吉馍，有着中式汉堡的美誉，扬名中外，深受人们喜爱。

肉夹馍价格低廉而食之不厌，是典型的民间小吃，传入北京后被称为"东方的汉堡包"。2016 年 1 月，肉夹馍入选陕西省第五批非物质文化遗产名录。

肉夹馍满嘴香醇可口的腊汁肉和白吉馍的诱人味道，令人满口生津，真是人生一乐，由此有一言：身居长安，随处可见，不觉其可贵；人在异乡，最勾魂的却是这满口留香的肉夹馍。

肉夹馍的吃法也是有讲究的。正宗吃肉夹馍的姿势为水平持馍，从两侧咬起。水平持馍，可以使腊汁肉肉汁充分浸入馍中，不致流出。陕西有个词叫“扎势”，即故作姿态的意思。但在老陕的眼里，吃肉夹馍有必要的讲究，不是“扎势”，而是正确享受这一美味。每到一地，初涉新奇事物，当入乡随俗，留意请教。这样不仅能增长阅历，更可体验地方风土人情。

词汇笔记

- **marinate** ['mærɪneɪt] *v.* If you marinate food or it marinates, you leave it in a marinade before cooking it. 腌制，腌渍，浸泡（食物）
- **staple** ['steɪpəl] *adj.* forming a basic, large or important part of sth. 主要的，常用的
- **glutinous** ['ɡlu:tənəs] *adj.* sticky 黏的，胶质的
- **reputation** [ˌrepju'teɪʃn] *n.* the opinion that people have about what sb./sth. is like, based on what has happened in the past 名誉，名声
- **intangible** [ɪn'tændʒəbl] *adj.* (business) that does not exist as a physical thing but is still valuable to a company （资产，利益）无形的
- **gravy** ['ɡreɪvi] *n.* a brown sauce made by adding flour to the juices that come out of meat while it is cooking 肉汁

Pita Bread Soaked in Beef/Lamb Soup 牛羊肉泡馍

必用三句

1 Pita Bread Soaked in Beef/Lamb Soup is one of the most distinctive and influential delicacies in Shaanxi province. 牛羊肉泡馍是陕西最有特色、最有影响的美食之一。

2 For Pita Bread Soaked in Beef/Lamb Soup, the soup is the signature, and the meat adds richness, but the key of its good taste attributes to the baked bun. 吃牛羊肉泡馍，汤是招牌，肉添光彩，但关键还在馍的提携。

3 Like many special snacks in Xi'an, Pita Bread Soaked in Beef/Lamb Soup can be seen everywhere, and the price is reasonable, so it is actually a national food. 它和西安的许多特色小吃一样，在街上随处可见，而且价格公道，是一种全民食品。

双语赏析

Pita Bread Soaked in Beef/Lamb Soup is one of the most distinctive and influential delicacies in Shaanxi province.

Pita Bread Soaked in Beef/Lamb Soup with a pleasant finish and the function of warming the stomach, as a perfect combination of staple food and soup, is featured by the rich seasoning and the mellow taste, the braised meat and the thick soup. In this way, Pita Bread Soaked in Beef/Lamb Soup is always beloved by the people of Shaanxi, and foreign guests also come to Shaanxi to taste it to satisfy their appetites, making it "the general representative" of Shaanxi's cuisines.

For Pita Bread Soaked in Beef/Lamb Soup, the soup is the signature, and the meat adds richness, but the key of its good taste attributes to the baked bun. "Paomo", another staple food in Xi'an, originated from the baked buns. Based on their own preference, people can tear a bun into different sizes. As for Xi'an natives, this process is not a trouble but what they enjoy very much.

In fact, Pita Bread Soaked in Beef/Lamb Soup enjoys great popularity in Xi'an not just because of its great taste. Like many special snacks in Xi'an, Pita Bread Soaked in Beef/Lamb Soup can be seen everywhere, and the price is reasonable, so it is actually a national food. As long as you want to eat, you can afford it regardless of your status.

Pita Bread Soaked in Beef/Lamb Soup is a typical delicacy of Shaanxi province and that of Xi'an is the most famous. The manufacturing skill of Pita Bread Soaked in Beef/Lamb Soup of "Tong Sheng Xiang" which is regarded as the representative of Pita Bread Soaked in Beef/Lamb Soup in Xi'an, has been included in the second batch of the State-level Non-material Cultural Heritage List.

With the development of history to this day, Pita Bread Soaked in Beef/Lamb Soup which has never really lost its appeal has become a delicacy that ordinary people have eaten for a long time. In the streets of Xi'an, there are many restaurants offering Pita Bread Soaked in Beef/Lamb Soup, which has fully consolidated and carried forward this delicacy. Since the well-known brand, Fang Shang Ren, is recognized as a "Chinese Famous Snack" by China Cuisine Association, "Paomo" has become the "national brand" and reached a new level.

牛羊肉泡馍是陕西最有特色、最有影响的美食之一。

牛羊肉泡馍是主食和汤的完美融合，其特点是料重味醇，肉烂汤浓，香气诱人，食后余味无穷，又有暖胃之功能。因它暖胃耐饥，素为陕西人民所喜爱，外宾来陕也争先品尝，以饱口福。牛羊肉泡馍因此成为陕西名吃的“总代表”。

吃牛羊肉泡馍，汤是招牌，肉添光彩，但关键还在馍的提携。泡馍也是从馍变化出来的一种西安主食。每个人根据自己喜好的口感，掰出大小、形状不一的馍块。对西安人来说，这个过程不是麻烦，而是弥足享受。

事实上，牛羊肉泡馍在西安广受欢迎并不只是因为它的美味。它和西安的许多特色小吃一样，在街上随处可见，而且价格公道，是一种全民食品。不管身份高低贵贱，只要想吃，就能吃得起。

牛羊肉泡馍作为陕西的风味美馔，尤以西安的牛羊肉泡馍最享盛名。西安“同盛祥”牛羊肉泡馍制作技艺作为西安牛羊肉泡馍的代表，被列入了第二批国家级非物质文化遗产名录。

历史发展到今天，牛羊肉泡馍已成为市井百姓久吃不衰的美食。在西安的大街小巷，经营牛羊肉泡馍的饭店星罗棋布，使这一美食充分得到了巩固和发扬，特别是知名品牌“坊上人”清真饭庄的牛羊肉泡馍被中国烹饪协会认定为“中华名小吃”，使泡馍一跃披上了“国字号”战袍，升华到了一个新的高度。

词汇笔记

- **soak** [səʊk] *v.* to put sth. in liquid for a time so that it becomes completely wet 浸泡
- **distinctive** [dɪ'stɪŋktɪv] *adj.* having a quality or characteristic that makes sth. different and easily noticed 独特的，与众不同的

- **pleasant** ['plezənt] *adj.* enjoyable, pleasing or attractive 令人愉快的，惬意的
- **braised** [breɪzd] *adj.* to cook meat or vegetables very slowly with a little liquid in a closed container 炖熟的；焖熟的
- **signature** ['sɪgnətʃər] *n.* a particular quality that makes sth. different from other similar things and makes it easy to recognize 鲜明特色，明显特征
- **preference** ['prefrəns] *n.* a greater interest in or desire for sb./sth. than sb./sth. else 偏爱，偏好

Hanzhong Hot Mianpi 汉中热面皮

必用三句

1 Hanzhong people eat Mianpi regardless of the season and the sale of Mianpi can be found on the street all year round. 汉中人吃面皮不分时节，无论是春夏秋冬，在街上都有做面皮生意的。

2 For everyone from Hanzhong who is away from home, the first thing to do is to eat a bowl of Mianpi fresh from the food steamer when he returns to his hometown. 每一个在外的汉中人，回到家乡的第一件事就是先吃上一碗刚出笼的面皮。

3 A bowl of Mianpi, the taste of a city; a bowl of Mianpi, a yearning for the hometown. 一份面皮，一座城市的味道；一份面皮，一种家乡的思念。

双语赏析

Hanzhong Hot Mianpi is a special dish in Hanzhong, Shaanxi province. It is said that the history of this dish began in the Qin and Han Dynasties.

The method of making Hanzhong Hot Mianpi is generally to soak the rice and grind it into rice milk, steam it into paper skins, smear them with rapeseed oil while they are still hot, then cut them into strips, and add chili oil, monosodium glutamate, refined salt, soy sauce, vinegar, etc. Finally side dishes are added, which are called "Di Dian Zi" locally, such as soybean sprouts, shredded potatoes, celery, spinach, etc, mix well and serve. Hanzhong Hot Mianpi tastes soft and glutinous, spicy and hot, which makes people want more.

It is many families' custom to treat relatives and friends to Mianpi in Hanzhong. Hanzhong people eat Mianpi regardless of the season and the sale of Mianpi can be found on the street all year round. Hanzhong is geographically close to Sichuan and Chongqing, so spicy flavor is crucial, but each Mianpi shop has its own unique recipe for making chili oil, which turns out to be their own characteristics, thus attracting different fans. Each county and district of Hanzhong has its own peculiarities in making Mianpi, showing different styles of Hanzhong Mianpi, which greatly enriches the flavor of Mianpi. In 2011, "the manufacturing skills of Hanzhong Mianpi" was included in the Third Batch of Intangible Cultural Heritage List of Shaanxi Province.

Hanzhong people can't do without Mianpi, just like Chongqing people can't do without Hot Pot, and Beijingers can't do without "Zhajiangmian (Zha Jiang Noodles)". Hot Mianpi is the food most Hanzhong people grow up on, so it represents the flavor of their hometown. For everyone from Hanzhong who is away from home, the first thing to do is to eat a bowl of Mianpi fresh from the food steamer when he returns to his hometown.

"A bowl of Mianpi, the taste of a city; a bowl of Mianpi, a yearning for the hometown." For people who have been away from Hanzhong for a long time, the moment they return to Hanzhong to eat Hot Mianpi, their fatigue, sadness, and homesickness will all be released immediately.

汉中热面皮，是陕西省汉中市的一道特色小吃，相传该菜品的历史始于秦汉时期。

汉中热面皮的做法一般是把大米浸泡后磨成米浆，上笼蒸成薄皮儿，趁热抹上菜籽油，切成条状，依个人口味调入油辣子、味精、精盐、酱油、醋等佐料，再加入配菜，在当地都称其为“底垫子”，比如黄豆芽、土豆丝、芹菜、菠菜等，拌匀即可食用，口感软糯，香辣，让人欲罢不能。

在汉中很多家庭都有用面皮招待亲友的习惯。汉中人吃面皮不分时节，无论是春夏秋冬，在街上都有做面皮生意的。在味型上，汉中因地近川渝，故辣味是主角，但每家面皮店又都有独门的油辣子制作配方，变化出各自不同的特点，因而有各自不同的拥趸。汉中各县区面皮各有自己的特色，分别代表了汉中面皮的不同流派，极大丰富了面皮的风味。2011 年，“汉中面皮制作技艺”列入陕西省第三批非物质文化遗产名录。

汉中人离不开面皮，就像重庆人离不开火锅、北京人离不开炸酱面一样。大多数汉中人吃面皮从小吃到大，因此热面皮对他们而言代表着家乡的味道。每一个在外的汉中人，回到家乡的第一件事就是先吃上一碗刚出笼的面皮。

“一份面皮，一座城市的味道；一份面皮，一种家乡的思念。”离开汉中太久的朋友，回到汉中吃到热面皮的一刹那，出门在外的疲劳、心酸，以及对汉中的思乡之情，都会在顷刻间全部释放。

词汇笔记

- **rapeseed** ['reɪpsiːd] *n.* seed of rape plants 油菜籽
- **vinegar** ['vɪnɪgər] *n.* a liquid with a bitter taste made from malt (= a type of grain) or wine, used to add flavour to food or to preserve it 醋
- **recipe** ['resəpi] *n.* a set of instructions that tells you how to cook sth. and the ingredients 烹饪法，食谱
- **peculiarity** [pɪˌkjuːli'ærəti] *n.* a feature that only belongs to one particular person, thing, place, etc. 特点，特性
- **enrich** [ɪn'rɪtʃ] *v.* to improve the quality of sth., often by adding sth. to it 使充实，使丰富；使富裕，使富有
- **fatigue** [fə'tiːg] *n.* a feeling of being extremely tired, usually because of hard work or exercise 疲乏，厌倦

Daoxiao Noodles 刀削面

必用三句

1 It is the signature food of Shanxi province and is listed as one of the Top Five Noodles together with Beijing Zha Jiang Noodles, Henan Braised Noodles,

Hubei Hot Dry Noodles, and Sichuan Dandan Noodles. 它与北京的炸酱面、河南的烩面、湖北的热干面、四川的担担面，同称为中国五大面食，享有盛誉，是山西美食最具代表性的名片之一。

2 It tastes smooth and chewy, soft but not mushy. It tastes better as you give it more chewing. 入口外滑内筋，软而不黏，越嚼越香。

3 The authentic version of the Datong Daoxiao Noodles uses a paste that consists braised pork, eggs, dried bean curd and meat balls. 正宗山西大同刀削面的卤汁是卤肉酱加鸡蛋、豆腐干和肉丸子一起卤制而成。

双语赏析

As the saying goes, the best cooked wheaten food in the world is found in China, while the best cooked wheaten food in China is found in Shanxi. Legend has it that the Daoxiao Noodles were created by the son-in-law of the emperor, hence it is also called Fuma (son-in-law in Chinese) noodles. It is popular in Shanxi province and its surrounding areas. There is a wide choice of pastes and condiments. Among all the Daoxiao Noodles, Datong noodles are the most famous. It is the signature food of Shanxi province and is listed as one of the Top Five Noodles together with Beijing Zha Jiang Noodles, Henan Braised Noodles, Hubei Hot Dry Noodles and Sichuan Dandan Noodles.

The name Daoxiao, which means knife-shaved in Chinese, can be best presented in the making process of the noodles, which is rather entertaining. The most authentic technique for making Daoxiao Noodles, which is called "fly cutter shaving the dough", is to hold a large block of dough downwards with one hand at about a 30-degree angle. The other hand, clutching a sharp knife that's specially made for this purpose, shaves the noodles directly into a large pot of boiling water. It takes years of practice to achieve such craftsmanship: to hold the dough in the left hand and the knife in the right hand with perfect hand-eye coordination so as to cut the noodles quickly, move the wrist flexibly, and exert the force evenly. It is believed that a top chef can shave 200 noodle strips a minute, each of which is exactly 20 centimeters long. The noodle strips are in the shape of willow leaves, thick in the middle and thin on both sides. It tastes smooth and chewy, soft but not mushy. It tastes better as you give it more chewing.

There is a great choice of paste to coat the noodles with, such as tomato egg paste, fried meat paste, assorted meat broth, mutton broth, egg plant and cubed meat paste, needle mushroom and egg paste, fungus and egg paste, etc. When served, top the noodles with sliced cucumber, leek flower, green sprouts, chopped garlic sprouts, and sprinkle stewed soybeans, chili powder, and a few drops of the famed Shanxi mature vinegar, which is absolutely tasty. The authentic version of the Datong Daoxiao Noodles uses a paste that consists braised pork, eggs, dried bean curd and meat balls.

俗话说：世界面食在中国，中国面食在山西。山西名声最大、影响最广的面食是刀削面，别称“驸马面”，据传是由驸马所创。刀削面流行于山西省及其周边地区，配以各种口味的臊子、调料食用，以山西大同刀削面最为著名。它与北京的炸酱面、河南的烩面、湖北的热干面、四川的担担面，同称为中国五大面食，享有盛誉，是山西美食最具代表性的名片之一。

刀削面全凭刀削而得名，以刀功和削技的绝妙而被称为“飞刀削面”，传统的操作方法是一手托面，一手拿刀，直接削到开水锅里。刀削面之妙妙在刀功。刀，一般不使用菜刀，要从特制的弧形削刀。操作时左手托住揉好的面团，右手持刀，手腕要灵，出力要平，用力要匀，手眼一条线。高明的厨师，每分钟能削二百刀左右，每个面叶的长度，恰好都是六寸。刀削面中厚边薄，形似柳叶；入口外滑内筋，软而不黏，越嚼越香。

山西刀削面的“浇头”品种繁多，有西红柿鸡蛋酱、肉炸酱、肉丝什锦卤汤、羊肉汤、茄子肉丁卤、金针木耳鸡蛋卤等，再配上黄瓜丝、韭菜花、绿豆芽、青蒜末等应时鲜菜，撒入煮黄豆、辣椒面，再滴上几滴山西老陈醋，绝对是一级棒的可口美味。正宗山西大同刀削面的卤汁是卤肉酱加鸡蛋、豆腐干和肉丸子一起卤制而成。

词汇笔记

- **craftsmanship** [ˈkræftsmənʃɪp] *n.* Craftsmanship is the skill that someone uses when they make beautiful things with their hands. 手艺
- **flexibility** [ˌfleksəˈbɪləti] *n.* the property of being flexible; easily bent or shaped 柔韧性
- **mushy** [ˈmʌʃi] *adj.* Vegetables and fruit that are mushy are soft and have lost most of their shape. （蔬菜和水果）软塌塌的
- **sprout** [spraʊt] *n.* the small white stem from a bean seed that is eaten as a vegetable 豆芽

Sauteed Boiled Pork 过油肉

必用三句

1 Legend has it that it originated from the Ming Dynasty (1368–1644), a government dish that made its way to the commoners' dinner table and thus became popularized. 相传起源于明代（1368—1644 年），原是一道官府菜，后来慢慢流传到民间才被人们广为流传。

2 The dish uses the most common ingredients, yet is cooked in the most meticulous way. 此菜虽然用料简单，做法却非常讲究。

3 The meat tastes extremely tender and smooth after being sauteed. With the combination of vegetables, it goes particularly well with rice and works up your appetite. 肉过完油后鲜嫩无比，再配上青菜，与米饭是绝配，十分开胃。

双语赏析

Sauteed Boiled Pork is a signature food of Shanxi province, being called "the first delicacy of Shanxi", one of the top ten classic dishes of Shanxi in 2018, and an indispensable part in the banquet menu and people's diet. Legend has it that it originated from the Ming Dynasty (1368–1644), a government dish that made its way to the commoners' dinner table and thus became popularized. Once one of the so-call eight ying dishes–meat featured dishes aimed to entertain guests or satisfy the craving for meat–of old Datong city in the 1980s, it symbolizes an epoch that brings back nostalgic recollections of the old days. It used to be a criteria of eating well. Nowadays, as the diet becomes increasingly diversified, people feel less attached to the meat-based dishes. But people's craving for Sauteed Boiled Pork remains unabated for its unique flavor.

The dish uses the most common ingredients, yet is cooked in the most meticulous way. Sauting and vinegar-sprinkling is the key to success. The meat should be first marinated in the seasonings before it is coated in beaten eggs. Only the boiled leaf fat can bring out the special flavor of the dish. Bring the oil to a boil and let the meat slide in. Drain the meat when it changes color to make sure the meat is smooth, tender, juicy. Vinegar sprinkling and a touch of ginger can enhance the flavor by removing the unpleasant smell of the meat yet not overpowering it. The accompaniments varies from place to place, but the most common practice and the most popular is to go with garlic sprouts. The meat tastes extremely tender and smooth after being sauteed. With the combination of vegetables, it goes particularly well with rice and works up your appetite.

过油肉是最地道的山西代表菜之一，被人们称为“三晋第一味”，在 2018 年被评为了山西十大经典名菜之一，无论是宴请聚会还是日常饮食，山西过油肉都是一道不可或缺的特色菜肴。相传起源于明代（1368—1644 年），原是一道官府菜，后来慢慢流传到民间才被人们广为流传。到了 20 世纪 80 年代，过油肉更是成为以肉为主的老大同“八大件”之一，作为一个时代的象征，承载着老大同人的回忆，是记忆中“吃得好”的标志。如今，随着饮食日益丰富，人们不再执着“八大件”硬菜，但是过油肉凭其“一招鲜，吃遍天”，格外受人青睐。

此菜虽然用料简单，做法却非常讲究。“过油”和“点醋”是关键。肉要先用调料腌制，再裹上蛋清。必须用洁净的熟猪板油，才能使菜肴发挥出应有的风味。待油热时入锅划油，待肉片变色后捞出沥干，以使肉片达到平整舒展、光滑利落、不干不硬、色泽金黄的效果。此菜在加热调味过程中，采取了点醋的方法调味，姜的加入也只是画龙点睛，达到“有姜不吃姜，有醋不吃醋”的意境，去腥同时还不能盖过肉自然的香味，这道过油肉才算是完美。配菜上因地区稍有区别，不过还是蒜薹配过油肉最为常见，也最受人们欢迎。肉过完油后鲜嫩无比，再配上青菜，与米饭是绝配，十分开胃。

词汇笔记

- **Indispensable** [ˌɪndɪ'spensəbl] *adj.* If you say that someone or something is indispensable, you mean that they are absolutely essential and other people or things cannot function without them. 必不可少的
- **unabated** [ˌʌnə'beɪtɪd] *adj.* If something continues unabated, it continues without any reduction in intensity or amount. （程度，数量）不减的
- **meticulous** [mə'tɪkjələs] *adj.* If you describe someone as meticulous, you mean that they do things very carefully and with great attention to detail. 细致的，小心谨慎的
- **appetite** ['æpɪtaɪt] *n.* Your appetite is your desire to eat. 胃口

Fried Leek Dumplings 韭菜盒子

必用三句

1 Fried Leek Dumplings, as a very popular traditional snack in Shandong, Henan, Hebei, Shanxi, Shaanxi and Northeast three provinces in northern China, are made with leeks, eggs and flour as the main ingredients. 韭菜盒子是中国北方地区山东、河南、河北、山西、陕西、东北三省等地非常流行的传统小吃。它是以韭菜、鸡蛋、面作为主要食材制作而成的传统美食。

2 Fried Leek Dumplings have different names in different regions. 韭菜盒子在不同的地区享有不同的称呼。

3 As a delicacy, Fried Leek Dumplings also enjoy its unique festival connotations.
韭菜盒子作为一种美食，亦享有独特的节日内涵。

双语赏析

Fried Leek Dumplings, as a very popular traditional snack in Shandong, Henan, Hebei, Shanxi, Shaanxi and Northeast three provinces in northern China, are made with leeks, eggs and flour as the main ingredients, which are good to eat in spring. Fried Leek Dumplings are both with vegetarian filling and meat filling. And Fried Leek Dumplings stuffed with vegetables are not greasy and taste good, and are nutritious. Fried Leek Dumplings with meat also have a flavor. And the skin of the Fried Leek Dumplings is golden and crisp; the filling of them with leeks smell is fresh. In a word, Fried Leek Dumplings have the most exquisite taste.

Fried Leek Dumplings have different names in different regions. In Jiaodong area (Yantai, Weihai), they are also called “Ha bing”; in some areas of Linyi, the dumpling-shaped Fried Leek Dumplings are called “Ta bing”, which is a kind of dumpling with flour, leeks and dried shrimps or pork, and eggs as main ingredients.

As a delicacy, Fried Leek Dumplings also enjoy its unique festival connotations. In northern areas such as Tianjin, during the Spring Festival, there is a saying that “Eat dumplings on the first day and noodles on the second day; Fried Leek Dumplings are made on the third day.” Therefore, the Fried Leek Dumplings are also a festival food on the third day of the Lunar New Year in Tianjin and some other places.

On February 14, 2022, the well-known athlete, the frog princess Eileen Gu, went viral on the Internet when she ate a fried leek dumpling in the break of the game during the Beijing Winter Olympics, which is dubbed by netizens as “the gold medal in the left hand and the fried leek dumpling in the right hand”. This interesting and classic scene makes Fried Leek Dumplings, as a Chinese delicacy, not only known and loved by the Chinese, but also concerned and loved by people all over the world.

韭菜盒子是中国北方地区山东、河南、河北、山西、陕西、东北三省等地非常流行的传统小吃。它是以韭菜、鸡蛋、面作为主要食材制作而成的传统美食，适宜于春季食用。韭菜盒子既有素馅的，也有肉馅的。素馅的韭菜盒子不肥腻，口感很好，而且很有营养。肉馅的韭菜盒子也别有一番风味。韭菜盒子表皮金黄酥脆，馅心韭香脆嫩。总体而言，韭菜盒子滋味优美，是适时佳点。

韭菜盒子在不同的地区享有不同的称呼。在胶东地区（烟台、威海），韭菜盒子也称“哈饼”；临沂部分地区将形如饺子的韭菜盒子称“塌饼”，是一种以面粉、韭菜加海米或猪肉，以及鸡蛋为主要原料加工制作而成的食品小吃。

韭菜盒子作为一种美食，亦享有独特的节日内涵。在天津等北方地区有“初一饺子初二面，初三盒子锅里转”之说法，因而韭菜盒子也是天津等地农历大年初三的节日食品。

2022 年 2 月 14 日，深受大家欢迎的著名运动员——青蛙公主谷爱凌在北京冬奥会比赛间隙吃韭菜盒子的一幕走红网络，被网友戏称为“左手金牌，右手韭菜盒子”。这有趣而又经典的一幕使作为中华美食的韭菜盒子不仅为中国人所熟知并喜爱，也受到全世界人民的关注和喜爱。

词汇笔记

- **ingredient** [ɪn'gri:diənt] *n.* one of the things from which sth. is made, especially one of the foods that are used together to make a particular dish （食品的）成分，原料
- **greasy** ['gri:si] *adj.* covered in a lot of grease or oil 油腻的
- **crisp** [krɪsp] *adj.* pleasantly hard and dry 爽口的，脆生的，脆的，易碎的
- **nutritious** [nju'trɪʃəs] *adj.* very good for you; containing many of the substances which help the body to grow 有营养的，营养丰富的
- **allusion** [ə'lu:ʒən] *n.* something that is said or written that refers to or mentions another person or subject in an indirect way 典故
- **delicacy** ['delɪkəsi] *n.* a type of food considered to be very special in a particular place 美味，佳肴

Braised Pork Balls in Gravy 四喜丸子

必用三句

1 As its name carries an auspicious sense which symbolizes good fortune, prosperity, longevity, and happiness, it is often used as the final course at wedding feasts and birthday banquets. 因其名字“讨喜”，寓意人生福、禄、寿、喜四大喜事，常用作喜宴、寿宴等宴席中的压轴菜，以取其吉祥之意。

2 The four meat balls, with attractive color, aroma and flavor, is made of minced meat from the pork belly, mixed thoroughly with a beaten egg and scallion water. 四喜丸子从外观上来说，由四个色香味俱佳的肉丸组成，主要用料为五花肉肉馅，加入鸡蛋、葱花水等调料。

3 The dish has since become popular and is served during festivals as a tasty, lovely and lucky symbol of Chinese people's pursuit of happiness. 自此，四喜丸子深受人们的喜爱，逢年过节搬上餐桌，好吃好看好彩头。

双语赏析

Braised Pork Balls in Gravy is a classic dish belonging to the Shandong cuisine. As its name carries an auspicious sense which symbolizes good fortune, prosperity, longevity, and happiness, it is often used as the final course at wedding feasts and birthday banquets. Not to be confused with Stewed Pork Ball in Brown Sauce from Huiyang Cuisine, which has one meat ball instead of four and much bigger in size, the four meat balls, with attractive color, aroma and flavor, is made of minced meat from the pork belly, mixed thoroughly with a beaten egg and scallion water. Give it a good whipping clockwise for a chewy texture. Then add diced water chestnuts and stir it well. Roll the meat paste into balls of 90 grams each, deep fry them until golden in color and set them aside. Arrange the blanched pak choi in a plate, top it with the meat balls and pour the gravy over the top before everything goes into a steaming pot and steamed for saturation of flavor and the dish is done.

Braised Pork Balls in Gravy dates back to the Tang Dynasty (618–907) over 1300 years ago. Legend has it that Zhang Jiuling, before he was the famous chancellor for Emperor Xuanzong of Tang Dynasty, was one of the many scholars who attended the imperial examination held in the capital city. Despite his humble appearance and shabby clothes, he came out first in the exam. The emperor was impressed by his talent and married his daughter to him. On the big day of the wedding, Zhang Jiuling was told the whereabouts of his long-lost parents in a hometown flood and welcomed them to the capital city. To celebrate the many happy occasions happening simultaneously, Zhang ordered the cook to make an auspicious dish. And viola, the four meat balls coated with gravy. When asked the implied meaning of the dish, the cook explained as the celebration of the four complete cycles of life achievements, namely, the top ranking in the imperial exam, the reunion of parents and son, the happy marriage and the start of a career, and being the son-in-law to the Emperor. Zhang rejoiced and modified the name from four cycles to four happiness which sounds more sonorous. The dish has since become popular and is served during festivals as a tasty, lovely and lucky symbol of Chinese people's pursuit of happiness.

四喜丸子是经典的中国名菜之一，属于鲁菜菜系。因其名字“讨喜”，寓意人生福、禄、寿、喜四大喜事，常用作喜宴、寿宴等宴席中的压轴菜，以取其吉祥之意。四喜丸子做法与属淮阳菜系的狮子头基本一致，只是四喜丸子要用四个肉丸，个头也小得多。四喜丸子从外观上来说，由四个色香味俱佳的肉丸组成，主要用料为五花肉肉馅，加入鸡蛋、葱花水等调料顺一个方向搅拌上劲儿，再加入马蹄丁拌匀，取约 90 克肉馅揉成团，在两手之间来回摔打，使之成形且肉馅更加紧致。用热油炸至微黄，捞出装盘，底下铺好油菜，上面浇个芡汁，再放入锅中蒸熟即可食用。

四喜丸子起源于唐代（618—907 年），距今已有 1300 多年的历史。传说张九龄，在他成为唐玄宗年代出名的宰相之前，也是赴京赶考众多考生中的一员。放榜之日，衣着寒酸的九龄中得状元，当朝皇帝欣赏他的才学，招他为驸马。当年九龄的老家正遭水灾，父母失散，不知音信。大婚当天，九龄得知双亲的下落，便使人将双亲接至京城。喜上加喜，九龄命厨师做一道吉祥的菜，以示庆贺。菜端上来一看，是四个炸透并浇以汤汁的大肉丸子。张九龄询问菜的含义，聪明的厨师答道：此菜为“四圆”。一喜，老爷金榜题名。二喜，阖家团圆。三喜，成家立业。四喜，做了乘龙快婿。张九龄听了之后大喜，连连称赞，便说：“四圆”不如“四喜”响亮好听，干脆叫它“四喜丸子”吧！自此，四喜丸子深受人们的喜爱，逢年过节搬上餐桌，好吃好看好彩头。

词汇笔记

- **auspicious** [ɔː'spɪʃəs] *adj.* Something that is auspicious indicates that success is likely. 吉利的；望成功的 [正式]
- **aroma** [ə'roʊmə] *n.* An aroma is a strong, pleasant smell. 芳香
- **simultaneously** [ˌsaɪm(ə)l'teɪniəsli] *adv.* happen or exist at the same time 同时地
- **sonorous** ['sɑːnərəs] *adj.* A sonorous sound is deep and rich. 洪亮的 [文学性]

Braised Intestines in Brown Sauce 九转大肠

必用三句

1. It soon gained regional fame and became the signature food of Shandong cuisine. 这一菜品名扬四方，成为鲁菜的经典。

2. It is cooked in a very delicate way, heavily seasoned and fully saturated. 此菜做法别具一格：下料狠，用料全，五味俱全。

3. It tastes tender and soft, fat but not greasy, so palatable and agreeable to the mouth that one just can't get enough of it. 吃起来质地软嫩，兼有酸、甜、香、辣、咸五味，肥而不腻，鲜香味美，异常适口，久食不厌。

双语赏析

Braised Intestines in Brown Sauce is one of the famous dishes of Shandong cuisine. In 2018, it was rated as one of the top 10 traditional dishes in Shandong province by the China Cuisine Association. The dish was created by the owner of Jiuhualin Restaurant in Jinan during the reign of Emperor Guangxu in the Qing Dynasty. It was initially called “braised intestines”. Some literati thought the dish was unique and tasteful and deserved a better name. In order to please the owner of the restaurant who had a fondness of the number “nine”, and praise the exquisite skills of the chef, they renamed it as “jiuzhuan intestines”. “Jiuzhuan” is a term used in alchemy, which literally means going through 9 times temperament and refinement for perfection. The dish won the popularity among the customers and invited the imitation among other restaurants. It is a groundbreaking dish in terms of using pork entrails as the main ingredient of a dish. It soon gained regional fame and became the signature food of Shandong cuisine.

It is cooked in a very delicate way, heavily seasoned and fully saturated. The intestines are first blanched, then deep fried, and stewed with 10 more condiments. When it is done, it gives a red and well lubricated luster, semitransparent and elastic with tier upon tier yet not sticky. It has a complex sour, sweet, aromatic, spicy and salty taste. It tastes tender and soft, fat but not greasy, so palatable and agreeable to the mouth that one just can’t get enough of it.

“九转大肠”是山东省济南市的一道传统名菜，属于鲁菜系。2018 年发布的“中国菜”中，“九转大肠”被中国食品协会评为山东十大经典名菜。相传是在清朝光绪初年，由济南九华林酒楼店主首创，开始名为“红烧大肠”。一些文人雅士食后，感到此菜确实与众不同，别有滋味，为取悦店家喜“九”之癖，并赞厨师制作此菜像道家“九炼金丹”一样精工细作，便将其更名为“九转大肠”。“九转”典出道家炼丹之说，为精烧九炼之意。从此以后，“九转大肠”开创了以猪下货为原料制作主菜上大席的先河，引得济南的酒楼纷纷效仿，使这一菜品名扬四方，成为鲁菜的经典。

此菜做法别具一格：下料狠，用料全，五味俱全。先将猪大肠焯水后油炸，再灌入十多种佐料，用微火炮制而成。色泽红润，通体半透明，柔韧异常，层层相叠又层层相分。吃起来质地软嫩，兼有酸、甜、香、辣、咸五味，肥而不腻，鲜香味美，异常适口，久食不厌。

词汇笔记

- **literati** [ˌlɪtəˈrɑːti] *n.* Literati are well-educated people who are interested in literature. 文学人士
- **alchemy** [ˈælkəmi] *n.* Alchemy was a form of chemistry studied in the Middle Ages, that was concerned with trying to discover ways to change ordinary metals into gold. 炼金术，炼丹术
- **groundbreaking** [graʊnd ˈbreɪkɪŋ] *adj.* You use groundbreaking to describe things which you think are significant because they provide new and positive ideas, and influence the way people think about things. 开拓性的
- **palatable** [ˈpælətəbl] *adj.* If you describe food or drink as palatable, you mean that it tastes pleasant. 美味的 [正式]

Stir-fried Kidney 爆炒腰花

必用三句

1 Stir-fried Kidney is one of the famous traditional delicacy of Shandong cuisine, with the pork kidney as its main ingredient. 爆炒腰花，为山东省特色传统名菜，以猪腰为主料。

2 The dish requires high skills of knife work and strict heating control. 这道菜对刀工和火候的要求极为严格。

3 When stir-frying, it's all about the oil temperature and the duration and degree of the heating, in order to finalize the shape without overcooking the meat. 入热油炸制，此时的油温和火候极为关键，既要定形，又不能过老。

双语赏析

Stir-fried Kidney is one of the famous traditional delicacies of Shandong cuisine, with the pork kidney as its main ingredient. In 2018, it was rated among the top 10 traditional dishes in Shandong province by the China Cuisine Association. Yaohua refers to the animal kidney. Pork kidney has high nutrient value which is rich in protein, vitamins B12, B6, C and H, myoinositol, folic acid, pantothenic acid, as well as minerals. According to Chinese medicine, taking animal kidneys nourishes the kidney and tonifies the energy. It helps the elderly to strengthen the body and resist aging. Keep in mind that the adrenal gland has to be removed thoroughly before it is cooked.

The dish uses pork kidney and water chestnuts as the main ingredients. After it is stir-fired, it tastes smooth and tender, palatable yet not greasy. The garnish and condiments vary from place to place. It comes in different flavors from sweet, sour, salty to spicy. The tricky part when making the dish is whether the unpleasant smell is completely removed, and whether the meat tastes tender and crisp. The dish requires high skills of knife work to make the criss-cross cuts and strict heating control. The criss-cross cuts not only better present the dish but also speed up the cooking time as it helps to absorb the heat evenly and thoroughly for a tender and crisp texture. When stir-frying, it's all about the oil temperature and the duration and degree of the heating, in order to finalize the shape without overcooking the meat.

爆炒腰花，为山东省特色传统名菜，以猪腰为主料。2018 年 9 月 10 日，“中国菜”正式发布，“爆炒腰花”被评为“山东十大经典名菜”之一。腰花指的是动物的肾脏，富含蛋白质，维生素 B12、B6、C、H，肌醇，叶酸，泛酸和各种微量元素。中医认为肾脏有养肾气、益精髓之功效，讲究脏补脏，老年人经常服用，有强身抗衰之奇效。但要注意的是，在食用之前，一定要将肾上腺割除干净。

制作时以猪腰、荸荠等为主料，经过爆炒制成。成品新嫩，味道醇厚，滑润不腻。配菜和佐料因地而异，口味也随之有偏甜、酸、咸、辣之分。这道菜的制作难度为臊味是否去除干净，口感是否鲜嫩带脆，这也是这道菜是否好吃的主要评判标准。

这道菜对刀工和火候的要求极为严格，需要厨师通过精湛的刀工将其处理成麦穗状，这种打花刀的烹饪技法其实不单是为了食材的美观，更主要的还是缩短食材成熟的时间，使热穿透均衡，达到食材内外老嫩一致。入热油炸制，此时的油温和火候极为关键，既要定形，又不能过老。

词汇笔记

- **tonify** ['toʊnɪfaɪ] *v.* impart tone to (the body or part of it) 使（身体或其部位）健康
- **gland** [glænd] *n.* A gland is an organ in the body which produces chemical substances for the body to use or get rid of. 腺
- **garnish** ['gɑːrnɪʃ] *v.* A garnish is a small amount of salad, herbs, or other food that is used to decorate cooked or prepared food. 装饰菜
- **condiment** ['kɒndɪmənt] *n.* A condiment is a substance such as salt, pepper, or mustard that you add to food when you eat it in order to improve the flavour. 调料

Sweet and Sour Carp 糖醋鲤鱼

必用三句

1 As the signature food of Shandong cuisine, it is much loved by the locals and is a must-have for visitors to Jinan. 糖醋鲤鱼作为鲁菜的代表菜之一，深受广大食客的喜爱，是到济南的必点菜品之一。

2 The dish comes in golden color, crisp on the outside and tender on the inside with a tangy, sweet and sour taste. 此菜色泽金黄，外脆里嫩，香鲜味美，酸甜可口。

3 As the one of the widely-known dishes, the Sweet and Sour Carp to some sense represents the elegance and magnanimity that are typical of the Shandong cuisine. 作为广为熟知的菜肴之一，糖醋鲤鱼一定程度上代表了鲁菜的雍容华贵、中正大气。

双语赏析

Sweet and Sour Carp is one of the traditional dishes in Shandong. It belongs to the Jinan branch of the Shandong cuisine. Because of its festive color and impressive style, it often appears on the banquet menu and wedding feasts. As the signature food of Shandong cuisine, it is much loved by the locals and is a must-have for visitors to Jinan.

The main ingredient is carp and a truly authentic Sweet and Sour Carp must use the local fish from the Yellow River. The city of Jinan lies to the south of the Yellow River where the carps have a fat and tender texture with golden scales and red tails, a perfect choice for banquets. The usual practice is to leave the fish in fresh water for 2 or 3 days to purify before it is cooked. The appropriate fish for cooking should weigh between 1.8 to 2 jin with the length between 38 to 40 centimeters and waistline of 10 centimeters. A male fish is preferable than a female, whose belly is too big for the curled-up shape.

The cooking of the fish requires exquisite techniques. Cross-hatch the meat and then deep fry it in hot oil. Hold the fish by the head and the tail in moderate heating for the first few seconds to set the shape, then heat up to fry the fish thoroughly till golden brown in color. When it is done, the fish curls up with both ends upturned, connoting the carp jumping over the dragon gate (meaning to pass successfully the imperial examination in the old times). When brought to the table, the bubbling sound of the hot gravy can still be heard. The dish comes in golden color, crisp on the outside and tender on the inside with a tangy, sweet and sour taste. As the one of the widely-known dishes, Sweet and Sour Carp to some sense represents the elegance and magnanimity that are typical of the Shandong cuisine.

糖醋鲤鱼是鲁菜的经典名菜，属于鲁菜当中的济南菜。糖醋鲤鱼作为鲁菜的代表菜之一，有浓厚的喜庆色彩，是婚宴流水席中的重要菜品之一，深受广大食客的喜爱，是到济南的必点菜品之一。

此菜以鲤鱼——尤以黄河鲤鱼为上品原料，济南北临黄河，黄河鲤鱼不仅肥嫩鲜美，肉质细嫩，而且金鳞赤尾，形态可爱，是宴会上的佳肴。黄河鲤鱼打捞上来后，先净养2～3天，吐净泥土味，再活杀。选体重1.8～2斤，长在38～40厘米之间，腰围要在10厘米左右的公鲤鱼，因为母鲤鱼的腹部较大，不利于造出鲤鱼跳龙门之形。

制作工艺也很讲究，用坡刀把鱼的两面解成瓦垄花纹，入热油锅炸透。炸鲤鱼的时候，为了其特殊的造型，鱼头、鱼尾要分由左右手持（也可用工具代替）。低温定型，高温炸制。成品头尾翘起，立而不倒，好似活的一样，恰似鱼跃龙门，寓意吉祥。上桌后其汁冒泡且“啪啪”作响，未尝其味先闻其声；色泽金黄，外脆里嫩，香鲜味美，酸甜可口。作为广为熟知的菜肴之一，糖醋鲤鱼一定程度上代表了鲁菜的雍容华贵、中正大气。

词汇笔记

- **festive** ['festɪv] *adj.* Something that is festive is special, colourful, or exciting, especially because of a holiday or celebration. 喜庆的
- **scale** [skeɪl] *n.* The scales of a fish or reptile are the small, flat pieces of hard skin that cover its body. 鳞
- **connote** [kə'noʊt] *v.* If a word or name connotes something, it makes you think of a particular idea or quality. 意味着［正式］
- **magnanimity** [ˌmægnə'nɪməti] *n.* Magnanimity is kindness and generosity toward someone, especially after defeating them or being treated badly by them. 宽宏大量，大方［正式］

Dezhou Braised Chicken 德州扒鸡

必用三句

1 A traditional delicacy of Shandong province and a classic dish of Shandong cuisine, the technique of making Dezhou Braised Chicken has been rated as National Intangible Cultural Heritage. 德州扒鸡是中国山东传统名吃，鲁菜经典，德州扒鸡制作技艺被列为国家非物质文化遗产。

2 Dezhou Braised Chicken has since enjoyed a national fame. It has been exported to overseas market and hailed as "the best chicken in the world". 德州扒鸡因而闻名全国，远销海外，被誉为"天下第一鸡"。

3 Dezhou Braised Chicken has a perfect combination of color, lustrous with golden yellow skins and juicy with tender meat. It tastes palatable and is fully saturated and rich in nutrition. 德州扒鸡形色兼优，色泽金黄，熟烂软嫩，卤香悠长，味透骨髓，鲜奇滋补。

双语赏析

Dezhou Braised Chicken, or boneless chicken in five spices is one of the three treasures of Dezhou along with water melons and golden thread jijithus. A traditional delicacy of Shandong province and a classic dish of Shandong cuisine, the technique of making Dezhou Braised Chicken has been rated as National Intangible Cultural Heritage. The origin of Dezhou Braised Chicken can be traced back to the Ming Dynasty, and became popular during the Qing Dynasty with a history of more than 300 years. With the development of canal transportation, Dezhou became the axis of the royal road that connected nine provinces to the capital city between the late Yuan Dynasty and early Ming Dynasty. The emergence of Braised Chicken came with the vent of the flourishing economy. Peddlers selling Braised Chicken in a basket were frequently seen hanging about the canal dock, water route and land route courier station, and the government office yamen. Dezhou Braised Chicken was listed as the tribute chicken to the royal court since the reign of Emperor Qianlong. In the 1950s, the vice president of the People's Republic of China, Song Qingling would make a stop in Dezhou as she commuted from Shanghai to Beijing to purchase the Braised Chicken as a gift for Chairman Mao. Dezhou Braised Chicken has since enjoyed a national fame. It has been exported to overseas market and hailed as "the best chicken in the world".

Legend has it that the dish was created by accident. In the 31st year of Emperor Kangxi's reign, there was a restaurant owner called Jia Jiancai whose family ran the business of making Braised Chicken that could sell a dozen or more chickens per day. One day, Jia was out on an errand, and asked his apprentice to watch over the chicken stewed in the pot. The apprentice fell asleep and the chicken was overcooked. When Jia came back, it was too late and he had no choice but to sell the chicken underpriced. To his surprise, the chicken was sold out immediately and the customers loved it as the meat was aromatic and savory, and even the bones were cooked thoroughly and tasted boneless. The chicken became popular instantly.

Dezhou Braised Chicken has a perfect combination of color, lustrous with golden yellow skins and juicy with tender meat. It tastes palatable and fully saturated and is rich in nutrition. The chicken is arranged in an amazing style in a prone position with a reddish golden color-the legs crossed, claws in the belly, the wings coming out of the mouth. It looks from afar like a duck swimming in the water, holding feathers in its mouth. It is presented in such an elegant way that it is more of an art than just food.

德州扒鸡又称德州五香脱骨扒鸡，是著名的德州三宝（扒鸡、西瓜、金丝枣）之一。德州扒鸡是中国山东传统名吃，鲁菜经典，德州扒鸡制作技艺被列为国家非物质文化遗产。德州扒鸡源于明代，盛于明末清初，距今已有300余年的历史。元末明初，随着漕运繁忙，德州成为京都通达九省的御路。经济开始呈现繁荣，市面上出现了烧鸡。挎篮叫卖烧鸡的人，经常出现在运河码头、水旱驿站和城内官衙附近。早在清朝乾隆年间，德州扒鸡就被列为山东贡品送入宫中供帝后及皇族们享用。五十年代，国家副主席宋庆龄从上海返京途中，曾多次在德州停车选购德州扒鸡送给毛泽东主席以示敬意。德州扒鸡因而闻名全国，远销海外，被誉为“天下第一鸡”。

“德州扒鸡”的诞生纯属意外。据传清康熙三十一年，有个叫贾建才的饭店掌柜，家传做烧鸡，每天卖上二三十只。一天，贾掌柜有急事外出，锅里煮着鸡，就嘱咐店小二压好火。可店小二在灶台前睡着了，一锅鸡煮过了火，掌柜的回来赶紧撤出锅底火，勉强端到门市上想低价卖出，哪知道过火的烧鸡不仅肉烂味香，就连骨头也入口即酥，吸引了过往的行人，眨眼间一锅鸡就卖完了。“德州扒鸡”就此成名。

德州扒鸡形色兼优，色泽金黄，熟烂软嫩，卤香悠长，味透骨髓，鲜奇滋补。造型上两腿盘起，爪入鸡膛，双翅经脖颈由嘴中交差而出，全鸡呈卧体，色泽金黄，黄中透红，远远望去似鸭浮水，口衔羽翎，十分美观，是上等的美食艺术珍品。

词汇笔记

- **courier** ['kʊriər] *n.* A courier is a person who is paid to take letters and packages direct from one place to another. 信使
- **tribute** ['trɪbjuːt] *n.* A tribute is something that you say, do, or make to show your admiration and respect for someone. 称赞；敬意；贡品
- **reign** [reɪn] *n.* When a king or queen reigns, he or she rules a country. 在位统治
- **lustrous** ['lʌstrəs] *adj.* Something that is lustrous shines brightly and gently, because it has a smooth or shiny surface. 有光泽的；闪亮的；光亮的

Chapter 05

The Cuisine in the Middle and Lower Reaches of the Yangtze River

长江中下游地区饮食

The Dietary Culture of the Middle and Lower Reaches of the Yangtze River

长江中下游地区饮食文化

The middle reaches of the Yangtze River mainly comprise Hubei, Hunan, and Jiangxi. The terrain is mainly hills and plains and this land of blessing enjoys abundant rainfall, rich produce, a temperate climate, and all kinds of lakes and rivers, which has led to a diverse diet and is now renowned throughout the country for its Chu culture.

The region's food production is of great importance in the country, especially from the end of the Ming Dynasty to the mid-Qing Dynasty, as the proverb says "When Huguang has a bumper crop, the country will be free from hunger". At the same time, there was a rapid development in the tastes of the food, with famous dishes, desserts, wines, teas, masters, restaurants, and banquets, and the skills of cooking food were constantly improved, resulting in a great fusion of food culture and a change in food customs.

The middle reaches of the Yangtze River are dominated by rice, freshwater fish, and pork dishes, and are famous for rice snacks. The restaurant specializes in the production of steamed dishes; the soup simmering technique is unique; the taste is savoury, salty and sweet, soft and fresh, with a watery atmosphere; there are extensive exchanges with domestic and international food cultures.

The lower reaches of the Yangtze River begin at Poyang Lake in Jiangxi, where the Yangtze River slows down, the terrain is open, and the topography is mostly plain and hilly; this area is mainly represented by Huaiyang, Suzhou and Hui cuisine, with an overall lighter taste and a colourful and distinctive shape. As the saying goes, "There is a paradise above and Suzhou and Hangzhou below." It is also safe to say that the food of Yangzhou, Suzhou and Hangzhou can also match with the fame.

Although, when examined in general, the food styles of the lower reaches of the Yangtze have much in common, the fact is: "The tastes are different from one another across the river." This is a vivid, graphic and accurate summary of the culinary flavours of places such as Yangzhou and Suzhou on both sides of the Yangtze River.

长江中游饮食文化区，主要包含湖北、湖南和江西，地形主要是丘陵、平原，雨量充沛，物产丰富，气候温润，湖泊河流密布，因此促成其多样的饮食，且以楚文化为底蕴，如今享誉全国。

这一地区的粮食生产在全国居于举足轻重的地位，特别是明末至清中叶，有"湖广熟，天下足"的谚语广为流传。同时区域内风味流派迅速发展，名菜、名点、名酒、名茶、名师、名店、名筵席层出不穷，饮食的技艺不断改进，产生了饮食文化的大融合与食俗的嬗变。

长江中游平原饮食文化亚区稻米占绝对优势，擅长烹淡水鱼鲜、猪肉菜，米制小吃闻名于世；擅长蒸菜制作；煨汤技术别具一格；口味重咸鲜、咸鲜回甜、软嫩、清鲜，具水乡灵气；与国内外饮食文化有广泛交流。

长江下游地区始于江西鄱阳湖，长江的水势放缓，地势开阔，地形多为平原和丘陵；此地主要以淮扬菜、苏州菜和徽菜为代表，口味整体偏清淡，并且造型绚丽多彩，颇具特色。俗话说："上有天堂，下有苏杭。"那么，我们也可以说扬州、苏州、杭州也是长江下游地区饮食的天堂。

虽然从总体上来考察，长江下游的饮食风格有许多相同之处，但事实上"一江之隔味不同。"这是对长江两岸的扬州、苏州等地的饮食风味所作的生动、形象、准确的概括。

Hot Dry Noodles 热干面

必用三句

1 Among the many cuisines of Wuhan, it is impossible not to mention the Hot Dry Noodles, which have become a part of the city. 在武汉的众多美食中，不能不提热干面，它已经和武汉融为一体。

2 Hot Dry Noodles, as the name implies, are mixed noodles without soup. 热干面，顾名思义，是不带汤的拌面。

3 Legend has it that Hot Dry Noodles were firstly made in the 1930s by a trader surnamed Li who dried them in oil and then heated them up with a variety of spices. 据传，热干面是由 20 世纪 30 年代的一姓李的商贩将面条过油烘干，继而烫热加上多种佐料而成。

双语赏析

Originating in Wuhan and then expanding to most of Hubei and then to many parts of China, Hot Dry Noodles are one of the most popular noodles in China, which would be no less famous than Shanxi Daoxiao Noodles, Henan braised Noodles, Sichuan Dandan Noodles and Beijing Zha Jiang Noodles.

Among the many cuisines of Wuhan, it is impossible not to mention the Hot Dry Noodles, which have become a part of the city. It has become one of Wuhan's calling cards. Hot Dry Noodles, as the name implies, are mixed noodles without soup. Authentic hot noodles do not need to be seasoned too much–smooth and strong lye noodle in a thick sauce, some minced chilies, chopped spring onions, minced garlic and some sour beans. The shimmering oil and the aroma of the sauce are mixed to form a bowl of thick, unctuous snacks that resemble the simple and varied flavours of life. In the morning, a bowl of Hot Dry Noodles is served with a cup of hot soya bean milk and you can enjoy the taste. Unlike cold noodles or noodles in soup, Hot Dry Noodles can be eaten in a variety of ways. It is a sophisticated dish in that the noodles are carefully selected from the chef who makes them to the raw materials used, while it is varied in that the noodles are served with a wide range of complex seasonings and side dishes, which can be mixed in to suit your own preferences. It can also be served with other soups, eggnog, milk and soya milk, making it even more nutritious and varied in taste.

Legend has it that Hot Dry Noodles were firstly made in the 1930s by a trader surnamed Li who dried them in oil and then heated them up with a variety of spices. The noodles were registered as "Hot Dry Noodles" in 1950 and have evolved from the original three main varieties: Hot Dry Noodles with barbecue pork, Hot Dry Noodles with whole ingredients and Hot Dry Noodles with shrimps, to the eight varieties that are now available to satisfy people's taste buds and bring a variety of choices.

热干面是武汉的汉族特色美食，起源于武汉后扩至湖北大部，继而又经湖北扩展到国内许多地方，是广受欢迎的面食之一。它可以与山西刀削面、河南烩面、四川担担面，北京炸酱面齐名并肩。

在武汉的众多美食中，不能不提热干面，它已经和武汉融为一体，成为武汉的名片之一。热干面，顾名思义，是不带汤的拌面。正宗的热干面不需要添加过多的调料，爽滑劲道的碱水面，浓汁浇的老酱，加上点辣椒末、葱花、蒜末，再配上酸豆角就成了。油光闪烁、酱香淳厚，搅拌均匀后汇聚成一碗浓而不腻的风俗小吃，像极了质朴而又五味杂陈的生活。每天清早，来上一碗热干面配搭一杯热豆浆就能够有滋有味地品味了。热干面既不同于凉面，也不同于汤面，它的吃法讲究而又千变万化。讲究，是指从做面的师傅到原材料的选取都经过精挑细选，而千变万化是指热干面有着复杂繁多的调料配菜，人们可根据自己的喜好拌入合适的配菜和调料。也可以搭配其他的汤、蛋酒、牛奶、豆浆等，使得营养更加丰富，口味更加多样。

据传，热干面是由 20 世纪 30 年代的一姓李的商贩将面条过油烘干，继而烫热加上多种佐料而成。1950 年工商登记为“热干面”，如今也推陈出新由最初的三个主要的品种：叉烧热干面、全料热干面，虾米热干面，发展到如今八个品种，满足人们的味蕾，带来多样的选择。

词汇笔记

- **imply** [ɪm'plaɪ] *v.* to suggest that sth. is true or that you feel or think sth., without saying so directly 暗示，暗指；意味着
- **unctuous** ['ʌŋktʃuəs] *adj.* smooth and greasy in texture or appearance 油质的
- **resemble** [rɪ'zembəl] *v.* to look like or be similar to another person or thing 像，与……相似
- **sophisticated** [sə'fɪstɪkeɪtɪd] *adj.* complicated and advanced in design 复杂巧妙的

Chopped Bell Pepper Fish Head 剁椒鱼头

必用三句

1 A traditional Han Chinese dish from Xiangtan, Hunan and the border area between Hunan and Jiangxi, the red and white fish head with minced pepper is a unique dish. 红白相间而色彩夺目的“剁椒鱼头”是湖南湘潭以及湘赣交界地方的一道汉族传统名菜，属于“湘菜”。

2 The white and tender fish head is covered in red chilies, hot and fragrant. 白嫩嫩的鱼头肉被火辣辣的红辣椒覆盖着，热腾腾而清香四溢。

3 The unparalleled aroma and flavour of Hunan cuisine are perfectly reflected in the Chopped Bell Pepper Fish Head, which is the hard power of the famous dish. 湘菜举世无双的香辣可口，在剁椒鱼头上得到了完美的体现，这是名菜的硬实力。

双语赏析

A traditional Han Chinese dish from Xiangtan, Hunan and the border area between Hunan and Jiangxi, the red and white fish head with minced pepper is a unique dish. It combines the freshness of fish head with the spiciness of chopped chilies to bring a unique flavour. The fish head dish has always been a classic dish in Hunan cuisine, and the key to making it is to use a bighead carp head of more than three kilos, in addition to the local Hunan chilies.

The capsaicin in chopped peppers has a stimulating effect on both the mouth and the intestines, enhancing peristalsis and promoting the secretion of digestive juices, which is important for improving appetite and aiding digestion. Some studies have found that the incidence of stomach ulcers is much lower in areas where chilies are commonly eaten than in other areas. Chopped peppers are rich in vitamins, especially vitamin C, which can convert excess cholesterol in the body into bile acids, thus playing a good role in preventing gallstones. Eating Chopped Bell Pepper Fish Head can promote blood circulation, slow down aging for beauty and skincare. It is also very effective for nourishing the body for people who have digestion problems.

The white and tender fish head is covered in red chilies, hot and fragrant. The unparalleled aroma and flavour of Hunan cuisine are perfectly reflected in the Chopped Bell Pepper Fish Head, which is the hard power of the famous dish. It is a dish that allows traditional Chinese culture to be incorporated into it. The red oil floating up represents the Chinese red, symbolizing the bright future of the motherland, which can be considered the soft power of this dish. The fish head has led to the formation and development of the food plaza of the second ring road in Changsha, and new approaches have gradually emerged, such as golden soup fish head, double-flavoured fish head, etc. Nowadays, the Chopped Bell Pepper Fish Head is served in Hunan restaurants of other provinces, modified to suit local tastes, and also named “Lucky Strike”.

红白相间而色彩夺目的“剁椒鱼头”是湖南湘潭以及湘赣交界地方的一道汉族传统名菜，属于“湘菜”。其集鱼头的“鲜”和剁辣椒的“辣”为一体，风味独具一格。在湘菜中鱼头菜历来是经典菜品，剁椒鱼头由于野鲜粗犷与辣味生猛的特点，制作的关键除了要选用三斤以上的鳙鱼鱼头之外，还要有湖南本地的剁辣椒。

剁椒中的辣椒素对口腔和肠胃均有刺激作用，能够增强肠胃的蠕动，促进消化液的分泌，对改善食欲、帮助消化具有重要的作用。有研究发现，普遍喜欢吃辣椒的地区，其居民胃溃疡的发病率远低于其他地区。剁椒里面含有丰富的维生素，尤其是维生素 C 的含量比较高，可以使人体内多余的胆固醇转化为胆汁酸，从而起到很好地预防胆结石的作用。吃剁椒鱼头可以促进血液循环、减缓老化、美容养颜等功效都是非常不错的，而身体瘦弱、食欲不振体质的人吃剁椒鱼头在开胃以及滋补身子上的疗效是不容小觑的。

白嫩嫩的鱼头肉被火辣辣的红辣椒覆盖着，热腾腾而清香四溢。湘菜举世无双的香辣可口，在剁椒鱼头上得到了完美的体现，这是名菜的硬实力。一道菜让中国传统文化融入其中，漂起的红油代表着中国红，象征着祖国江山一片红，可谓是这道菜的软实力。鱼头带动了长沙二环线美食带的形成和发展，也逐渐出现了新式的做法，比如黄金鱼头、双味鱼头等。而如今剁椒鱼头在外省的湘菜馆中，经过改良以适应当地人的口味，也有被命名为“鸿运当头”的。

词汇笔记

- **minced** [mɪnst] *adj.* food, especially meat,cut into very small pieces 切碎的
- **capsaicin** [kæp'seɪɪsɪn] *n.* a compound that is responsible for the pungency of capsicums [生化] 辣椒素
- **intestine** [ɪn'testɪn] *n.* a long tube in the body between the stomach and the anus （脊椎动物的）肠
- **peristalsis** [ˌperɪ'stælsɪs] *n.* the wave-like movements of the intestine, etc. caused when the muscles contract and relax （肠等的）蠕动
- **unparalleled** [ʌn'pærəleld] *adj.* used to emphasize that sth. is bigger, better or worse than anything else like it 无与伦比的，无双的

Chairman Mao's Red Braised Pork 毛氏红烧肉

必用三句

1 Chairman Mao's Red Braised Pork is a direct translation of the eight famous dishes served at the Chairman's banquet and is a unique dish in Hunan cuisine, also known as “Mao's braised pork” because of its consistent popularity with Chairman Mao. 毛家红烧肉，是主席宴上的八大名菜直译，也是湖南菜独树一帜的美食，因其受到毛主席的钟爱，故又名“毛氏红烧肉”。

2 Chairman Mao believed that braised pork could nourish the brain, enhance memory and energise people. 毛主席认为红烧肉可以补脑增强记忆力并且可以使人精力充沛。

3 The authentic Mao's Restaurant is located in Shaoshan, Xiangtan, Hunan province, and is pure and well-selected. 正宗的毛家饭店位于湖南湘潭韶山，其做法纯正，选料精良。

双语赏析

Chairman Mao's Red Braised Pork is a direct translation of the eight famous dishes served at the Chairman's banquet and is a unique dish in Hunan cuisine, also known as "Mao's braised pork" because of its consistent popularity with Chairman Mao. Chairman Mao believed that braised pork could nourish the brain, enhance memory and energise people. On 10 September 2018, the "Chinese Cuisine" was officially released and "Mao's Braised Pork" was named one of the "Chinese Cuisine" as one of the top 10 classic dishes in Hunan.

It is said to have a long history and was originally called "rebate meat", referring to the time when Su Shi, a great writer in the Northern Song Dynasty, built a dike to protect the city from floods and the people slaughtered livestock to show their gratitude; Su Shi gave back to the people after making red meat, that was the original meaning of its name. Su Shi gave back to the people after making red meat, that was the original meaning of its name. Nowadays, there are various ways to make braised pork in the eight major cuisines, the most famous of which is Mao's braised pork. This is because it is not just a simple dish, but also a reflection of the love and respect people have for Chairman Mao.

The authentic Mao's Restaurant is located in Shaoshan, Xiangtan, Hunan province, and is pure and well-selected. Mao's braised pork is also known as "triple-layer-pork", which is selected from the abdomen of the pig, with fat and lean meat intertwined with a good balance. The pork is steamed and then fried with sugar, star anise and cinnamon, and then cooked in a pot with fermented soya beans. The cooked Mao's braised pork is golden and oily in colour, fatty but not greasy, very aromatic and tasty, and has a rich sauce flavour with a salty and fresh taste. Pork is rich in high quality protein and essential amino acids, and also provides haemoglobin and promotes iron absorption, effectively improving iron deficiency anaemia.

毛家红烧肉，是主席宴上的八大名菜直译，也是湖南菜独树一帜的美食，因其受到毛主席的钟爱，故又名“毛氏红烧肉”。毛主席认为红烧肉可以补脑增强记忆力并且可以使人精力充沛。2018 年 9 月 10 日，“中国菜”正式发布，“毛氏红烧肉”被评为“中国菜”湖南十大经典名菜。

红烧肉历史悠久，据说最初被称为“回赠肉”，指的是北宋时期的大文豪苏轼在抗洪筑堤保城之后，百姓宰杀牲畜以示感激；苏轼在制成红烧肉之后又回馈给了百姓，因此而得名。现如今，红烧肉在八大菜系中有多种做法，其中最出名的当属毛氏红烧肉。因为它不只是一道菜那么简单，更体现出人们对毛主席的爱戴和尊崇。

正宗的毛家饭店位于湖南湘潭韶山，其做法纯正，选料精良。毛氏红烧肉所采用的五花肉又称为“三层肉”，选自猪的腹部，脂肪与瘦肉交织，肥瘦相间为宜。需要将五花肉辅以冰糖、八角、桂皮先蒸后炸，然后入锅放入豆豉进行烹制。做熟的毛氏红烧肉色泽金黄油亮、肥而不腻，十分香润可口；并且伴有浓郁的酱香味，咸鲜味突出。猪肉中富含优质蛋白质和人体必需的氨基酸，也能提供血红素和促进铁吸收，有效改善缺铁性贫血。

词汇笔记

- **rebate** ['ri:beɪt] *v.* an amount of money that is paid back to you because you have paid too much 退还
- **reflection** [rɪ'flekʃn] *n.* attitude towards sb. or sth. （尤指见诸语言的）想法，意见
- **abdomen** ['æbdəmən] *n.* the part of the body below the chest that contains the stomach, bowels, etc. 腹，腹部
- **lean** [li:n] *adj.* containing little or no fat（肉）瘦的，脂肪少的
- **haemoglobin** [ˌhi:mə'gləʊbɪn] *n.* a red substance in the blood that carries oxygen and contains iron 血红蛋白；血色素

Jiangxi Steamed Rice Powder and Pork 江西粉蒸肉

必用三句

1 Made with streaky pork with skin, rice flour and other seasonings, the dish is fragrant with the smell of rice and meat, presenting a soft and glutinous taste without being greasy. 以带皮五花肉、米粉和其他调味料制作，成菜之后，米香肉香，呈现出一种软糯入味，香而不腻的口感。

2 This way of cooking reflects the appreciation of nature's deliciousness and the desire not to use too many condiments to break the original goodness. 这种烹饪方式能够体现人们对于自然所赋予美味的珍惜，不忍心用过多的佐料打破最初的那份美好。

3 There are various ways to make it, including the traditional method, which uses large vegetable leaves as padding and is steamed on a steamer, and is widely seen at banqueting festivals. 粉蒸肉有多种做法，包括古法粉蒸肉，采用大菜叶为铺垫，蒸笼上蒸熟，广泛现身于宴席佳节中。

双语赏析

In *Suiyuan Food List*, the Qing Dynasty, more than 300 kinds of dishes from the north and south were introduced, among which Jiangxi Steamed Rice Powder and Pork was on the list, saying that "the meat is tender, and the dish all together is almost no water, but not dry at all". Made with streaky pork with skin, rice flour and other seasonings, the dish is fragrant with the smell of rice and meat, presenting a soft and glutinous taste without being greasy.

Steaming is a very good and distinctive cooking method in traditional Chinese cooking, with the following advantages: 1. heated by vapour, achieving yin and yang, no inflammation; 2. evenly heated, no frying, harmless, easy to digest and maintain nutrition; 3. moist heat sterilisation, the most hygienic;

4. original taste, greatly reducing the composition of cooking oil; 5. the selection of ingredients must be fresh, much stricter than the requirements of frying and stir-frying; 6. The form remains unchanged, the original taste is not lost, and the nutrients and moisture in the food can be maintained. This way of cooking reflects the appreciation of nature's deliciousness and the desire not to use too many condiments to break the original goodness.

There are various ways to make it, including the traditional method, which uses large vegetable leaves as padding and is steamed on a steamer, and is widely seen at banqueting festivals. In Jiangxi people usually eat it at special festivals, such as the summer festival (eaten on the first day of summer), the steamer feast and the Tasting New Rice. Steamed pork is served in different ways throughout the south, including Sichuan, and each has its own legend, further reflecting the diversity and popularity of the dish. The art of making steamed pork at Songhu in Jiangxi is included in the Nanchang Intangible Cultural Heritage List.

在清代的《随园食单》中介绍了当时流行的300多种南北各地的美食，其中江西粉蒸肉榜上有名，书中说江西粉蒸肉“不但肉美，菜亦美，以不见水，故味独全”，可谓是以米入菜的代表佳作。以带皮五花肉、米粉和其他调味料制作，成菜之后，米香肉香，呈现出一种软糯入味，香而不腻的口感。

蒸是中国传统烹饪中很好又很有特色的方式，其优点如下：1. 以水汽加热，阴阳共济，味道滋润，不上火；2. 受热均匀，无煎炸，既无害，又容易消化，保持营养；3. 湿热灭菌，最卫生；4. 原汁原味，大大减少食用油成分；5. 选料必须新鲜，比煎炸炒的要求要严格得多；6. 形态不变，原味不失，能够保持食物中的营养和水分。这种烹饪方式能够体现人们对于自然所赋予美味的珍惜，不忍心用过多的佐料打破最初的那份美好。

粉蒸肉有多种做法，包括古法粉蒸肉，采用大菜叶为铺垫，蒸笼上蒸熟，广泛现身于宴席佳节中。在江西，人们通常在一些特殊的节日中吃粉蒸肉，例如撑夏（立夏当天吃）、笼床宴和尝新节（吃新节）。粉蒸肉在南方各地，包括四川等地都有不同的做法，并且各有传说，更加体现出这道菜的多样性以及受欢迎程度。江西松湖粉蒸肉制作技艺已经列入了南昌市非物质文化遗产名录。

词汇笔记

- **steam** [stiːm] *v.* to place food over boiling water so that it cooks in the steam; to be cooked in this way 蒸（食物）
- **streaky** [ˈstriːki] *adj.* marked with lines of a different colour 有条纹的
- **vapour** [ˈveɪpər] *n.* a mass of very small drops of liquid in the air, for example steam 蒸汽，水汽
- **inflammation** [ˌɪnfləˈmeɪʃən] *n.* a condition in which a part of the body becomes red, sore and swollen 发炎，炎症，上火
- **intangible** [ɪnˈtændʒəbl] *adj.* that does not exist as a physical thing but is still valuable（资产，利益）无形的；非物质的

Beggar's Chicken 叫花鸡

必用三句

1 "Beggar's Chicken", also called Braised Chicken，is a traditional famous dish in Changshu, Jiangsu province. 叫花鸡又名"煨鸡"，是江苏常熟的特色名菜。

2 The chicken is not simply what the name implies, but the ingredients are very elaborate. 叫花鸡，不能单纯地顾名思义，其用料十分讲究。

3 It can be described as "fragrant, crispy, fresh, tender" in one with unique flavor, such an irreplaceable masterpiece. 真可谓是集"香、酥、鲜、嫩"于一体，风味独特，无可替代的佳作。

双语赏析

"Beggar's Chicken", also called Braised Chicken, is a traditional famous dish in Changshu, Jiangsu province, which applies mud and lotus leaves to cover prepared chick. The raw materials include fresh lotus leaves, yellow mud and live free ranch chicken etc. Although its name is not elegant, it is famous in China and abroad, making diners feel mouth-watering and unforgettable for a long time.

According to records, in the late Ming and early Qing dynasties, a beggar in Changshu got a chicken by chance, but he was suffering from the lack of cooking utensils and seasonings, so he thought hard about it and suddenly decided to remove the guts of the chicken and wrap it in a thick layer of mud. After simmering for a period, the dry mud shell will be baked, after being knocked down, a roast meat aroma immediately came to the nostrils. Then the beggar was beautifully satiated, attracting people passing by to wonder how to cook it so good. The method of making it gradually spread, and soon got highly recognized by the general public.

The chicken is not simply what the name implies, but the ingredients are very elaborate. The modern, improved versions usually include fresh meat, dried scallops, shrimp, diced ham and shiitake mushrooms in the chicken's chamber. The method of preparation still retains the traditional style: the chicken is wrapped in lotus leaves with feathers, then coated with yellow clay and simmered over the fire, allowing the original flavor of the ingredients to be gradually released. After being cooked, the outer layer of yellow mud is removed and what is presented in front of the diners is an all-round impact, with golden skin and overflowing aroma; a closer taste of the original flavor of the chicken, crispy and fatty, with nutritious ingredients hidden in the belly, and delicious. It can be described as “fragrant, crispy, fresh, tender” in one with unique flavor, such an irreplaceable masterpiece.

叫花鸡又名“煨鸡”，是江苏常熟的特色名菜。通常采用黄泥和荷叶作为外层的包装以及新鲜的散养鸡等。其名虽不雅，却蜚声中外，令食客感到口齿留香，久久难以忘却。

据记载，明末清初，在常熟地带的一个叫花子，偶然得到一只鸡，但他苦于没有炊具和调料，苦思冥想一番，忽然灵机一动、就决定将这只鸡直接去掉内脏，然后裹上一层厚厚的泥巴。煨制一段时间后，将烤得干裂的泥壳敲下去，一股烤肉的香气立马扑鼻而来，叫花子美美地饱餐了一顿，引得过往人们的争相询问，并逐渐流传开来，得到寻常百姓的高度认可。

叫花鸡，不能单纯地顾名思义，其用料十分讲究。现代改良版通常会在鸡膛里放入鲜肉、干贝、虾仁、火腿丁和香菇。制作方法仍然保留传统的别致做法：鸡不去毛就在外面包上荷叶，然后涂上黄泥放在火上煨烤，让食材的原汁原味逐渐释放出来。静待熟后，将外层的黄泥去掉，呈现在食客面前的就是全方位的冲击，鸡肉皮色金黄、香味四溢；细品一下尽是鸡肉的原汁原味，酥香肥嫩，腹藏营养的配料，鲜美异常。真可谓是集“香、酥、鲜、嫩”于一体，风味独特，无可替代。

词汇笔记

- **chamber** ['tʃeɪmbə(r)] *n.* a space in the body, in a plant or in a machine, which is separated from the rest（人体、植物或机器内的）腔，室
- **elaborate** [ɪ'læbərət] *adj.* very complicated and detailed; carefully prepared and organized 复杂的，详尽的；精心制作的
- **mouth-watering** ['maʊθ wɔːtərɪŋ] *adj.* (approving) Mouth-watering food looks or smells so good that you want to eat it immediately.（食物）令人垂涎的

Shanghai Pan-fried Pork Buns 上海生煎包

必用三句

1 Pan-fried Pork Buns are also known as Pan-fried Steamed Buns, which are a traditional Han Chinese snack, popular in Jiangsu, Zhejiang, Shanghai and Guangdong, in short called pan-fried. 生煎包又称生煎馒头，是流行于苏浙沪粤的一种传统汉族小吃，简称为生煎。

2 Shanghai is the most popular place for pan-fried dishes. 上海是生煎的执牛耳地。

3 Shanghai Pan-fried Pork Buns are fried golden brown on the bottom and sprinkled with some sesame seeds and scallions on the top half. 上海生煎包外皮底部煎得金黄色，上半部撒了一些芝麻、香葱。

双语赏析

Pan-fried Pork Buns are also known as pan-fried steamed buns, which are a traditional Han Chinese snack, popular in Jiangsu, Zhejiang, Shanghai and Guangdong, in short called pan-fried. It has been around for hundreds of years and was originally a part-time snack in teahouses and tiger stoves (i.e. boiling water shops). Shanghai is the most popular place for pan-fried dishes.

Shanghai Pan-fried Pork Buns are fried golden brown on the bottom and sprinkled with some sesame seeds and scallions on the top half. It smells good, and the bite of it is full of soup, which is popular among Shanghai people. It is white, soft and fluffy, with a tender meat filling and a marinade, with a sesame and spring onion flavour. It is said of it that "the skin is thin, not broken and not burnt, well baked, the fresh filling is full of soup, and if the bottom is thick and burnt it would be deemed failure." It not only introduces the merits of the pan-fried pork buns, but also reminds diners not to buy those with a "thick and burnt bottom", or even to "stop eating them".

From the 1930s onwards, shops specializing in pan-fried buns gradually emerged, and the variety of fillings expanded from fresh meat with meat jelly to include chicken and shrimp, offering people more choices and satisfying their discerning taste buds. They are best eaten hot, fresh from the pan, with a juicy aroma, and are best savoured carefully to prevent burns.

Each person will have a certain amount of it, served with laver soup, wonton, soy milk or a bowl of white congee, just the right amount to start the day. In the middle of winter, eating a freshly cooked pan-fried bun is even better for chasing away the cold, chewing the flavour and absorbing the nutrients. The black sesame seeds at the top of the bun also have a wonderful effect on the appetite and spleen, soothing the Qi, and calming the cough.

生煎包又称生煎馒头，是流行于苏浙沪粤的一种传统汉族小吃，简称为生煎。生煎已经有上百年的历史，最初是茶楼、老虎灶（即熟水店）兼营的小吃品种。上海是生煎的执牛耳地。

上海生煎包外皮底部煎得金黄色，上半部撒了一些芝麻、香葱。闻起来香香的，咬一口满嘴汤汁，颇受上海人喜爱。成品面白，软而松，肉馅鲜嫩，中有卤汁，咬嚼时有芝麻及葱香味。对它的评价是：“皮薄不破又不焦，二分酵头靠烘烤，鲜馅汤汁满口来，底厚焦枯是败品。”不仅介绍了生煎馒头的优点，也提醒食客，凡是“底厚焦枯”的可以不买，甚至“罢吃”。

20 世纪 30 年代之后，逐渐出现生煎包的专营店，馅心花色也从鲜肉加肉皮冻，拓展丰富到加入鸡肉、虾仁等多个品种，供人们挑选自己合宜的口味，满足人们挑剔的味蕾。生煎外皮底部煎至金黄，以刚出锅热吃为最佳，吃起来香气汁水四溢，最好细品，以防烫伤。

每个人吃生煎都会有标准的数量，配上紫菜汤、小馄饨、豆浆或者一碗白粥，吃得刚刚好，开启元气满满的一天。隆冬时节，吃上刚出锅的生煎包，更有利于驱走寒气，嚼出香味，吸收营养。包子顶部收口处的黑芝麻，还有开胃健脾、顺气和中、平喘止咳的奇妙作用。

词汇笔记

- **sprinkle** [ˈsprɪŋkəl] *v.* to shake small pieces of sth. or drops of a liquid on sth. 撒，洒；用……点缀
- **sesame** [ˈsesəmi] *n.* a tropical plant grown for its seeds and their oil that are used in cooking 芝麻
- **marinade** [ˌmærɪˈneɪd] *n.* a mixture of oil, wine, spices, etc., in which meat or fish is left before it is cooked in order to make it softer or to give it a particular flavour 腌泡汁；卤汁
- **discerning** [dɪˈsɜːnɪŋ] *adj.* (approving) able to show good judgement about the quality of sb./sth. 有辨识能力的
- **savour** [ˈseɪvər] *v.* to enjoy the full taste or flavour of sth., especially by eating or drinking it slowly 品尝；尽情享受

Ningbo Tangyuan 宁波汤圆

必用三句

1 As one of Ningbo's famous snacks and one of China's representative snacks, Tangyuan is said to have originated in the Song Dynasty and has a long history. 汤圆是宁波的著名小吃之一，也是我国的代表小吃之一。据传，汤圆起源于宋代，历史源远流长。

2 The traditional Ningbo Tangyuan seems to be very simple but rather complicated to make. 传统的宁波汤圆，结构看似简单，可制作起来颇为讲究。

3 Tangyuan can be made with sunflower seeds, walnuts, and brown sugar, making them sweet, soft, and sticky with a delicate texture and a slightly sweet soup. 汤圆当中可以加入瓜子、核桃仁以及红糖，制成之后香甜软糯，口感细腻，汤汁微甜。

双语赏析

As one of Ningbo's famous snacks and one of China's representative snacks, Tangyuan is said to have originated in the Song Dynasty and has a long history. Unlike the jiaozi eaten in the north, Ningbo people sit down to eat Tangyuan in the morning of Chinese New Year, so Tangyuan is not just a traditional snack in Ningbo, and has the same cultural bearing as jiaozi in the north. Ningbo people have a deep and sincere affection for Tangyuan, perhaps because it has been eaten for generations and it is in their genes–after all, Tangyuan has been with Ningbo people for 700 years.

The most famous Tangyuan in Ningbo is made by the old and famous restaurant "Gangyagou", made with lard to be fragrant, sweet, fresh, smooth and glutinous, and when you bite into the outer skin, the fragrance of lard overflows. The reason for its popularity is that it is made with the finest ingredients. Nowadays, if you want to eat Ningbo Tangyuan, you can get them in many places outside of Ningbo; and semi-finished Tangyuan and Tangyuan fillings are available in all major supermarkets nationwide, so you can buy them yourself and enjoy a bowl of authentic Ningbo Tangyuan with a little processing.

The traditional Ningbo Tangyuan seems to be very simple but rather complicated to make. Because the glutinous rice balls float and then sink in the pot, they were first called "floating balls", but some regions have since changed the name to "yuanxiao" (used in North China, similar to Tangyuan). Tangyuan can be made with sunflower seeds, walnuts, and brown sugar, making them sweet, soft, and sticky with a delicate texture and a slightly sweet soup. Nowadays, there are more and more varieties of Tangyuan, such as durian Tangyuan and matcha Tangyuan. Moderate consumption can definitely bring tons of health benefits, but excessive consumption can easily lead to indigestion.

汤圆是宁波的著名小吃之一，也是我国的代表小吃之一。据传，汤圆起源于宋代，历史源远流长。与北方过年吃饺子不同，宁波人在春节早上都全家聚坐共进汤圆，所以汤圆在宁波并非一般意义上的传统小吃，而是和北方的饺子具有一样的文化承载。宁波人对汤圆的情愫深沉而真诚，这或许是因为历代宁波人吃汤圆把这些味道都吃进了基因里，毕竟从历史上看，汤圆陪伴宁波人也有 700 年历史了。

宁波汤圆最出名的当属"缸鸭狗"这家老字号，其制作的猪油汤圆独具香、甜、鲜、滑、糯的特点，咬开外皮，油香四溢。之所以广受欢迎是因为一是用料讲究，二是制作精良。如今缸鸭狗的宁波汤圆在宁波之外的很多地方也可以吃得到；并且半成品的缸鸭狗的水磨汤圆和汤圆馅料在全国各大超市均有出售，可以自行采购稍作加工，就可以享受一碗正宗的宁波汤圆。

传统的宁波汤圆，结构看似简单，可制作起来颇为讲究。因为这种糯米球煮在锅里又浮又沉，所以它最早叫"浮元子"，后来有的地区把"浮元子"改称元宵。汤圆当中可以加入瓜子、核桃仁以及红糖，制成之后香甜软糯，口感细腻，汤汁微甜。如今汤圆的品种也越来越多，有榴莲汤圆、抹茶汤圆等，推陈出新，供食客们挑选。适度食用对身体益处多多，过度食用容易导致消化不良。

词汇笔记

- **representative** [ˌreprɪˈzentətɪv] *adj.* able to be used as a typical example of sth. 典型的，有代表性的

- **sincere** [sɪn'sɪər] *adj.* showing what you really think or feel 衷心的，诚挚的
- **affection** [ə'fekʃn] *n.* the feeling of liking or loving sb./sth. very much and caring about them 喜爱
- **lard** [lɑːd] *n.* a firm white substance made from the melted fat of pigs that is used in cooking 猪油
- **overflow** [ˌəʊvə'fləʊ] *v.* to be so full that the contents go over the sides 漫出

Crab Roe Soup Buns 蟹黄汤包

必用三句

1 The Crab Roe Soup Buns are thin-skin and almost translucent, full of soup and delicious, and look like a clock on a plate or a lantern on chopsticks. 蟹黄包皮薄透亮、汤多馅饱、味道鲜美的特点，放在盘里像座钟，夹在筷上像灯笼。

2 The ingredients used to make the Crab Roe Soup Buns are very delicate, with the filling being crab roe and crab meat and the soup being the original chicken soup. 蟹黄汤包的制作原料十分讲究，馅为蟹黄和蟹肉，汤为原味鸡汤，制作工艺精妙绝伦。

3 Crab is rich in protein and trace elements, and is a good tonic for the body. 螃蟹含有丰富的蛋白质及微量元素，对身体有很好的滋补作用。

双语赏析

The Crab Roe Soup Buns are thin-skin and almost translucent, full of soup and delicious, and look like a clock on a plate or a lantern on chopsticks. The ingredients used to make the Crab Roe Soup Buns are very delicate, with the filling being crab roe and crab meat and the soup being the original chicken soup. The Crab Roe Soup Buns are known throughout the country for their paper-thin skin, the fact that they are easy to break when blown, and the fact that they are “superb” in production, “beautiful” in form and “strange” in eating. The most famous ones are Nanjing Longpao Crab Roe Soup Buns, Jingjiang Crab Roe Soup Buns, Taixing Quxia Crab Roe Soup Buns, Zhenjiang Yanchun Crab Roe Soup Buns and Huaian Wenlou Crab Roe Soup Buns. Nanjing hosts a year-round food and cultural festival for Longpao Crab Roe Soup Buns.

Legend has it that the Crab Roe Soup Buns took shape during the Three Kingdoms because Zhuge Liang, made meat steamed buns as a sacrifice, and the people who made them added the crab meat and crab roe that Liu Bei’s wife Sun Shangxiang liked a lot, which is regarded as the very beginning of the Crab Roe Soup Buns. Nanjing Liuhe’s Longpao Crab Roe Soup Buns have been around for more than 140 years and were a tribute to the Qing government, thanks to Emperor Qianlong’s visit to Jiangnan where he tasted the Crab Roe Soup Buns, hence the people also called them “Qianlong soup buns”.

Crab is rich in protein and trace elements, and is a good tonic for the body. Crab also has an anti-tuberculosis effect, and eating crab can be very beneficial in recovering from tuberculosis. These days it is easy to see tourists from all over the world sampling this delicacy in many tourist spots in the south, queuing for hours just to taste this delicious crab bun. Take a straw, suck up the delicious soup and then dip the thin skin into the vinegar. Of course, you can also bite off the skin and then suck the soup. Don’t grab and eat hastily, otherwise the soup will spill all over. It’s worth waiting for and savouring slowly.

蟹黄汤包有皮薄透亮、汤多馅饱、味道鲜美的特点，放在盘里像座钟，夹在筷上像灯笼。蟹黄汤包的制作原料十分讲究，馅为蟹黄和蟹肉，汤为原味鸡汤，制作工艺精妙绝伦。蟹黄汤包因皮薄如纸，吹弹即破，制作“绝”、形态“美”、吃法“奇”而盛誉全国，蜚声四海。最出名的当属南京龙袍蟹黄汤包、靖江蟹黄汤包、泰兴曲霞蟹黄汤包、镇江宴春蟹黄汤包、淮安文楼蟹黄汤包。南京常年举办龙袍蟹黄汤包美食文化节。

传说，蟹黄汤包在三国时就有了雏形，是因为诸葛亮命人做肉馒头祭祀，制作的人将刘备夫人孙尚香喜欢吃的蟹肉蟹黄加入馅料，成就了蟹黄汤包的开端。南京六合的龙袍蟹黄汤包已经有 140 多年的历史，是清朝朝廷贡品，归功于乾隆皇帝当年下江南品尝了蟹黄蟹肉为馅的汤包，因此百姓们称之为“乾隆汤包”。

螃蟹含有丰富的蛋白质及微量元素，对身体有很好的滋补作用。螃蟹还有抗结核作用，吃蟹对结核病的康复大有补益。如今在南方多个旅游景点很容易看到各地游客品尝这一美味，排队数小时就为品尝蟹黄汤包。取吸管一根，吸完鲜美汤汁之后，然后将薄皮蘸醋食之。当然，也可用牙齿将薄皮咬下缺口，然后吸干汤汁食用。切不可抓而食之，不然则汤洒一身。美味值得等待也值得细细品味。

词汇笔记

- **roe** [rəʊ] *n.* the mass of eggs inside a female fish (hard roe) or the sperm of a male fish (soft roe), used as food 鱼卵，鱼子
- **translucent** [trænz'lu:sənt] *adj.* (formal) allowing light to pass through but not transparent 透明的；半透明的
- **superb** [su:'pɜ:b; sju:'pɜ:b] *adj.* excellent; of very good quality 极佳的，质量极高的
- **emperor** ['empərər] *n.* the ruler of an empire 皇帝
- **tonic** ['tɒnɪk] *n.* a medicine that makes you feel stronger and healthier, taken especially when you feel tired 补药

Mochi 麻糍

必用三句

1 Mochi, also known as mazi, is a traditional snack. 麻糍又称麻子，是一种传统的小吃。

2 Popular in most of Jiangxi, Zhejiang and southern Fujian provinces, it is made from glutinous rice and other ingredients to be round in shape and nearly transparent. 流行于江西大部地区、浙江省和福建闽南地区等地，该小吃由糯米等食材制作而成，呈圆形，几近透明。

3 Mochi is sweet and savoury, with a sweet, smooth texture, and is soft and slightly icy. 麻糍香甜可口，有着甜、滑的口感，且软韧、微冰。

双语赏析

Mochi, also known as mazi, is a traditional snack. Popular in most of Jiangxi, Zhejiang and southern Fujian provinces, it is made from glutinous rice and other ingredients to be round in shape and nearly transparent. There are many different kinds, and when it is well cooked, it is as white as snow, soft as cotton, smooth and delicate. It does not glue to the bowl, or stick to the teeth and mouth, and is suitable for people of all ages.

Mochi is a distinctive glutinous rice food in Dongyang and Yongkang, and is eaten by almost every household for building houses, planting fields and in the middle of the seventh month of the lunar calendar. They are also often sold in the market, but only the Mochi on the outskirts of the city is the most famous. Mochi can be dried and steamed, fried, roasted or stir-fried. Mochi is also a famous snack in southern Fujian, made from good glutinous rice, lard, sesame seeds, peanuts and rock sugar. Mochi is sweet and savoury, with a sweet, smooth texture, and is soft and slightly icy. The finished product is bright white in colour, smooth and transparent. It is customary to celebrate the Mochi Festival in the tenth month of the lunar calendar in Jiangshan, Zhejiang province. In Jinhua, Zhejiang province, it is customary to eat Mochi on the winter solstice.

Mochi is one of the most important foods during the Chinese New Year, and can be eaten at home or as a treat for guests, and is an essential gift for visiting relatives in the New Year. It can also be offered as an offering to ancestors during the Qingming Festival. Mochi used to be made to fill the stomach, but now the consumer market has long since shifted from filling the stomach to tasting the culture and feeling the history.

麻糍又称麻子，是一种传统的小吃。流行于江西大部地区、浙江省和福建闽南地区等地，该小吃由糯米等食材制作而成，呈圆形，几近透明。其种类很多，成品洁白如雪，柔软如绵，光滑细腻，不粘碗，不钉牙糊口，老少皆宜，食者无所禁忌。

麻糍在东阳、永康等地是别具一格的一种糯米食品，民间建房、种田和农历七月半几乎家家户户都要食用。市场上也常有出售，但唯独城郊的田宅麻糍最负盛名。

麻糍阴干后蒸、煎、火烤、砂炒皆宜。麻糍也是闽南著名小吃，其原料为上好糯米、猪油、芝麻、花生仁、冰糖等。麻糍香甜可口，有着甜滑的口感，且软韧、微冰。成品色泽鲜白，滑韧透明。浙江省江山市有每年农历十月份过麻糍节的风俗。浙江金华一带有冬至吃麻糍的风俗。

麻糍在春节期间是重要的食物之一，既可以自家食用，也可招待客人，更是拜年走亲戚的必备礼物。清明时节祭祀祖先也可以奉上。以前做麻糍是为了填饱肚子，而现在的消费市场早已从吃饱肚子转为品尝文化、感受历史。

词汇笔记

- **cotton** ['kɒtn] *n.* a plant grown in warm countries for the soft white hairs around its seeds that are used to make cloth and thread 棉，棉花
- **glue** [glu:] *v.* to join two things together 胶合，粘贴
- **household** ['haʊshəʊld] *n.* all the people living together in a house 家庭
- **lunar** ['lu:nər] *adj.* connected with the moon 阴历的
- **solstice** ['sɒlstɪs] *n.* either of the two times of the year at which the sun reaches its highest or lowest point in the sky at midday, marked by the longest and shortest days 至，至日

Jinhua Ham 金华火腿

必用三句

1 Jinhua Ham is both a precious food and a high-grade nutritional tonic and medicinal food. It is known as one of the top three famous hams in the world. 金华火腿既是珍贵的食品，又是一种高档营养滋补品和药膳食品，堪称世界三大名腿之一。

2 Jinhua Ham is a specialty of Jinhua, Zhejiang province, and a National Geographical Indication Product of China. 金华火腿，浙江省金华市特产，中国国家地理标志产品。

3 Jinhua is the origin of Jinhua Ham for its own specific climate and conditions.
金华是金华火腿的原产地，有其特定的气候和条件。

双语赏析

Jinhua Ham is both a precious food and a high-grade nutritional tonic and medicinal food. It is known as one of the top three famous hams in the world. Jinhua Ham is a specialty of Jinhua, Zhejiang province, and a National Geographical Indication Product of China. When stir-fried in soup, mixed with a few thin slices of Jinhua Ham, the dish is instantly transformed and upgraded, with a strong fragrance and a richer soup; therefore, a spoonful of taste will make you never forget it, and no other condiments can compare with it. Jinhua Ham is brightly coloured, red and white, salty with sweetness for the lean, fragrant without being greasy for the fat, being rich in protein, fat, vitamins and minerals.

The origin of Jinhua Ham varies, but it is generally believed to have originated in the Tang or Song dynasties; during the Yuan dynasty, Marco Polo introduced the way of making ham to Europe, thus making Jinhua Ham the king of hams; during the Qing dynasty, it had become one of the products that generated foreign exchange and was sold to many parts of the world.

Jinhua Ham is made from local Jinhua pigs, with blacks on the head and tail, which are cured in winter and then air-dried over a period of a few months. Authentic Jinhua Ham can be stored at natural temperatures for three or four years and still retain its original quality because a rather long time has passed since the curing stage. The Jinhua Ham coming into its existence is the result of the hard work and wisdom of the Jinhua people. Jinhua is the origin of Jinhua Ham for its own specific climate and conditions. According to the *Gleanings from Compendium of Materia Medica* compiled by Zhao Xuemin in the Qing Dynasty, Jinhua Ham is beneficial to the kidneys, nourishes the stomach, strengthens the yang, consolidates the bone marrow, and strengthens the feet.

In everyday life, it is a great way for the sick to regain vitality, for the elderly to prolong their lives, and for women to nourish themselves after giving birth.

金华火腿既是珍贵的食品，又是一种高档营养滋补品和药膳食品，堪称世界三大名腿之一。金华火腿，浙江省金华市特产，中国国家地理标志产品。煲汤炒菜，拌几片薄薄的金华火腿，菜肴顿时转型升级，浓香四溢，汤汁愈发浓郁，品一勺鲜得眉毛都要掉下来了，其他调味品很难与之相比。金华火腿色泽鲜艳，红白分明，瘦肉香咸带甜，肥肉香而不腻，美味可口；内含丰富的蛋白质和脂肪，多种维生素和矿物质。

金华火腿的历史起源，众说纷纭，一般认为起源于唐朝或者宋朝；元朝，由马可波罗将制作火腿的方式传到了欧洲，因此金华火腿乃火腿之王；清朝时，其已经成为出口创汇的产品之一，销往世界多地。

金华火腿精选金华当地土猪“两头乌”为原料，立冬后开始腌制，再经月风干。地道的金华火腿，因为腌制阶段就有时间的积淀，所以在自然温度下能够储存三四年，仍保持原来品质。金华火腿的形成，是金华人民勤劳与智慧的结晶，源远流长。金华是金华火腿的原产地，有其特定的气候和条件。据清代赵学敏编纂的《本草纲目拾遗》记载，金华火腿有益肾、养胃、生津、壮阳、固骨髓、健足力等功能。在日常生活中，病人恢复元气，老人益寿延年，妇女产后养身，吃点火腿都是很好的选择。

词汇笔记

- **ham** [hæm] *n.* the top part of a pig's leg that has been cured (= preserved using salt or smoke) and is eaten as food 火腿
- **indication** [ˌɪndɪˈkeɪʃn] *n.* a remark or sign that shows that sth. is happening or what sb is thinking or feeling 指示，标示
- **vitamin** [ˈvɪtəmɪn] *n.* a natural substance found in food that is an essential part of what humans and animals eat to help them grow and stay healthy 维生素
- **generate** [ˈdʒenəreɪt] *v.* to produce or create sth. 产生
- **cure** [kjʊər] *v.* to treat food or tobacco with smoke, salt, etc. in order to preserve it（用熏、腌等方法）加工贮藏（食物或烟草）

Salted Duck 盐水鸭

必用三句

1 Salted Duck is a famous specialty of Nanjing, and is one of the representatives of Jinling cuisine. 盐水鸭是南京的著名特产，属金陵菜，是金陵菜的代表之一。

2 Nanjing is located in the middle and lower reaches of the Yangtze River, with many lakes and a dense network of waterways, which provides a natural advantage for duck farming, and has even been given the name “Duck Capital”. 南京地处长江中下游，湖泊、水道众多，水网密布，为鸭子的养殖提供了天然的有利因素，甚至被冠以“鸭都”的名号。

3 Jiangsu Salted Duck has a long-standing reputation and has a history of more than 2,500 years. People have accumulated rich production experience during this long period of time. 江苏盐水鸭久负盛名，至今已有两千五百多年历史。盐水鸭制作历史悠久，积累了丰富的制作经验。

双语赏析

Salted Duck is a famous specialty of Nanjing, and is one of the representatives of Jinling cuisine. It is also known as sweet-scented osmanthus duck, and a National Geographical Indication Product of China. It is also called “Jinling Slated Duck” because of its nickname “Jinling”. Nanjing people love to eat duck, and the rise and prosperity of Nanjing's duck culture cannot be separated from the natural conditions. Nanjing is located in the middle and lower reaches of the Yangtze River, with many lakes and a dense network of waterways, which provides a natural advantage for duck farming, and has even been given the name “Duck Capital”. Nanjing has a long history of duck farming, and the same goes for duck production.

Jiangsu Salted Duck has a long-standing reputation and has a history of more than 2,500 years. People have accumulated rich production experience during this long period of time. The produced Salted Duck has tender skin and white meat, fat but not greasy, fragrant and delicious, and enjoys the features of being fragrant, crisp and tender. Before and after the Mid-Autumn Festival, the Salted Duck made in the blooming season of sweet-scented osmanthus has the best color and taste, and it is called sweet-scented duck. The cooking process of this dish seems to be very simple, but the chef needs to be very experienced. If the heat is insufficient, the meat is not mature enough, and the meat is not well cooked. If the heat is too high, the meat will be less juicy and the texture will be hard.

Salted Duck can best reflect the original taste of duck meat. Through the method of marinating, the grease and the smelly of the meat can be covered. Salted Duck is very suitable for people who are weak and easily tired because duck meat can play a role in nourishing blood, and the therapeutic effect is obvious, especially for those with dry skin, duck soup is highly recommended. The sweet-scented osmanthus duck soup not only has the elegant aroma of sweet-scented osmanthus, but also the delicious mellow duck meat, which can whiten the skin, nourish the body and stomach.

盐水鸭是南京的著名特产，属金陵菜，是金陵菜的代表之一，又叫桂花鸭，是中国地理标志产品。因南京有“金陵”别称，故也称“金陵盐水鸭”。南京人喜欢吃鸭子，南京鸭肴文化的兴起与繁盛离不开自然条件的支持。南京地处长江中下游，湖泊、水道众多，水网密布，为鸭子的养殖提供了天然的有利因素，甚至被冠以“鸭都”的名号。南京养鸭有悠久的历史，制鸭也是同样。

江苏盐水鸭久负盛名，至今已有两千五百多年历史。盐水鸭制作历史悠久，积累了丰富的制作经验。生产的盐水鸭皮白肉嫩、肥而不腻、香鲜味美，具有香、酥、嫩的特点。而以中秋前后，桂花盛开季节制作的盐水鸭色味最佳，名为桂花鸭。该菜品看似简单的烹调过程，却对制作经验的要求非常高，火候不足则不够成熟，肉质不烂，火候过大，则肉质汁水较少，质感柴硬。

盐水鸭最能体现鸭肉的本味，用卤制的方法可以过滤油腻，驱除腥气。盐水鸭很适合身体虚弱疲乏者，因为鸭肉正可以起到补血的功效，食疗效果明显，特别是皮肤干燥者，可以经常喝些鸭汤。而桂花鸭汤，不仅有桂花的清雅香气，还有醇厚的鸭肉鲜美，能够起到美白肌肤、养生润燥，和胃生津的作用。

词汇笔记

- **prosperity** [prɒ'sperəti] *n.* the state of being successful 繁荣，成功
- **reach** [riːtʃ] *n.* a straight section of water between two bends on a river 河段
- **waterway** ['wɔːtəweɪ] *n.* a river, canal, etc. along which boats can travel 水路
- **experienced** [ɪk'spɪəriənst] *adj.* having knowledge or skill in a particular job or activity 熟练的，有经验的
- **insufficient** [ˌɪnsə'fɪʃənt] *adj.* not large, strong or important enough for a particular purpose 不充分的，不够重要的

Braised Pork Ball in Brown Sauce 红烧狮子头

必用三句

1 Braised Pork Ball in Brown Sauce is a famous Huaiyang dish. 红烧狮子头是一道淮扬名菜。

2 The fatty and lean meat is combined with water chestnuts and mushrooms to make balls, which are then fried and boiled. 将有肥有瘦的肉配上荸荠、香菇等材料，做成丸子，然后先炸后煮。

3 The nutritional value of Braised Pork Ball in Brown Sauce is relatively high and it is easily absorbed, making it ideal for the elderly, young, women and children, as well as the infirm. 红烧狮子头的营养价值相对比较高，也易于吸收，非常适合老幼妇孺，体弱多病者。

双语赏析

Braised Pork Ball in Brown Sauce is a famous Huaiyang dish. The fatty and lean meat is combined with water chestnuts and mushrooms to make balls, which are then fried and boiled. The fragrance of the meat is so strong that the mellow smell of the meat and the juices are super delicious. The late master painter Zhang Daqian taught his wife a special dish called "Braised Pork Ball in Brown Sauce", which is made of pork of 70% lean meat and 30% fat, finely cut and roughly chopped to be the size of a grain of rice, not too finely chopped to keep the gaps between the meat to contain the juices.

According to the legend, it was made during the Ming Dynasty when Zhu Di saw the stone lions on the Lugou Bridge in his fiefdom of Beijing and was reminded of his mother. He ordered his cook to make 50 meatballs to celebrate his mother's 50th birthday and to wish for a reunion with his mother in the future. The dish later spread to the people and became a delicacy enjoyed by young and old alike. There are many legends about the origin of the dish, so here is just one of them.

The nutritional value of Braised Pork Ball in Brown Sauce is relatively high and it is easily absorbed, making it ideal for the elderly, young, women and children, as well as the infirm.

红烧狮子头是一道淮扬名菜。将有肥有瘦的肉配上荸荠、香菇等材料，做成丸子，然后先炸后煮。出锅后香味扑鼻，光闻起来就引动食欲，醇香味浓的肉块与汁液超级美味。已故国画大师张大千传授夫人的一道拿手好菜就是"红烧狮子头"，大千先生的做法是七分瘦肉，三分肥肉，细切粗斩，大小要如米粒，不能剁太细，让肉质间保持缝隙，才能含汁。

相传，红烧狮子头是明朝时期朱棣在自己的封地北京看到卢沟桥上的石狮子，触景生情，不禁想起自己的母亲。于是令厨子做了 50 个肉圆，一来为母亲祝五十大寿，二来预祝将来母子骨肉团圆。后来这道菜就传到了民间，成为老少皆宜的美味。关于其起源的传说比较多，这里只选择其中一条。

红烧狮子头的营养价值相对比较高，也易于吸收，非常适合老幼妇孺，体弱多病者。

词汇笔记

- **braised** [breɪzd] *adj.* to cook meat or vegetables very slowly with a little liquid in a closed container 炖熟的

- **grain** [greɪn] *n.* a small hard piece of particular substances 颗粒，细粒
- **fiefdom** ['fiːfdəm] *n.* (old use) an area of land, especially a rented area for which the payment is work, not money 领地；（尤指）采邑，封地
- **infirm** [ɪn'fɜːm] *n.* people who are weak and ill/sick for a long period 病弱的人；体弱的

Jiaxing Zongzi 嘉兴粽子

必用三句

1 Zongzi, a food made from steamed glutinous rice wrapped in Zongzi leaves, is one of the traditional Chinese festive foods. 粽子，由粽叶包裹糯米蒸制而成的食品，是中国传统节庆食物之一。

2 As one of the traditional foods that has been inherited from ancient time in China, Zongzi has spread far and wide. 粽子作为中国历史文化积淀最深厚的传统食品之一，传播亦甚远。

3 Jiaxing Zongzi is now world famous, especially the pork Zongzi, known as the "king of Zongzi", which tastes light, soft, salty and sweet, easy to carry, quick to eat and perfectly suited to today's fast-food culture. 嘉兴粽子如今已经闻名世界，尤其是鲜肉粽，被誉为"粽子之王"，口感清香软糯，咸甜适中，而且便于携带，食用快捷，完全能够适应当今的快餐文化。

双语赏析

Compared with the north, the south has a greater variety of Zongzi and a greater reputation, and the Zongzi from the south of the Yangtze River is most famous for being produced in Jiaxing. Jiaxing Zongzi is a generic term for a range of Zongzi, including bean paste Zongzi, pine nut Zongzi, ham Zongzi and pork Zongzi. Zongzi is not only a festive food in Jiaxing, but also an everyday food, and is made in a sophisticated way. Zongzi, a food made from steamed glutinous rice wrapped in Zongzi leaves, is one of the traditional Chinese festive foods. As one of the traditional foods that has been inherited from ancient time in China, Zongzi has spread far and wide. For thousands of years, the custom of eating Zongzi has been prevalent in China and has spread to Korea, Japan and Southeast Asian countries.

Zongzi has a long history and was originally used as a tribute to ancestral spirits. They are called different in the north and the south, but in the north, they are made of millet, which is horn-shaped and was called "horned millet" in the north of ancient times. Due to the differences in eating habits around the country, Zongzi has developed north and south flavours; in terms of taste, there are two categories of Zongzi: salty and sweet Zongzi. The history of Jiaxing Zongzi can be traced back as far as the *County Annals of Xiushui in WanLi* in Ming Dynasty, where it was recorded: "Dragon Boat Festival stickers and mugwort hanged, horn millet eaten, Pu Huang wine drunk..." In the Qing Dynasty, it was also recorded that "village people gather to watch and share horned millet". By the end of the Qing Dynasty, in the Jiaxing area, people would wrap their own Zongzi during the New Year, Qingming Festival and Dragon Boat Festival, and they could also be given as gifts to friends and relatives.

Jiaxing Zongzi is now world famous, especially the pork Zongzi, known as the "king of Zongzi", which tastes light, soft, salty and sweet, easy to carry, quick to eat and perfectly suited to today's fast-food culture.

相比于北方，南方的粽子花样更多，名声也更大，江南的粽子又以嘉兴出产的最为出名。嘉兴粽子是一系列的粽子的总称，包括豆沙粽、松仁粽、火腿粽、鲜肉粽等。粽子在嘉兴不仅是节庆食品，更是一种日常饮食，做法也是比较讲究。粽子，由粽叶包裹糯米蒸制而成的食品，是中国传统节庆食物之一。粽子作为中国历史文化积淀最深厚的传统食品之一，传播亦甚远。端午食粽的风俗，千百年来，在中国盛行不衰，而且流传到朝鲜、日本及东南亚诸国。

粽子由来久远，最初是用来祭祀祖先神灵的贡品。南北叫法不同，北方产黍，用黍米做粽，角状，古时候在北方称“角黍”。由于各地饮食习惯的不同，粽子形成了南北风味；从口味上分，有咸粽和甜粽两大类。嘉兴粽子的历史最早可以追溯到明代的《万历秀水县志》，其中曾记载："端午贴符悬艾啖角黍蒲黄酒……"。在清代也曾记载："村人聚观，分享角黍"。到清末时期，在嘉兴一带，人们在过年、清明节、端午节都要自己包粽子，也可以作为礼品馈赠亲友。

嘉兴粽子如今已经闻名世界，尤其是鲜肉粽，被誉为"粽子之王"，口感清香软糯，咸甜适中，而且便于携带，食用快捷，完全能够适应当今的快餐文化。

词汇笔记

- **generic** [dʒə'nerɪk] *adj.* shared by, including or typical of a whole group of thing 一般的，通用的
- **festive** ['festɪv] *adj.* typical of a special event or celebration 节日的
- **prevalent** ['prevələnt] *adj.* that exists or is very common at a particular time or in a particular place 盛行的，普遍的
- **tribute** ['trɪbjuːt] *n.* a gift that is intended to show your respect or admiration, especially for a dead person 贡品

Dongpo Pork 东坡肉

必用三句

1 Dongpo Pork is also known as Rolled Pork and Braised Pork. With pork as the main ingredient, it is a traditional famous dish in the south of the Yangtze River, belonging to Zhejiang cuisine. 东坡肉又名滚肉、红烧肉。它是江南地区传统名菜，属于浙菜系，以猪肉为主要食材。

2 Dongpo Pork is not only perfect in color, aroma and taste, but also has high nutritional value. 东坡肉不仅色香味俱全，营养价值也比较高。

3 The earliest birthplace of Dongpo Pork is Xuzhou of Jiangsu province. 东坡肉最早的发源地是江苏徐州。

双语赏析

Dongpo Pork is also known as Rolled Pork and Braised Pork. With pork as the main ingredient, it is a traditional famous dish in the south of the Yangtze River, belonging to Zhejiang cuisine. The main ingredients and shapes of Dongpo Pork are similar. The main ingredients are half-fat and half-thin pork, which is stewed with other ingredients. The finished dish is neatly arranged mahjong-shaped pieces of pork with agate-like color, red and translucent. If you taste one piece, it is soft but not overcooked, fat but not greasy. The lean meat is soft and tender, and it does not stick to the teeth at all. The fatty meat is not greasy, serving as a great complement to the lean meat. The last part you eat is the pork skin, which is very chewy, but not hard at all. When chewing slowly, you get a strong aroma in your mouth.

Dongpo Pork is not only perfect in color, aroma and taste, but also has high nutritional value. Pork is rich in high-quality protein and essential fatty acids, and provides heme and cysteine, which can improve iron-deficiency anemia, nourish Yin and strengthen the kidney.

The origin of Dongpo Pork is quite interesting. In 1090 AD, Su Dongpo, a great writer in the Song Dynasty, served as the governor of Hangzhou. He often led the people of Hangzhou to dredge the West Lake and restored the West Lake to its youth. The people of Hangzhou were so grateful that they carried pork and wine to his house. Then the chefs in the house were ordered to cut the pork into cubes and use in the cooking the method of stewing pork legs in Meishan of Sichuan province which was Su Dongpo's hometown. Catering to the taste of Hangzhou people, the chefs cooked the meat until it was tender and aromatic, and distributed the meat to the local people, who found it very distinctive, and called it "Dongpo Pork".

The earliest birthplace of Dongpo Pork is Xuzhou of Jiangsu province. It is said that when Su Dongpo was the governor of Xuzhou, there was a flood besieging Xuzhou. Su Dongpo led the local people in building dams and fighting the flood, and finally saved the city. The people were very grateful to him, and they went to thank him with wine and pork, which they made Su Shi have to accept. After that, he instructed his family in person to make braised pork, and gave it back to the people who had been engaged in fighting the flood. After eating the braised pork, the people found that it was fat but not greasy, crispy and delicious, and they unanimously called it "Reward Pork", which was the prototype of Dongpo Pork.

The braised pork cooked by Su Dongpo in Xuzhou only had local influence and was not well-known in the whole country. The braised pork that was really famous all over the country was his "Dongpo Pork" when he was in Hangzhou.

东坡肉又名滚肉、红烧肉。它是江南地区传统名菜，属于浙菜系，以猪肉为主要食材。东坡肉的主料和造型大同小异，主料都是半肥半瘦的猪肉，加入配料焖制而成。成品菜都是码得整整齐齐的麻将块儿，红得透亮，色如玛瑙，夹起一块尝尝，软而不烂，肥而不腻。瘦肉松松嫩嫩，一点也不塞牙。肥肉一点儿也不腻，和瘦肉一起吃，便有了一种相得益彰的感觉，最后吃的是肉皮，很有嚼劲，但一点儿也不硬，慢慢咀嚼，会有一股浓浓的香味。

东坡肉不仅色香味俱全，营养价值也比较高。猪肉含有丰富的优质蛋白质和人体必需的脂肪酸，并提供血红素和半胱氨酸，能改善缺铁性贫血，具有补肾养血、滋阴润燥的功效。

东坡肉的来历颇为有趣。公元 1090 年，宋代大文豪苏东坡在杭州任知州，常带领杭州人民疏浚西湖，使西湖重返青春，杭州百姓感激不尽，纷纷抬猪担酒送到知州府，苏东坡推辞不掉，只好收下，命府上厨师把肉切成方块，用自己家乡四川眉山炖肘子的方法，结合杭州人的口味，将肉煮得香嫩酥烂，并将肉分送给民工。民工们吃着苏东坡送的肉，觉得十分与众不同，纷纷称其“东坡肉”。

东坡肉最早的发源地是江苏徐州。话说苏轼在任徐州知州期间，有一年洪水围困徐州，苏轼身先士卒，率领徐州城的军民筑堤抗洪保城，保住了徐州城。全城百姓对他十分感激，纷纷携美酒及猪肉前去谢恩。苏轼推辞不掉，收下猪肉后，他亲自指点家人制成红烧肉，又回赠给一起抗洪的百姓。百姓吃了这肉之后，觉得肥而不腻、酥香味美，一致称他为“回赠肉”，这便是东坡肉的原型。

苏轼在徐州时烹制的红烧肉，只是在当地有影响，在全国并没有多大名气。真正叫得响并闻名全国的红烧肉，是苏轼在杭州时的“东坡肉”。

词汇笔记

- **ingredient** [ɪnˈɡriːdiənt] *n.* one of the things from which sth. is made, especially six of the foods that are used together to make a particular dish 成分；（尤指烹饪）材料
- 2. stew [stuː] *v.* to cook sth. slowly, or allow sth. to cook slowly, in liquid in a closed dish 炖；煨
- 3. dredge [dredʒ] *v.* to remove mud, stones, etc. from the bottom of a river, canal, etc. using a boat or special machine, to make it deeper or to search for sth. 疏浚；清淤；挖掘
- 4. distribute [dɪˈstrɪbjuːt] *v.* to give things to a large number of people; to share sth. between a number of people 分发；分配
- 5. engage [ɪnˈɡeɪdʒ] *v.* to succeed in attracting and keeping sb's attention and interest 吸引住（注意力、兴趣）

Chapter 06

The Cuisine in the Southeast Region

东南地区饮食

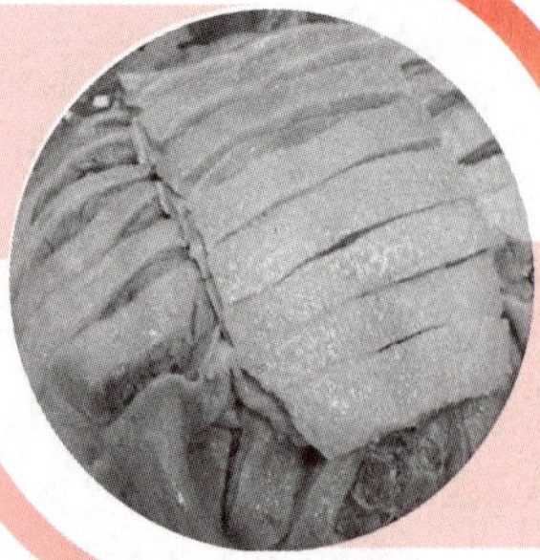

The Dietary Culture of the Southeast Region
东南地区饮食文化

The southeastern diet culture circle roughly includes Fujian, Guangdong, Taiwan, Hainan and some parts of Zhejiang, Jiangxi, Hunan and Guangxi, with Fujian and Guangdong as the center area.

The southeastern region is surrounded by mountains and seas, and has superior natural resources. It has been the pioneering land of China's food sources since ancient times. Rice is the staple food in this area, and vegetables, fruits, seafood, livestock and poultry are abundant. Prosperous overseas trade and convenient transportation outside the region, as well as a relatively long-term and stable social environment and rich products, have formed the regional characteristics of the diet culture in this region: people here like eating rice, focus on fresh food, enjoy drinking tea; vegetables and fruits seafood account for a large proportion. In the meanwhile, Hong Kong, Macau, Taiwan and other places have long been infected by European diet styles, and are more obviously influenced by Western diet, gradually forming a distinctive diet culture combining Chinese and Western styles.

The southeastern diet culture circle includes "Cantonese cuisine", one of the four major Chinese cuisines, which brings together the essence of the southeast diet culture. It is a culture, a kind of atmosphere, a kind of harmony, a kind of folk custom, a kind of color and also a manifestation of health standards.

东南饮食文化区大致包括闽、粤、台、琼以及浙、赣、湘、桂局部，以闽粤为中心地区。

东南地区依山傍海，有着优越的自然资源，自古即是中国食源的开拓地。该地区以稻米为主食，蔬菜水果海产畜禽都很丰饶。繁盛的海外贸易和便利的域外交通，以及相对长久稳定的社会环境，丰富的物产，形成了这一地区饮食文化的区域特点：喜食稻米、重鲜活、尚茶饮，蔬果与海产比重高。同时，香港、澳门、台湾等地长期受欧美食风的侵染，受西方饮食的影响较为明显，逐渐形成中西相结合的特色饮食文化。

东南地区饮食文化圈包含了我国四大菜系之一的“粤菜”，荟萃了东南饮食文化的精华，一种文化，是一种气氛、一种和谐、一种民俗、一种色彩，也是一种健康标准的体现。

Roast Suckling Pig 烤乳猪

必用三句

1 Among the barbecues in Guangdong enjoying great popularity at home and abroad, Roast Suckling Pig is a wonder. 在誉满中外的广东烧烤中，此菜堪称一绝。

2 This excellent taste made Roast Suckling Pig the favorite "top grade" of the noble and royal in the old days. 绝佳的口感让烤乳猪在旧时就成为了皇宫贵族最爱的"上上品"。

3 Cantonese people usually provide Roast Suckling Pig on the festivals to worship the gods. 广东人逢年过节上香拜神都会摆上烤乳猪。

双语赏析

Roast Suckling Pig is the most famous speciality in Guangzhou and one of the main dishes in the "Manchu Han Imperial Feast". Among the barbecues in Guangdong enjoying great popularity at home and abroad, Roast Suckling Pig is a wonder.

Roast Suckling Pig has a long history. In China, as early as the Southern and Northern Dynasties, Jia Sixie had recorded Roast Suckling Pig as an important cooking technique achievement in *Qi Min Yao Shu*. As early as the Western Zhou Dynasty, this dish was listed as one of the "Eight Treasures", and it was called "pao tun" at that time. In the Qing Dynasty, Roast Suckling Pig became Kangxi's favorite and was listed as the most important main dish in the "Manchu Han Imperial Feast".

The roasted suckling pig is ruddy in color and complete in shape, and the outer skin is fried to golden. In sharp contrast to the crispy texture, the roasted suckling tastes tender. Take a bite, the skin is crispy and the meat is fresh, fat but not greasy, palatable. And this excellent taste made Roast Suckling Pig the favorite "top grade" of the noble and royal in the old days.

Among the many origins of roasted suckling pig, Guangdong cannot be ignored. There is such a wedding custom in Guangdong. On the third day after marriage, the bridegroom accompanies the bride to visit the father-in-law and mother-in-law, which is called "hui men". And this is where a traditional wedding really ends. The essential gift for "hui men" that the bridegroom brings is Roast Suckling Pig. The emphasis on Roast Suckling Pig at the banquet also makes other ceremonies follow suit. Cantonese people usually provide Roast Suckling Pig on the festivals to worship the gods. In the old days, Roast Suckling Pig was often given as prizes at the major competitions in Cantonese. Even during the opening ceremony of a company, they like to cut Roast Suckling Pig, symbolizing the prosperity of their bodies and careers, and for auspiciousness. In addition, Roast Suckling Pig has been the highlight of ancestor worship for Cantonese people for many years. It is an indispensable festive item in almost every family. After using it to sacrifice ancestors, relatives will gather for having a big meal.

Have a bite of Roast Suckling Pig and take a sip of wine. Isn't it a pleasure in the world?

烤乳猪是广州最著名的特色菜，并且是"满汉全席"中的主打菜肴之一。在誉满中外的广东烧烤中，此菜堪称一绝。

烤乳猪历史久远。在我国，早在南北朝时，贾思勰已把烤乳猪作为一项重要的烹饪技术成果而记载在《齐民要术》中了。早在西周时此菜已被列为"八珍"之一，那时称为"炮豚"。等到了清朝时期，烤乳猪更是成为康熙的最爱，被列为"满汉全席"里最重要的主菜。

烤乳猪色泽红润，形态完整，外表的皮被炸至金黄，与酥脆口感形成鲜明对比的是烤乳猪鲜嫩的肉质。一口咬下去，皮酥肉嫩，肥而不腻，入口奇香。绝佳的口感让烤乳猪在旧时就成为了皇宫贵族最爱的"上上品"。

在诸多"烤乳猪"的产地里，自然无法忽略广东。广东有这样一个婚俗，婚后第三天新郎陪同新娘去拜见岳父、岳母，称为"回门"。一场传统的婚礼到此才算真正结束。新郎官"回门"的必备礼物就是烤乳猪。回门宴上对于"烤乳猪"的重视，也令其余仪式典礼效法。广东人逢年过节上香拜神都会摆上烤乳猪。旧时粤地重大竞技比赛，也常将烤乳猪作为奖品。甚至公司企业开业庆典时，亦喜切烤乳猪，象征身体、事业红当赤壮，以图吉利。同时，烤乳猪是许多年来广东人祭祖的重头戏，几乎是家家都少不了的应节之物，用烤乳猪祭完先人后，亲戚们再聚会大吃一顿。

趁热吃一口乳猪，呷一口酒，岂非人间一桩乐事乎？

词汇笔记

- **roast** [rəʊst] *v.* to cook food, especially meat, without liquid in an oven or over a fire; to be cooked in this way 炙，烘（食物，尤指肉）
- **suckling** ['sʌklɪŋ] *adj.* a baby or young animal that is still drinking milk from its mother 尚未断奶的，哺乳的
- **wonder** ['wʌndər] *n.* something that fills you with surprise and admiration 令人惊讶的事物，令人难以置信的事物
- **palatable** ['pælətəbəl] *adj.* having a pleasant or acceptable taste 美味的，可口的

Claypot Rice 煲仔饭

必用三句

1 The history of Claypot Rice can be traced back to the Eight Treasures of the Zhou Dynasty recorded in *The Book of Rites* and other books more than 2,000 years ago. 煲仔饭的历史渊源可以追溯到两千多年前的《礼记》等书记载的周代八珍。

2 Rice crust is the soul of Claypot Rice, the crispy and tender taste of which has conquered everyone who came to taste it. 锅巴，是煲仔饭的灵魂。煲仔饭的锅巴以外酥里嫩的口感，征服了每一个前来品尝它的人。

3 Claypot Rice is always asked for over and over by Cantonese people and the local people often think about it. 煲仔饭让广东人百吃不厌、常常惦记。

双语赏析

Claypot Rice is a famous cuisine in Guangzhou, Guangdong province. And it belongs to Cantonese cuisine.

Claypot Rice uses a casserole to cook rice. Usually, first brush the casserole with lard, then put the washed rice into the pot, measure the amount of water, cover, cook the rice until it is seven mature, add the ingredients, and then switch to a slow cooker. Because casserole is called claypot in Guangdong, it is called Claypot Rice.

The history of Claypot Rice can be traced back to the Eight Treasures of the Zhou Dynasty recorded in *The Book of Rites* and other books more than 1,000 years ago. Today, Claypot Rice has its own place in many regions, such as Guangzhou, Hefei, Shenzhen, Shandong, etc. Claypot Rice in each region has its own characteristics, among which the most famous is surely in Guangdong.

Delicious Claypot Rice has two characteristics that cannot be ignored. One is the sauce that is served with the pot, and when you lift the lid and pour it on the rice, there is a sizzling sound, which is the finishing touch; the other is a layer of golden rice crust cooked by the crystal-clear rice at the smooth bottom of the claypot. Different from ordinary rice, the rice crust is not only crispy but also has a deep taste and it is the essence of Claypot Rice. Rice crust is the soul of Claypot Rice, the crispy and tender taste of which has conquered everyone who comes to taste it. The soft rice attached to the inner side of the rice crust enhances the chewy texture.

Every city has its own street food, which not only fills the hungry stomachs of people walking on the streets, but also supports a variety of deepest memories about the cities. And the most down-to-earth and the most common sense of belonging in Guangdong is Claypot Rice.

Claypot Rice is always asked for over and over by Cantonese people and the local people often think about it. Friends from the whole world, if you have time, welcome to Guangdong to taste Claypot Rice!

煲仔饭，是广东省广州市的一道特色名菜，属于粤菜系。

煲仔饭是以砂锅作为器皿煮米饭，通常是先将锅中刷猪油，再把淘好的米放入煲中，量好水量，加盖，把米饭煲至七成熟时加入配料，再转用慢火煲熟。因广东称砂锅为煲仔，所以称为煲仔饭。

煲仔饭的历史渊源可以追溯到一千多年前的《礼记》等书记载的周代八珍。时至今日，煲仔饭在许多地区都有自己的一席之地，比如广州、合肥、深圳、山东等，各个地区的煲仔饭均有各自的特色，其中最负盛名的还是广东的煲仔饭。

好吃的煲仔饭有两个不容忽视的特征，一是跟煲上桌的调味汁，揭开盖子浇在饭上，有嗞嗞的响声，此为画龙点睛之笔；另一处是晶莹剔透的大米被光滑的煲底烧出的一层金黄的锅巴，与普通米饭不同的是不但脆而且滋味深长，实为一煲之精华。锅巴，是煲仔饭的灵魂。煲仔饭的锅巴以外酥里嫩的口感，征服了每一个前来品尝它的人。那些附着在锅巴内侧柔软的大米，更是升级了咀嚼的口感。

每座城市都有独属于自己的市井美食。它们不仅填饱了游走在街头的人们的饥肠辘辘的胃，也支撑起五花八门关于城市最深处的记忆。而这份归属感之于广东，最接地气也是最常见的，非煲仔饭莫属。

煲仔饭让广东人百吃不厌、常常惦记。八方来客、四面来宾，大家有空来广东吃煲仔饭。

词汇笔记

- **Cantonese** [ˌkæntəˈniːz] *adj.* of or relating to people who speak cantonese, or their language or culture 广州的，广州人的
- **lid** [lɪd] *n.* a cover over a container that can be removed or opened by turning it or lifting it （容器的）盖，盖子
- **sizzle** [ˈsɪzl] *v.* to make the sound of food frying in hot oil（油煎食物时）发嘶嘶声
- **conquer** [ˈkɒŋkər] *v.* to take control of a country or city and its people by force 占领，攻克，征服

Oyster Omelet 蚵仔煎

必用三句

1 In Taiwan, Oyster Omelet is a traditional snack known to the older generation in the Anping area of Tainan. 在台湾，它是台南安平地区一带的老一辈的人都知道的传统点心。

2 Oyster Omelet first appeared in Fujian and spread to Taiwan because of its unique taste. 蚵仔煎最早是出现于福建地区的，因口味独特而流传至台湾。

3 Today, Oyster Omelet has become a delicacy that people on both sides of the Taiwan Strait love. 如今，蚵仔煎已成为海峡两岸人民共同喜爱的美味佳肴。

双语赏析

Oyster Omelet is a common home-cooked dish, a specialty snack in coastal cities in Fujian, Taiwan and Chaoshan, which is said to be a creative dish invented in a poor society. It is an alternative food invented by the ancestors when they were poor and could not eat enough and a symbol of a poor life.

Where does the name of Oyster Omelet come from? Its pronunciation is "e-a-jian" in Southern Fujian Dialect. "E-a" comes from Hakka, referring to oysters. Cantonese people call oysters "hao", while in southern Fujian, Chaoshan and Taiwan, people call them "e-a". There is a saying in southern Fujian, "fat oysters, fat leeks.", which means that the second month of the lunar calendar when the leeks grow very well is also the season when the oysters are the most plump. And Oyster Omelet is a wonderful combination of the two. In Taiwan, Oyster Omelet is a traditional snack known to the older generation in the Anping area of Tainan. As a classic delicacy in Taiwan, Oyster Omelet is now known to everyone.

The ingredients for making Oyster Omelet are mainly oysters and sweet potato powder. The method of cooking is simple; the taste is salty, fresh and crispy; and the fillings are palatable and smooth. Although the Minnan area, Taiwan, and Chaoshan have basically the same origin, due to regional differences, individual inheritances are different, and of course there are some differences in flavor. Oyster Omelet first appeared in Fujian and spread to Taiwan because of its unique taste. Oyster Omelet is a pan-fried cake made of oysters, eggs, small cabbage, leeks and other ingredients wrapped in sweet potato batter after adding water, which is truly delicious.

Oyster Omelet from any region has captured the hearts of many diners with their unique flavors. Today, Oyster Omelet has become a delicacy that people on both sides of the Taiwan Strait love.

蚵仔煎，是一道常见的家常菜，是福建沿海城市、台湾和潮汕地区的特色小吃。蚵仔煎据传是一种在贫穷社会之下所发明的创意料理，是先民困苦，在无法饱食下所发明的替代粮食，是一种贫苦生活的象征。

蚵仔煎的名字从何而来呢？蚵仔为闽南语，指牡蛎。广东人称牡蛎为“蚝”，而在闽南潮汕及台湾一带称之为“蚵仔”。闽南有句俗谚叫“肥蚵仔肥韭菜”，意思是农历二月，韭菜的生长最为旺盛的时候，也是蚵仔最为肥硕的季节。蚵仔煎则是两者奇妙的黄金组合。在台湾，它是台南安平地区一带的老一辈的人都知道的传统点心。作为一道经典美食，蚵仔煎的名声现已无人不知无人不晓。

制作蚵仔煎的食材以海蛎、地瓜粉为主，做法简单，味道咸、鲜，口感香脆，内馅香滑。闽南、台湾、潮汕三地虽然基本同根同源，但因为地域差别，个体传承不同，风味当然有些许区别。蚵仔煎最早是出现于福建地区的，因口味独特而流传至台湾。蚵仔煎是以加水后的番薯粉浆包裹蚵仔、鸡蛋、小白菜、韭菜等食材所煎成的饼状物，口味鲜香。

无论哪个地区的蚵仔煎，都以自己独有的风味俘获了众多食客的心。如今，蚵仔煎已成为海峡两岸人民共同喜爱的美味佳肴。

词汇笔记

- **plump** [plʌmp] *adj.* having a soft, round body; slightly fat 胖乎乎的，丰满的
- **filling** ['fɪlɪŋ] *n.* food put inside a sandwich, cake, pie, etc.（糕点或馅饼里的）馅，夹心
- **capture** ['kæptʃər] *v.* to make sb interested in sth. 吸引，引起
- **diner** ['daɪnər] *n.* a person eating a meal, especially in a restaurant 进餐者，食客

Hakka Stuffed Tofu 客家酿豆腐

必用三句

1 So it is fair to say that Stuffed Tofu is one of the most representative dishes in Hakka diet culture. 恰当地说，酿豆腐是客家地区美食文化最具代表性的菜肴之一。

2 Stuffed Tofu is indeed a typical food that combines the traditional eating habits of the Central Plains with the special way of life in the migration area. 酿豆腐是中原传统饮食习惯与迁徙地特殊生活方式相结合的典范食品。

3 In 2015, Huizhou Hakka Stuffed Tofu cooking skills were included in the Intangible Cultural Heritage List of Guangdong Province. 2015 年，惠州客家酿豆腐烹饪技艺入列广东省级非物质文化遗产名录。

双语赏析

Stuffed Tofu (Yong Tau Foo) is a famous dish in Hakka whose ingredients include tofu, green onions, pork, mushrooms, etc. Stuffed Tofu soup is mellow, tender and smooth, and it really tastes delicious. So it is fair to say that Stuffed Tofu is one of the most representative dishes in Hakka diet culture.

There is a legend about Hakka Stuffed Tofu. It is said that a long time ago, a man from Wuhua and a man from Xingning were sworn brothers. And a disagreement occurred when they were ordering food. One wanted pork and the other wanted tofu. Then a smart restaurant owner came up with a good way to best of both worlds–making Stuffed Tofu. This also shows the wisdom of the Hakka people and the profound Hakka diet culture.

Stuffed Tofu is indeed a typical food that combines the traditional eating habits of the Central Plains with the special way of life in the migration area. Hakka Stuffed Tofu has a beautiful flavor. And the white and tender tofu is stuffed with pork, fish, shrimps, etc., which increases the taste and makes Stuffed Tofu more chewier. In 2015, Huizhou Hakka Stuffed Tofu cooking skills were included in the Intangible Cultural Heritage List of Guangdong Province.

Stuffed Tofu is so important to the Hakka people that in the life of Hakka people, whenever there is a banquet, there must be this dish. Because Stuffed Tofu is tender, fragrant, and nutritious, usually during the festivals, the Hakka people will carefully prepare a large plate of Stuffed Tofu to celebrate the festival and entertain relatives and friends, and it will always be favored by everyone.

On a winter night, sitting around the fireplace with the family, chatting about everyday things, and eating hot Stuffed Tofu is definitely a great pleasure in the world.

酿豆腐是一道客家名菜，制作材料需要豆腐、大葱、猪肉、香菇等，其汤汁醇厚，鲜嫩滑润，口味鲜美。恰当地说，酿豆腐是客家地区美食文化最具代表性的菜肴之一。

关于客家酿豆腐，还有一个传说。相传很久以前，一个五华人和一个兴宁人是结拜的好兄弟，后来因为在点菜的时候出现了矛盾，一个要吃猪肉，一个要吃豆腐，后来，聪明的饭店老板想出了一个两全其美的办法，制作出了酿豆腐。这也表现了客家人的智慧和深厚的客家饮食文化。

酿豆腐是中原传统饮食习惯与迁徙地特殊生活方式相结合的典范食品。客家酿豆腐味道鲜美，在白嫩的豆腐中酿入肉馅、鱼肉、虾米等，增加了口感，更有嚼头。2015 年，惠州客家酿豆腐烹饪技艺入列广东省级非物质文化遗产名录。

酿豆腐对客家人是非常重要的。在客家人的生活中，但凡有宴席必有此道菜。

酿豆腐鲜嫩滑香、营养丰富，是客家人过年的保留菜式，一般逢年过节的时候，客家人都会精心地制作上满满一大盘的酿豆腐，用来庆祝节日、招待好友，也总会得到大家的青睐。

冬天的夜晚，和家人围炉而坐，一边聊家常，一边吃着热腾腾的酿豆腐，不得不说是人间一大美事。

词汇笔记

- **legend** ['ledʒənd] *n.* a story from ancient times about people and events, that may or may not be true; this type of story 传说，传奇故事
- **sworn** [swɔːn] *adj.* made after you have promised to tell the truth, especially in court 发过誓的，宣誓过的
- **disagreement** [ˌdɪsə'griːmənt] *n.* a situation where people have different opinions about sth. and often argue 分歧，争论
- **favor** ['feɪvər] *v.* promote over another 较喜欢

Hainan Coconut Eight-treasure Rice 海南椰子八宝饭

必用三句

1 Rice, as an indispensable staple food on the table of Hainan people, has contributed to various innovations. 米饭，作为海南人餐桌上不可或缺的主食，被玩出种种花样。

2 Coconut Eight-treasure Rice has a unique method of cooking and unique flavor, and it is a rare natural food. 椰子八宝饭做法独特，风味别具一格，实为难得的天然食品。

3 In addition, the shape and sweetness of Eight-treasure Rice are also a symbol of completeness and sweetness. 八宝饭的造型及甜味还有圆圆满满、甜甜蜜蜜的寓意。

Rice, as an indispensable staple food on the table of Hainan people, has contributed to various innovations. Hainan coconut Eight-treasure Rice is one of the most common delicacies in Hainan. And it is named after eight foods, including lotus seeds, lily, red dates, candied melon, peanut kernels, and red bean paste.

Coconut Eight-treasure Rice has a unique method of cooking and unique flavor, and it is a rare natural food. Eight-treasure Rice is soft, waxy and smooth, beautiful in shape and sweet in taste. It is indeed an indispensable dish for family reunions and wedding banquets. In addition, the shape and sweetness of Eight-treasure Rice are also a symbol of completeness and sweetness.

Why do Hainan people like eating Coconut Eight-treasure Rice so much? First, Eight-treasure Rice is often served at the end of the banquet, which is similar to western desserts, and Hainan people prefer sweet foods. Second, Eight-treasure Rice has auspicious meaning, because whether it is the name of "eight treasures" or the "lily" (meaning a harmonious union lasting a hundred years), "red dates" (meaning early birth in China), "lotus seeds" (meaning continuous birth in China), expresses good wishes and auspicious meanings.

What does Coconut Eight-treasure Rice mean to Hainan people?

Mr. Xu, a Hainan person in a foreign land, once wrote a poem about this:

"When you go to study outside the land, nostalgia is a bowl of sweet rice.

I'm on the other side of the strait and it ends at the wedding feast.

It is not necessarily so popular with the general public.

Because children are afraid that Eight-treasure Rice stick to their teeth; young people think that it is too sweet; it seems that only the older generation has a fondness for it.

But in terms of its own beautiful meaning, it has become an indispensable landscape.

How can it be crystal clear, there is a lot of efforts in it.

It requires many making processes and considerable patience.

Although Eight-treasure Rice is not recommended to eat too much, but if you put a piece of sweetness into your mouth, you still admire the pioneering work of the laboring people from the bottom of your heart."

米饭，作为海南人餐桌上不可或缺的主食，被玩出种种花样。海南椰子八宝饭是海南最常见的美食之一，因饭中有莲子、百合、红枣、冬瓜糖、花生仁、豆沙等八种食物而得名。

椰子八宝饭做法独特，风味别具一格，实为难得的天然食品。八宝饭软糯黏滑，造型美观，口味清甜，是家庭团聚、婚嫁喜宴必不可少、既可当菜又可当饭的一道美食。此外，八宝饭的造型及甜味还有圆圆满满、甜甜蜜蜜的寓意。

海南人为何特别独爱八宝饭？其一，八宝饭在宴席上往往是较后上，其类似于西方的餐后甜食，而海南人较喜欢甜食。其二，取其吉祥含义，因无论是"八宝"之名还是其用料中的"百合"（有百年好合的寓意）、"红枣"（有早生贵子的寓意）、"莲子"（有"连生贵子"的寓意），都表达着美好的祝愿和寓意。

椰子八宝饭于海南人而言，是怎样的一种存在呢？

身在异乡的海南人徐先生曾为此作诗一首：

外出求学的时候，乡愁是一碗甜甜的八宝饭。

我在海峡那头，它在喜宴酒席压轴。

它并不见得那么深受广大人民群众欢迎。

小孩怕粘牙，年轻人怕太甜，似乎只有老一辈人对它情有独钟。

但是就其本身的美好寓意，它成了必不可少的一道风景。

问它哪得晶莹剔透，很多功夫在里头。

它的亮相，需要很多道工序，还需要相当的耐心。

虽然不建议多食，但是夹一块甘甜送入嘴中，你还是发自肺腑地敬佩劳动人民的创举。

词汇笔记

- **waxy** ['wæksi] *adj.* looking or feeling like wax 质地光滑的，柔软的
- **coconut** ['kəʊkənʌt] *n.* the large nut of a tropical tree called a coconut palm. it grows inside a hard shell and contains a soft white substance that can be eaten

and juice that can be drunk 椰子

- **auspicious** [ɔːˈspɪʃəs] *adj.* showing signs that sth. is likely to be successful in the future 吉利的，吉兆的
- **pioneering** [ˌpaɪəˈnɪərɪŋ] *adj.* introducing ideas and methods that have never been used before 首创的，先驱的

Hong Kong Curry Fish Balls 香港咖喱鱼蛋

必用三句

1 The historical background where Chinese and foreigners coexist makes Hong Kong's diet rich and compatible. 华洋杂处的历史背景，让香港的饮食蔚为大观、东西兼容。

2 In addition, because curry contains spices, fish eggs with curry powder look good, smell good and taste good. 此外，由于咖喱含有香料，经咖喱烹调后的鱼蛋变得色香味俱全。

3 For foodies, fish balls are always indispensable when they come to Hong Kong. Whether you are happy or not, have a Curry Fish Balls! 对于吃货而言，来香港，这一口总是少不了的。开不开心的，来一份咖喱鱼蛋吧！

双语赏析

Hong Kong people, like Cantonese people, enjoy good food and know how to eat delicious food. The historical background where Chinese and foreigners coexist makes Hong Kong's diet rich and compatible. Whether it is a flamboyant restaurant, tea house, porridge shop or congee restaurant on the street, or a popular small shop hidden deep in the alley, there will never be a shortage of diners. In the pots of fish balls, refreshments, and food stalls, the soup is always boiling, cook never stops and regardless of your preference, you can always find something to your liking here.

Curry is a traditional food in India. After the British ruled the Indian subcontinent in the 19th century, the British established British India. Therefore, the Indians followed the British to British Hong Kong, which was also a British colony. They also brought curry from their native Indian cuisine to Hong Kong. Fish balls are popular in Chaoshan area, but in Hong Kong, where Chinese and foreigners coexist, the two have been combined into a classic snack.

To produce fish balls, the first step is to make fish paste. The fish meat used to make fish balls is generally made of cheap fish species. In the process of making fish paste, flour is usually added. After the fish balls are formed, they will be fried. Therefore, fish balls are usually golden in appearance and have a springy texture. In addition, because curry contains spices, fish eggs with curry powder look good, smell good and taste good.

Curry Fish Balls were sold at first in Hong Kong by the street vendors around the 1950s, and have now become the mainstay of Hong Kong street food. Fish balls are a food many Hong Kong people grow up on. There are stalls around many schools, specializing in Lou Mei (dishes made by braising in a sauce known as a master stock or lou sauce), fish balls, etc. During recess or after school, they will buy a few fish balls at first and dip them in sweet chilli sauce or curry to relieve their cravings. Therefore, fish balls are honored as one of the favorite snacks of Hong Kong students.

For foodies, fish balls are always indispensable when they come to Hong Kong. Whether you are happy or not, have a Curry Fish Balls!

香港人和广东人一样，爱吃也会吃。华洋杂处的历史背景，让香港的饮食蔚为大观、东西兼容。不论是街边招摇的酒楼、茶餐厅、粥店还是甜品店，还是藏匿于巷子深处的人气小店永远不缺少食客，鱼蛋、茶点，大排档的锅里永远汤水沸腾，明炉快炒，丰俭由人。

咖喱是印度的传统食品。英国在 19 世纪统治印度次大陆后建立英属印度。印度人因此跟随英国人来到同样是英国殖民地的英属香港，他们亦把印度家乡菜的咖喱带到香港；鱼蛋则流行于潮汕地区。在华洋杂处的香港，两者结合成为一种经典小吃。

生产鱼蛋首先要将鱼肉打成鱼浆，用来制作鱼蛋的鱼肉一般都选用廉价鱼种，在制作鱼浆的过程中，通常会加入面粉，鱼蛋在成型后会经过油炸处理，因此鱼蛋外表通常都是金黄色的，而且有弹牙口感。此外，由于咖喱含有香料，经咖喱烹调后的鱼蛋变得色香味俱全。

咖喱鱼蛋约于 20 世纪 50 年代在香港街头流动熟食小贩开始售卖，现已成为香港街头小食的台柱。鱼蛋是很多香港人从小吃到大的，很多学校周围都会有档车仔，专卖卤味、鱼蛋等等，课间时间或是放学，先来几串鱼蛋，蘸着甜辣酱或是咖喱酱，解馋得很。鱼蛋也因此光荣入围香港学生最喜爱的零食之一。

对于吃货而言，来香港，这一口总是少不了的。开不开心的，来一份咖喱鱼蛋吧！

词汇笔记

- **flamboyant** [flæmˈbɔɪənt] *adj.* different, confident and exciting in a way that attracts attention 炫耀的
- **refreshment** [rɪˈfreʃmənt] *n.* drinks and small amounts of food that are provided or sold to people in a public place or at a public event 茶点，点心
- **curry** [ˈkʌri] *n.* a type of food from india consisting of meat or vegetables covered in a thick liquid with hot taste 咖喱
- **craving** [ˈkreɪvɪŋ] *n.* a strong desire for sth. 渴望；热望

Braised Pork with Salted Vegetables (Mei Cai) 梅菜扣肉

必用三句

1 The combination of Mei Cai and fatty pork belly can really be said to be just right. 梅菜和肥五花肉的搭配真的可以说是恰到好处。

2 Mei Cai has a long history and is well-known at home and abroad. It is one of the three famous vegetables in Lingnan area, which is a famous traditional specialty of Lingnan area. 梅菜历史悠久，闻名中外，是岭南三大名菜之一，为岭南著名传统特产。

3 In the eyes of the Hakka people, Mei Cai is indeed a perfect match of the pork belly. 在客家人看来，梅菜和扣肉是“天仙配”。

双语赏析

Braised Pork with Salted Vegetables (Mei Cai), a dish of braised and then steamed pork belly, is a traditional famous cuisine with full of color, aroma and taste. It is a Hakka specialty in Huizhou, Guangdong province.

When it comes to Braised Pork with Salted Vegetables (Mei Cai), the melt-in-the-mouth, fat but not greasy taste and the sweet and refreshing aroma of Mei Cai will immediately make many Hakka people salivate. This dish is mainly made of pork belly, Mei Cai (also known as mei gan cai, a type of dried pickle made with either Chinese cabbage or mustard greens that have undergone quite an elaborate production process that takes several weeks), scallion stalk, ginger slices and other ingredients. The pork belly is wrapped in Mei Cai stuffing, and if you put a piece in your mouth, the soft and mellow aroma of the pork belly collides with the rich aroma of the Mei Cai, and the delicious taste bursts between the lips and teeth. And this moment represents the supreme delicacy. Mei Cai absorbs oil, and the pork belly usually has the fragrance clearance of Mei Cai. The combination of Mei Cai and fatty pork belly can really be said to be just right.

Mei Cai has a long history and is well-known at home and abroad. It is one of the three famous vegetables in Lingnan area, which is a famous traditional specialty of Lingnan area. Historically, it was called “Tribute Cuisine of Huizhou” as a court food, and Huizhou was awarded the “Hometown of Chinese Mei Cai” by the State Council. Huizhou, an old city surrounded by mountains and rivers in Lingnan area, has gone through the baptism of time, but still remains true to its original aspiration. It has completely retained the Hakka flavor, and has formed a unique Dongjiang cuisine.

Braised Pork with Salted Vegetables (Mei Cai) is known as one of the three treasures of Hakka. In the eyes of the Hakka people, Mei Cai is indeed a perfect match of the pork belly. In the restaurants of Hakka, Braised Pork with

Salted Vegetables (Mei Cai) is an indispensable signature dish. This seemingly ordinary dish is indispensable for both wedding banquets and family banquets. The delicious Mei Cai and the pork belly paired with a bowl of rice can be described as an excellent dish, which makes people linger.

As the saying goes, “Live for love, love for food”, and Braised Pork with Salted Vegetables (Mei Cai)makes people salivate and give them a good appetite. Braised Pork with Salted Vegetables (Mei Cai) is really a treat for the taste buds.

梅菜扣肉，将五花肉先烧后蒸的一道菜，是一道色香味俱全的传统名肴，是广东惠州客家特产。

提到梅菜扣肉，那入口即化、肥而不腻的口感和香甜爽口的梅菜香气，立即会让很多客家人忍不住咽口水。这道菜主要由五花肉、梅菜（也叫梅干菜，一种用大白菜或芥菜制成的干泡菜，经过精心制作，需要数周时间）、葱白、姜片等材料制作而成。五花肉包着梅菜馅，夹一块放入嘴里，扣肉的软烂醇香与梅菜的浓郁芳香相互碰撞，鲜美的口感在唇齿间迸发。这一刻，是至高的美味。梅菜吸油，五花肉又会带着梅菜的清香。梅菜和肥五花肉的搭配真的可以说是恰到好处。

梅菜历史悠久，闻名中外，是岭南三大名菜之一，为岭南著名传统特产。历史上梅菜作为宫廷食品而被称为“惠州贡菜”，而惠州被国务院授予“中国梅菜之乡”的称号。惠州，这座山水酿出来的岭南老城，历经时光洗礼，依然初心不改，完整地保留着客家风味，形成了独特的东江菜系。

梅菜扣肉被称为客家三件宝之一。在客家人看来，梅菜和扣肉是“天仙配”。在客家菜馆，梅菜扣肉更是不可缺少的招牌菜。而梅菜扣肉这道看似平凡的一道菜，无论是喜宴还是家宴都少不了它的身影。入味的梅菜和五花肉搭配一碗米饭，可谓上等佳肴，让人流连忘返。

俗话说，唯有美食和爱不可辜负，而梅菜扣肉则是让人垂涎之口水天上来，奔流到胃不复回。食梅菜扣肉，着实是味蕾上的一种享受。

词汇笔记

- **pickle** ['pɪkl] *n.* a vegetable that has been preserved in vinegar or salt water and has a strong flavour, served cold with meat, salads, etc. 泡菜，腌菜

- **mustard** ['mʌstəd] *n.* a small plant with yellow flowers, grown for its seeds that are crushed to make mustard 芥菜
- **baptism** ['bæptɪzəm] *n.* a Christian ceremony in which a few drops of water are poured on sb or they are covered with water, to welcome them into the Christian Church and often to name them 洗礼
- **linger** ['lɪŋgər] *v.* to stay somewhere for longer because you do not want to leave; to spend a long time doing sth. 流连，逗留

Buddha Jumping over the Wall 佛跳墙

必用三句

1 Fujian, with its geographical features of being close to the mountains and the sea, has created a sense of taste enjoyment of Fujian cuisine that integrates table delicacies from land and sea. 福建依山傍海的地理特征造就了闽菜集山珍与海味于一体的味觉享受。

2 Buddha Jumping over the Wall is well-deserved to say the first of Fujian cuisine. 说到闽菜之首，佛跳墙当之无愧。

3 Buddha Jumping over the Wall, with its distinguished status, has become the business card of Fuzhou. 佛跳墙以其尊贵的地位成为了福州这座城市的名片。

双语赏析

Fujian, with its geographical features of being close to the mountains and the sea, has created a sense of taste enjoyment of Fujian cuisine that integrates table delicacies from land and sea. Buddha Jumping over the Wall is well-deserved to say the first of Fujian cuisine.

Buddha Jumping over the Wall is a famous dish in Fuzhou, Fujian province, belonging to Fujian cuisine. Buddha Jumping over the Wall is like a "spiritual beacon" in Fujian cuisine. When it comes to Fujian cuisine, both Fujianese and foreigners will think of "Buddha Jumping over the Wall".

Buddha Jumping over the Wall was founded in Ju Chun Yuan, Fuzhou, with a history of more than 100 years. Just like Fuzhou's compatible attitude, Buddha Jumping over the Wall selected a wide range of ingredients, such as abalone, trepang, fish lips, yak-skin gelatin, king oyster mushrooms, tendons, flower mushrooms, cuttlefish, dried scallops, quail eggs, etc. Add the stock and Fujian old wine and simmer gently. "When the lid is removed, the scent of wine combing with the smell of meat fills the surrounding air, and the Buddha is attracted, abandons Zen and jumps over the wall." Buddha Jumping over the Wall is to simmer dozens of ingredients in a jar, which not only has a common meat flavor, but also maintains its own characteristics. It tastes soft, tender, and is rich in meat fragrance, and meaty but not greasy; each ingredient penetrates each other, and the taste is wonderful. It is indeed the best representative of Chinese stews.

After the improvement of several generations of famous chefs in Ju Chun Yuan, Buddha Jumping over the Wall gradually entered Beijing, attended the state banquet, and served as the main dish many times to serve the head of state. In 1990, Buddha Jumping over the Wall won the Jinding Award, the highest national quality product award. In 2008, Buddha Jumping over the Wall was listed in the National Intangible Cultural Heritage List, demonstrating its distinguished status.

When guests from all over the world come to Fuzhou, they will come here to taste this wonderful dish and enjoy the cultural feast. Buddha Jumping over the Wall, with its distinguished status, has become the business card of Fuzhou.

福建依山傍海的地理特征造就了闽菜集山珍与海味于一体的味觉享受。说到闽菜之首，佛跳墙当之无愧。

佛跳墙是福建省福州市的一道特色名菜，属闽菜系。佛跳墙好似闽菜里的“精神灯塔”，一说到闽菜，不管是福建人还是外地人，都会说出“佛跳墙”这三个字。

佛跳墙始创于福州聚春园，距今已有一百多年的历史。正如福州海纳百川的情怀一般，佛跳墙取材广泛，通常选用鲍鱼、海参、鱼唇、牦牛皮胶、杏鲍菇、蹄筋、花菇、墨鱼、瑶柱、鹌鹑蛋等汇聚到一起，加入高汤和福建老酒，文火煨制而成。“坛起荤香飘四邻，佛闻弃禅跳墙来”。佛跳墙是把几十种原料煨于一坛，既有共同的荤味，又保持各自的特色。吃起来软嫩柔润，浓郁荤香，又荤而不腻；各料互为渗透，味中有味，妙不可言，堪称是中国菜炖品中的极品代表之作。

佛跳墙经过聚春园几代名厨的改良，逐渐地进了北京，上了国宴，并多次作为国宴的主菜招待国家元首。1990 年，佛跳墙荣获国家优质产品最高奖——金鼎奖。2008 年，“聚春园佛跳墙制作技艺”荣列国家级非物质文化遗产名录，彰显了其尊贵的地位。

世界各地的嘉宾来到福州，都会慕名前来品尝这道美食盛宴、文化大餐。佛跳墙以其尊贵的地位成为了福州这座城市的名片。

词汇笔记

- **simmer** ['sɪmər] *v.* to cook sth. by keeping it almost at boiling point; to be cooked in this way 炖，煨
- **buddha** ['bʊdə] *n.* a person who has achieved enlightenment 佛陀；佛像
- **compatible** [kəm'pætəbl] *adj.* able to exist or be used together without causing problems 兼容的
- **banquet** ['bæŋkwɪt] *n.* a formal meal for a large number of people, usually for a special occasion, at which speeches are often made 宴会，盛宴

Chapter 07

The Cuisine in the Southwest Region

西南地区饮食

The Dietary Culture of the Southwest Region
西南地区饮食文化

Southwest China is an ecological region with a suitable climate and rich organisms. Except for the regions including Sichuan Basin, most of the southwest region is high mountains and valleys. The mountainous land is barren with low yield. Rice is the main crop in the dam and river valley area, and corn is mainly on the mountains. Due to the underdeveloped planting industry, people are not particular about raw materials for cooking. Due to the humid air in the mountainous areas, there are many miasmas. In order to dispel cold and dampness, people in the southwest region have been fond of drinking and eating spicy food, such as pepper, cornel, ginger, etc. since ancient times. People in this area are generally addicted to spicy food, “it is better to have no vegetables than to lack spicy food”; most people like sour, “if you haven’t eat sour food for three days, you cannot walk steadily”; the food is generally characterized by high quality and low price, and has a strong regional and cultural characteristics. Sichuan cuisine is the most representative one in the region and one of the four major cuisines in China. Sichuan is rich in seasoning and fond of spicy taste, which is similar to other regions in the southwest. Although the cuisines of different places in the southwest have their own characteristics, the taste is generally spicy and sour.

西南地区是气候适宜、生物丰厚的生态区域。除了四川盆地等地区以外，西南地区大部分区域是高山峡谷。山区土地贫瘠，产量较低，在坝区和河谷地带多种稻米，山上以玉米为主。由于种植业不发达，人们在食物原料上的禁忌很少。由于山区空气潮湿，多有瘴气，为了散寒祛湿，避秽解毒，西南地区的人们自古以来就爱饮酒和吃辛香刺激之物，如花椒、茱萸、生姜等。这一区域人们普遍嗜辣，“宁可无菜，不可缺辣”；大多喜酸，“三天不吃酸，走路打转转”；食物一般都具有物美价廉的特点，且具备浓厚的地域饮食文化色彩。川菜是该区域的最具代表性的菜系，也是我国四大菜系之一。巴蜀“好滋味”，调味丰富；“尚辛香”，嗜好辛香刺激之味，这点与西南其他地区相似。尽管西南地区不同地方的饮食各有特点,但口味总体上以麻辣、酸辣为主。

Kung Pao Chicken 宫保鸡丁

必用三句

1 Kung Pao Chicken is made of chicken (the main ingredient) with peanuts, chilies and other condiments. 宫保鸡丁选用鸡肉为主料，佐以花生米、辣椒等辅料烹制而成。

2 The so-called "Kung Pao" was actually the honorary title of Ding Baozhen. 所谓“宫保”，其实是丁宝桢的荣誉官衔。

3 In September 2018, it was rated as one of the top ten classic dishes in Guizhou and Sichuan. 2018 年 9 月，被评为“中国菜”之贵州十大经典名菜、四川十大经典名菜。

双语赏析

Kung Pao Chicken is a famous dish in Sichuan, Guizhou, Shandong and other places. It originated from the sauce fried chicken in Shandong cuisine and the spicy chicken in Guizhou cuisine. Later, it was said that when he was the governor of Shandong during Qing Dynasty, Ding Baozhen improved the dish and formed a new dish–Kung Pao Chicken, which was categorized as a Palace Cuisine and widely spread. Kung Pao Chicken is made of chicken (the main ingredient) with peanuts, chilies and other condiments. The dish is spicy but not dry in taste; the strong aroma and crisp chicken offer a pleasant mouth enjoyment; the freshness and tenderness of chicken is matched with the crispness of peanuts, which is deeply loved by the world.

Kung Pao Chicken was created by Ding Baozhen who was an expert in cooking and enjoyed eating chicken and peanuts, especially spicy food. When he was an official in Shandong, he ordered the chef to improve the Shandong cuisine "sauce fried chicken" by adding chilli, and created a delicious dish by stir-frying chicken, red chilies and peanuts. Later, when he was the governor of Sichuan, this dish was popularized. This delicacy was originally a private dish of Ding's family, but it was later widely spread and became known as Kung Pao Chicken. The so-called "Kung Pao" was actually the honorary title of Ding Baozhen. Ding Baozhen governed Sichuan for ten years, and he was an upright official with many achievements. When he died in office, the Qing government awarded him the "Prince Taibao" in recognition of his achievements. "Prince Taibao" was one of the "Kung Pao", so in order to commemorate Ding Baozhen, the dish he invented was named "Kung Pao Chicken".

Because this dish is so widely spread, there are many different cooking styles in various places, and there is even a "Kung pao pork" that replaces chicken with pork. After the Kung Pao Chicken was introduced to the West, Westerners also made some improvements according to their own tastes, making it western-style Kung Pao Chicken in line with Western tastes. In 1986, China participated in the 5th Gourmet Exhibition in Luxembourg for the first time with this dish, which won praise, and Kung Pao Chicken went to the world. In September 2018, it was rated as one of the top ten classic dishes in Guizhou and Sichuan.

宫保鸡丁是四川、贵州、山东等地的著名风味菜肴。该菜品起源于鲁菜中的酱爆鸡丁、贵州菜中的胡辣子鸡丁，后传被清朝时任山东巡抚丁宝桢改良发扬，形成了一道新菜式——宫保鸡丁，并被归为北京宫廷菜而广为流传。宫保鸡丁选用鸡肉为主料，佐以花生米、辣椒等辅料烹制而成。口感红而不辣、辣而不燥、香辣味浓、肉质滑脆，其入口鲜辣，鸡肉的鲜嫩可以配合花生的香脆，深得世人喜爱。

宫保鸡丁为四川总督丁宝桢所创，他对烹饪颇有研究，喜欢吃鸡和花生米，并尤其喜好辣味。他在山东为官时曾命家厨改良鲁菜“酱爆鸡丁”为辣炒，创制了一道将鸡丁、红辣椒、花生米下锅爆炒而成的美味佳肴。后来在任职四川总督时将这道菜推广开来。这道美味本来是丁家的私房菜，但后来广为流传，成为了人们熟知的宫保鸡丁。所谓“宫保”，其实是丁宝桢的荣誉官衔。丁宝桢治蜀十年，为官刚正不阿，多有建树，于光绪十一年死在任上，清廷为了表彰他的功绩，追赠“太子太保”。“太子太保”是“宫保”之一，于是，为了纪念丁宝桢，他发明的这道菜得名“宫保鸡丁”。

由于这道菜流传太广，在各地有很多不同的做法，甚至还出现了将鸡丁演变为肉丁的“宫保肉丁”。宫保鸡丁传到西方后，西方人还根据自己的口味进行了一些改良，使之成为了符合西方口味的“西式宫保鸡丁”。1986 年，中国第一次参加卢森堡第五届美食展览就是以这道菜打头阵，赢得赞赏，宫保鸡丁因此走向了世界。2018 年 9 月，被评为“中国菜”之贵州十大经典名菜、四川十大经典名菜。

词汇笔记

- **categorize** ['kætəgəraɪz] *v.* to put people or things into groups according to what type they are 将……分类，把……列作
- **palace** ['pæləs] *n.* the official home of a king, queen, president, etc. 王宫，（官位极高者的）府邸
- **condiment** ['kɒndɪmənt] *n.* a substance such as salt or pepper that is used to give flavour to food 调味品；佐料
- **commemorate** [kə'meməreɪt] *v.* to remind people of an important person or event from the past with a special action or object 纪念，用以纪念
- **upright** ['ʌpraɪt] *adj.* behaving in a moral and honest way 正直的，诚实的
- **exhibition** [ˌeksɪ'bɪʃən] *n.* the act of showing sth., for example works of art, to the public 展览，展出

Sour Soup Fish 酸汤鱼

必用三句

1 The dish attracts the diners with its slightly sour, savory, fresh and refreshing taste. 口味略带酸味、幽香沁人、鲜嫩爽口开胃。

2 Sour Soup Fish can be regarded as the trump card in the Guizhou Sour Soup series, among which Kaili Sour Soup is the most authentic. 酸汤鱼在贵州酸汤菜系列中算得上是王牌菜式，尤以凯里酸汤最为正宗。

3 The Miao people invented the dietary custom of "replacing salt with sour taste", thus lessening the lack of salt to a certain extent. 苗族同胞发明了“以酸代盐”的饮食方法，在一定程度上摆脱了缺盐的困境。

双语赏析

Sour Soup Fish of Guizhou is a traditional dish of the Miao people, and it belongs to the "Qianjia specialty" of Guizhou. The main ingredients of the dish are fish, Sour Soup, litsea cubeba, etc. The dish attracts the diners with its slightly sour, savory, fresh and refreshing taste. With its long history, Sour Soup Fish is famous all over the country and mentioned in the CCTV documentary *A Bite of China*. Up to now, Sour Soup Fish has become the representative of Guizhou cuisine, and it can also be said to be the most recommended dish of Guizhou. The carefully prepared Sour Soup presents a sour and spicy taste. The fish is slightly mushy in the Sour Soup, granting the diners fantastic enjoyment with delicious fish and proper Sour Soup.

Sour Soup Fish can be regarded as the trump card in the Guizhou Sour Soup series, among which Kaili Sour Soup is the most authentic. There is a saying among local Miao people that "you won't find a husband if you can't make Sour Soup", which shows the importance of Sour Soup dishes in the dietary customs in some areas of Guizhou. There is a folk legend about the Sour Soup. It is said that in ancient times, the ancestor of the Miao people was Chiyou who had 81 brothers. They were all very brave and good at fighting. They ever fought with the two tribes of Yandi and Huangdi for the Central China. In the end, Chiyou was defeated and killed, and his descendants also suffered ruthless conquests and exiles many times during the periods of Yao, Shun and Yu. Later, some of them moved to western Hunan and southeastern Guizhou which is mainly mountainous areas. Salt was very scarce due to the inconvenient transportation. Finally, the Miao people invented the dietary custom of "replacing salt with sour taste", thus lessening the lack of salt to a certain extent. It is also a very effective way to prevent the decay of food, enriching the taste of the diet as well. This is the story of Sour Soup.

贵州酸汤鱼是苗族的一道传统菜肴，属于贵州“黔家特色菜”。菜品主要材料为鱼肉、酸汤、山仓子等。口味略带酸味、幽香沁人、鲜嫩爽口开胃。贵州酸汤鱼历史悠久，全国闻名，央视纪录片《舌尖上的中国》提到的美食中就有这道贵州酸汤鱼。发展到现在，贵州酸汤鱼已经成为了黔菜中的代表，也可以说是贵州的招牌菜。千锤百炼之后的酸汤，汤底味道醇厚，酸中带辣。鱼肉在酸汤中已经煮得微烂，舀一勺酸汤，夹一块鱼肉，鱼块肉质鲜美，酸汤酸得恰到好处，混合着调料中的香辣，口感刺激，带来多层次的美味感受。

酸汤鱼在贵州酸汤菜系列中算得上是王牌菜式，尤以凯里酸汤最为正宗。当地苗民有“做不来酸汤嫁不了人”的俗语，可见酸汤菜式在贵州一些地区饮食习俗中的位置。关于酸汤，民间有一个传说，据说在上古时期，苗民的祖先蚩尤有 81 个兄弟，他们都非常的英勇善战，曾与炎帝和黄帝两大部落为争夺中原而开战。最后蚩尤战败被杀，他的后裔在尧、舜、禹时期也多次遭受了无情的征伐、放逐。后来就有一些辗转到湘西、黔东南这一带。而这一带都以山区为主，交通运输非常不方便，食盐也非常匮乏。最后苗族同胞发明了“以酸代盐”的饮食方法，在一定程度上摆脱了缺盐的困境。这有效地防止了食物的腐烂，还丰富了饮食的品味。这就是酸汤的故事。

词汇笔记

- **refreshing** [rɪ'freʃɪŋ] *adj.* making you feel less tired or hot 令人耳目一新的；使人精神振作的
- **sour** ['saʊər] *adj.* having a taste like that of a lemon or of fruit that is not ready to eat 酸的，酸味的
- **documentary** [ˌdɒkju'mentəri] *n.* a film or a radio or television programme giving facts about sth. 纪实节目，纪录片
- **mushy** ['mʌʃi] *adj.* soft and thick, like mush 糊状的
- **lessen** ['lesn] *v.* to become or make sth. become smaller, weaker, less important, etc.（使）缩小，（使）减少
- **tribe** [traɪb] *n.* a group of people of the same race, and with the same customs, language, religion, etc., living in a particular area and often led by a chief 部落，宗族

Spicy Hot Pot 麻辣烫

必用三句

1 Spicy Hot Pot originated along the banks of the Yangtze River in Sichuan, and was originally created by boatmen and boat trackers. 麻辣烫起源于四川长江之滨，最初是船工和纤夫创造了这种吃法。

2 The vegetables cooked with Sichuan pepper, chili and other seasonings tasted very delicious. It could not only fill the stomach, but also dispelled coldness and dampness. 各种蔬菜放入花椒、辣椒等调料，涮烫后食用，滋味美不可言。既可果腹，又可驱寒、祛湿。

3 Today, Spicy Hot Pot has been improved several times, and the formula is more concerned with health topics. 时至今日，麻辣烫几经改良，配方更加关注健康话题。

双语赏析

Spicy Hot Pot is a Sichuan specialty snack. The main feature is that all can be used as its ingredients and it is abundant in taste, which makes it deeply loved by many diners. Spicy Hot Pot originated along the banks of the Yangtze River in Sichuan, and was originally created by boatmen and boat trackers.

There is rapid flow from Yibin, Sichuan to Wushan Mountain in the Three Gorges area, where the climate is cloudy, humid and foggy. The boatmen and boat trackers who had worked there for many years picked up a few stones on the riverside to set up a clay pot, and scooped up water from the river. Making fire with dry wood, they cooked vegetables in the pot. They plucked wild vegetables if there were no vegetables. The vegetables cooked with Sichuan pepper, chili and other seasonings tasted very delicious. It could not only fill the stomach, but also dispelled coldness and dampness. This custom of cooking food gradually spread along the riverside. In view of the profitability, the peddlers on the wharf improved the dishes and cooking utensils which were placed on both ends of the shoulder pole and peddled on the bank. Because of the high quality and low price, they attracted boat trackers. Therefore, the boat trackers no longer made this kind of snacks by themselves, but instead bought from those peddlers. It was a unique view of the eaters enjoying Spicy Hot Pot along the river. Spicy Hot Pot gradually moved from the riverside to other places. Later, it developed into Spicy Hot Pot that we often see in the streets today.

Spicy Hot Pot is the predecessor of Sichuan Hot Pot, and it can also be said to be a simplified version of Hot Pot, except that the meat and vegetables are skewered with bamboo sticks. The authentic way to eat is to grab a large handful, gently stroke it into a sesame oil dish with chopsticks one after another, and then eat happily. The cooking of Spicy Hot Pot has been improved continuously, and many traditional Chinese medicines have been included into the recipe. Not only can it dispel dampness and drive cold, but it is also delicious. Because of its low price, this delicacy quickly becomes popular in Sichuan and is popular among students and office workers. Today, Spicy Hot Pot has been improved several times, and the formula is more concerned with health topics. The shops aim at making healthy food, using fresh ingredients and less additives.

麻辣烫是一道四川特色小吃。其主要特点是无可不烫，无味不有，深受众多食客的喜爱。麻辣烫起源于四川长江之滨，最初是船工和纤夫创造了这种吃法。

从四川宜宾到三峡内的巫山一带水流湍急，气候阴湿多雾，在此路段长年劳作的船工和纤夫在拉纤之余，在江边拾上几块石头，支起瓦罐，舀几瓢江水，撸上把干柴生火。在罐里加入蔬菜，没有蔬菜便就地取材，拔些野菜。各种蔬菜放入花椒、辣椒等调料，涮烫后食用，滋味美不可言。既可果腹，又可驱寒、祛湿。这种煮食涮烫食品的习俗便渐渐开始在江边沿袭。码头上的小贩见这种饮食方式有利可图，便将菜品和炊具加以改良，置于挑担两头，边走边吆喝，因其物美价廉，吸引了当地的纤夫！所以纤夫们不再自行做这种小食，转而购买附近的小商贩提供的小吃，江边桥头卖劳力的食客围着担子享用麻辣烫，也是江边的一道独特的景色。麻辣烫渐渐从江边走到了岸上。后来发展成了今天我们在大街小巷经常看到的麻辣烫了。

麻辣烫是四川火锅的前身，也可说是火锅的简装版，只是肉和菜都穿在竹签上，正宗的吃法可不是一串一串地吃，而是一抓一大把，用筷子轻轻一捋，菜就纷纷掉落香油碟中，然后开怀大吃！麻辣烫的做法一再被改良，配方加入了很多中药调料。不仅可以祛湿驱寒，而且又美味无比。因其价格低廉，这种美食很快便在四川流行开来，是很多学生和上班族的最爱。时至今日，麻辣烫几经改良，配方更加关注健康话题。商家都主打少添加剂、菜品新鲜的健康美食！

词汇笔记

- **snack** [snæk] *n.* a small meal or amount of food, usually eaten in a hurry 零食，点心，小吃；快餐
- **scoop** [skuːp] *v.* to move or lift sth. with a scoop or sth. like a scoop 用勺舀，用铲子铲；挖出，挖空；
- **predecessor** [ˈpriːdəsesər] *n.* a thing, such as a machine, that has been followed or replaced by sth. else （被取代的）原有事物，前身
- **peddle** [ˈpedəl] *v.* to try to sell goods by going from house to house or from place to place 沿街叫卖
- **simplify** [ˈsɪmplɪfaɪ] *v.* to make sth. easier to do or understand 使简易，简化
- **chopstick** [ˈtʃɒpstɪk] *n.* a pair of thin sticks that are used for eating with, especially in some asian countries 筷子

Mapo Tofu (Stir-fried Tofu in Hot Sauce) 麻婆豆腐

必用三句

1 The surface of the tofu is covered with a layer of light red chili oil, which can keep the heat in the tofu from dissipating quickly. 豆腐表面盖有一层淡红色的辣油，可保持豆腐内的热度不会很快散失。

2 When it comes to the history of Mapo Tofu, we can’t miss “Chen Mapo Tofu Shop” in Chengdu, Sichuan. 说起麻婆豆腐的历史，就不得不提起四川成都的“陈麻婆豆腐店”。

3 Due to its outstanding reputation, Mapo Tofu has spread all over the country and even the world. All tourists who come to Sichuan will try it as a pleasure.
由于名声卓著，麻婆豆腐已流传全国乃至全世界，凡到四川的游客莫不以一尝为快事。

双语赏析

Mapo Tofu is one of the famous dishes of traditional Sichuan cuisine. Together with garlic sprouts and minced beef, the main ingredient tofu is cooked with bean paste, chili powder and pepper powder, soy sauce, light soy sauce, dark soy sauce, sugar, starch and other seasonings. The color of the dish is light yellow, and the tofu is soft and lusters. It tastes tongue-numbing, spicy, crisp, savory, tender, fresh and hot. The surface of the tofu is covered with a layer of light red chili oil, which can keep the heat in the tofu from dissipating quickly. It tastes better when eaten hot.

When it comes to the history of Mapo Tofu, we can't miss "Chen Mapo Tofu Shop" in Chengdu, Sichuan. In 1824, the famous Sichuan Chen Mapo Tofu Restaurant opened at Wanfu Bridge in Chengdu. At that time, it was just a mom-and-pop shop selling plain dishes. Mrs. Liu was in charge of the cooking in the restaurant. Because her husband's family name was Chen and her face was pock-marked, people called her "Chen Mapo" behind her back. Wanfu Bridge was a good place for a restaurant, and there were constant merchants going by. One day, a "youzuzi" (a porter who sold oil) coming to the restaurant bought two pieces of tofu and a bit of beef, scooped a spoonful of rapeseed oil from his own oil basket, and asked Chen Mapo to cook for him. Chen Mapo immediately agreed. When the savory and attractively colored roasted tofu with minced beef was served on the table, the dish made the mouths of other "youzuzi" water. They also bought tofu and beef, scooped some rapeseed oil and asked Chen Mapo to cook for them. Because of the high oil temperature, the white and soft tofu, and the fresh and tender beef, the tofu cooked by Chen Mapo was very delicious. Since then, the dish was spread over though word of mouth. Not only "youzuzi", but also some literati and wealthy businessmen went to taste the tofu cooked by Chen Mapo. Over time, the tofu cooked by Chen Mapo become a famous dish with unique flavor in Sichuan. For convenience, people call the tofu cooked in the restaurant "Mapo Tofu".

On September 10, 2018, Mapo Tofu was rated as one of the top ten classic dishes of Sichuan in "Chinese Cuisine". Due to its outstanding reputation, Mapo Tofu has spread all over the country and even the world. All tourists who come to Sichuan will try it as a pleasure.

麻婆豆腐是传统川菜的名菜之一，主料为豆腐，加入蒜苗、牛肉沫后，用豆瓣、辣椒面和花椒面、酱油、生抽、老抽、糖、淀粉等调料配制而成。此菜色泽淡黄，豆腐软嫩而有光泽，其味麻、辣、酥、香、嫩、鲜、烫。豆腐表面盖有一层淡红色的辣油，可保持豆腐内的热度不会很快散失。这道菜趁热吃滋味更佳。

说起麻婆豆腐的历史，就不得不提起四川成都的"陈麻婆豆腐店"。1824 年，闻名中外的四川陈麻婆豆腐饭店在万福桥头开业了。当时这只是一个经营素饭小菜的夫妻店，饭铺由刘氏掌灶，因为她夫家姓陈，脸上又有麻子，人们背地里都叫她陈麻婆。万福桥头是开饭馆的好去处，南来北往的客商不断。一天，一位来万福桥歇脚的"油脚子"（贩油的脚夫）买来两块豆腐和一点牛肉，从自己的油篓子里舀上一勺菜油，请求陈麻婆代为加工。陈麻婆立即应允。当香气四溢，颜色诱人的牛肉沫烧豆腐端上饭桌时，其他"油脚子"也馋涎欲滴，纷纷买来豆腐和牛肉，并也舀上一勺子菜油请陈麻婆代为烹制。因为油大火旺，豆腐雪白绵软，下锅不烂，牛肉又鲜又嫩，所以陈麻婆烧制的豆腐异常可口。从此，一传十，十传百，不但"油脚子"，后来连一些文人雅士，富商巨贾也慕名前来这里品尝陈麻婆烧制的豆腐了。久而久之，陈麻婆烧制的豆腐遂成为四川一道风味独特的名菜。人们为了称呼方便，便把陈麻婆店烧制的豆腐称作"麻婆豆腐"。

2018 年 9 月 10 日，麻婆豆腐被评为"中国菜"四川十大经典名菜。由于名声卓著，麻婆豆腐已流传全国乃至全世界，凡到四川的游客莫不以一尝为快事。

词汇笔记

- **mince** [mɪns] *v.* to cut food, especially meat, into very small pieces using a special machine（用机器）切碎，绞碎

- **luster** ['lʌstər] vi. be very bright and shine 有光泽；发亮
- **savory** ['seɪvəri] *adj.* having a pleasant taste or smell 可口的；风味极佳的；味美的
- **dissipate** ['dɪsɪpeɪt] *v.* to gradually become or make sth. become weaker until it disappears（使某事物）消散，消失
- **mom-and-pop** [ˌmɒm ən 'pɒp] *adj.* owned and run by a husband and wife, or by a family 夫妻经营的；家庭经营的
- **pock-marked** ['pɒk mɑːkt] *adj.* covered with hollow marks or holes 有痘疤的

Three Cannons 三大炮

必用三句

1 Three Cannons (Glutinous Rice Balls) is one of the Chengdu-style snacks, also known as glutinous rice cake. 三大炮是成都风味小吃之一，又名糍粑。

2 Three Cannons is a food made through performance. 三大炮为表演型美食。

3 Of course, Three Cannons not only entertains customers with performances, but also appeals to them with its softness, sweetness and savory taste. 当然，三大炮红糖糍粑不光以表演取悦顾客，其软糯、甜美和喷香也让食者久久难以忘怀。

双语赏析

Three Cannons (Glutinous Rice Balls) is one of the Chengdu-style snacks, also known as glutinous rice cake. Because of the peculiar and interesting cooking, it enjoys a high reputation. The ingredients are glutinous rice, soybeans and sesame seeds. Its cooking process comes as follows: wash the glutinous rice, steam it in a steamer for one hour, pour it into a treadle-operated tilt hammer after drying, and pound it into a glutinous rice dough for later use;

stir-fry soybeans and sesame seeds, and grind them into flour; the cook shapes it into a ball the size of an egg, oil and throw it into a shallow basket containing soybeans and sesame flour to coat it evenly; place the balls into a copper plate and drizzle them with syrup. Because the sound “dang, dang, dang” is made when the cook throws glutinous rice balls, it is named “Three Cannons”.

Three Cannons is a food made through performance. On traditional lantern shows, temple fairs, flower fairs and other lively occasions, Three Cannons comes on stage as the representative of Chengdu’s traditional snacks. The more people there are, the more eye-catching it is. In addition to mobilizing people’s sense of smell, it can also stimulate people’s hearing and vision. There are not many tools for making Three Cannons, and the key lies at the maker’s proficient mastery of skills. First, a wooden board is put up, and 12 copper plates are placed on the wooden board, which are stacked on top of each other in two rows. Beneath the wooden board is a large iron pot containing cooked sticky rice pounded with a mallet. The maker pulls out a handful of glutinous rice from the pot, knead it into three glutinous rice cakes and punch them out rhythmically. The glutinous rice cakes bounce from the wooden board, jump into the shallow basket with soybean flour above the wooden board, making three sounds of “dang, dang, dang”. Then put three glutinous rice cakes into a plate one time and sprinkle with brown sugar and sesame flour. Of course, Three Cannons not only entertains customers with performances, but also appeals to them with its softness, sweetness and savory taste.

三大炮是成都风味小吃之一，又名糍粑。由于做法奇特，又饶有风趣，故享有盛名。它以糯米、黄豆、芝麻为食材。其制作方法：糯米洗净，放笼屉中急火蒸 1 小时，稍晾后倒入石碓中，舂成糯米面团待用；黄豆、芝麻炒熟，研成细面；而后由厨师根据顾客的需要将糯米团捏成鸡蛋大小的圆球形、抹上油扔到盛黄豆、芝麻面的簸箩中使其均匀裹上，再盛入铜碟里，淋上浓糖汁即好。由于在抛扔糯米团时如“弹丸”发出“当、当、当”的响声，故名“三大炮”。

三大炮为表演型美食。每逢传统的灯会、庙会、花会等热闹场合，作为成都传统小吃代表的三大炮便粉墨登场。越是人多的地方，它越吸引眼球。除了能调动人们的嗅觉外，它还可以刺激人们的听觉和视觉。制作三大炮的工具不多，关键在于制作者能熟练地掌握操作技巧。首先支起一块木板，木板上摆放 12 个铜盘，两两相叠，排成两行。木板下面放着一口热气腾腾的大铁锅，装着蒸好又用木槌舂黏的糯米饭。制作者要不断地从锅里扯出一把糯米饭揉糍粑，分摘三坨，有节奏地打出来。糍粑从木板中弹跳而过，跃进放于木板上方的装有黄豆面的簸箕内，发出发出“当、当、当”三响。再把糍粑团每三个拣为一盘，浇上红糖，撒上芝麻即可。当然，三大炮红糖糍粑不光以表演取悦顾客，其软糯、甜美和喷香也让食者久久难以忘怀。

词汇笔记

- **peculiar** [pɪ'kjuːliər] *adj.* (to sb./sth.) belonging or relating to one particular place, situation, person, etc., and not to others 特别的，独特的
- **pound** [paʊnd] *v.* to hit sth. many times in order to break it into smaller pieces 捣碎；击碎
- **grind** [graɪnd] *v.* to break or crush sth. into very small pieces between two hard surfaces or using a special machine 磨碎；碾碎；把……磨成粉
- **drizzle** ['drɪzəl] *v.* to pour a small amount of liquid over the surface of sth. 洒上
- **lively** ['laɪvli] *adj.* full of interest or excitement 热闹的，激烈的
- **mastery** ['mɑːstəri] *n.* great knowledge about or understanding of a particular thing 精通，熟练掌握

Twice-cooked Pork 回锅肉

必用三句

1 There is a saying “if you don't eat Twice-cooked Pork when you visit Sichuan, you haven't really been to Sichuan.” 人们常说“入蜀不吃回锅肉，等于没有到四川”。

2 The main ingredient of Twice-cooked Pork is pork, which is preferably streaky pork. 回锅肉的主料是猪肉，以肥瘦相连的为佳。

3 Twice-cooked Pork has always been considered to be the epitome of Sichuan cuisine. When it comes to Sichuan cuisine, one must think of Twice-cooked Pork. 回锅肉一直被认为是川菜之首，川菜之化身，提到川菜必然想到回锅肉。

双语赏析

Twice-cooked Pork is a traditional Sichuan dish, and it is also a popular dish today. Every household in Sichuan can make Twice-cooked Pork. When you go to Sichuan, you can't miss Twice-cooked Pork. There is a saying "if you don't eat Twice-cooked Pork when you visit Sichuan, you haven't really been to Sichuan." For Sichuan people who have lived in other places for a long time and come back to visit relatives and friends, the first thing that comes to mind is the Twice-cooked Pork.

The main ingredient of Twice-cooked Pork is pork, which is preferably streaky pork; other ingredients are selected according to the season, including green garlic sprouts, green peppers, ginger, garlic sprouts, cabbage, Chinese cabbage, spring onions, bamboo shoots, etc. Pixian County Bean Paste, sweet bean sauce, fermented black bean, soy sauce and some cooking oil are needed. The cooking process comes as follows: cook pork, green onion, ginger and Sichuan pepper in a pot until the meat is cooked; after the pork has cooled thoroughly, cut it into thin slices and fry it in a pan; then add garlic sprouts, Pixian County Bean Paste and soy sauce, fry until the pork is oily and savory; serve the dish in a plate.

It is called Boiled Pork in the area of Chengdu in western Sichuan, and it is called Twice-cooked Pork in the area of Chongqing in east Sichuan. Its characteristics are as follows: unique flavor, red and bright color, fat but not greasy taste, and strong aroma. The so-called "twice-cooked" means cooking again. Twice-cooked Pork has always been considered to be the epitome of Sichuan cuisine. When it comes to Sichuan cuisine, one must think of Twice-cooked Pork. As the first choice for a good meal, it is a perfect integration of color, aroma and taste. So, do you know the story behind Twice-cooked Pork?

It is said that Sichuan people in the past used boiled pork belly as a sacrificial offering. When the pork was cool after the sacrificial ceremony, people recooked it by stir-frying it in the pot. Later, this cooking evolved into a dish called “Twice-cooked Pork”. At the late Qing Dynasty, there was a Hanlin (a member of the Imperial Academy) surnamed Ling in Chengdu, who retired to his home because of his disappointment in his official career and devoted himself to the study of cooking. He changed the cooking of Twice-cooked Pork by steaming it in a water-proof container before stir-frying. Because of the long time steaming, the loss of soluble protein is reduced; the rich and fresh flavor of the pork is maintained without losing the original flavor; and the color is bright red. Since then, Twice-cooked Pork made in this way spread to other places.

回锅肉是一道传统川菜，也是现如今深受大众喜欢的一道菜。四川每家每户都能做回锅肉，到四川不能不吃回锅肉。人们常说“入蜀不吃回锅肉，等于没有到四川”。久居外乡的四川人，回川探亲访友，首先想到要吃的就是回锅肉。

回锅肉的主料是猪肉，以肥瘦相连的为佳。辅料随季节选用，有青蒜苗、青椒、生姜、蒜薹、卷心菜、大白菜、京葱、笋等。调料用正宗的郫县豆瓣、甜面酱、豆豉、酱油，还需要些食用油。其制作方法是：将猪肉、葱、姜、花椒一起放入锅里煮，至肉熟皮软捞出；冷透后，切成薄片，放入油锅炒；再加入蒜苗、郫县豆瓣、酱油，炒至肉冒油，出香味；起锅装盘，回锅肉就做成了。

在川西成都一带称作熬锅肉，川东重庆一带称为回锅肉。其特点是：口味独特，色泽红亮，肥而不腻，入口浓香。所谓回锅，就是再次烹调的意思。回锅肉一直被认为是川菜之首，川菜之化身，提到川菜必然想到回锅肉。它色香味俱全，是下饭菜之首选。那么，你知道这样美味的回锅肉有着怎样的典故吗?

据说以前川人每月初一和十五要家祭，以煮熟的五花肉作为祭品。当仪式完成后祭肉已凉，食用时要再放锅里炒一炒，回回锅。后来这种做法演变成一道菜，名为“回锅肉”。清末时成都有位姓凌的翰林，因宦途失意退隐家居，潜心研究烹饪。他将回锅肉做法改为先将猪肉去腥味，以隔水容器密封的方法蒸熟后再煎炒成菜。因为久蒸至熟，减少了可溶性蛋白质的损失，保持了肉质的浓郁鲜香，原味不失，色泽红亮。自此，久蒸回锅肉便流传开来。

词汇笔记

- **slice** [slaɪs] *n.* a thin flat piece of food that has been cut off a larger piece（切下的食物）薄片，片
- **epitome** [ɪ'pɪtəmi] *n.* a perfect example of sth. 典型，缩影；摘要，概要
- **devote** [dɪ'vəʊt] *v.* to give most of your time, energy, attention, etc. to sb./sth. 献身，致力；用于
- **evolve** [ɪ'vɒlv] *v.* to develop gradually, especially from a simple to a more complicated form 进化，演化；逐步发展，逐渐演变
- **integration** [ˌɪntɪ'greɪʃən] *n.* the act or process of combining two or more things so that they work together 结合，融合
- **original** [ə'rɪdʒənəl] *adj.* existing at the beginning of a particular period, process or activity 起初的，原先的

Fish Flavored Shredded Pork 鱼香肉丝

必用三句

1 It is definitely one of the most popular must-order dishes. 它绝对是最具人气的必点菜品之一。

2 In fact, the name of this dish has nothing to do with the raw materials, but it has something to do with the seasonings used to cook it. 其实，这道菜的得名确实与原料没有关系，但与烹制它的调料有关。

3 Although there is no fish in the raw materials for the dishes named in this way, the seasonings are those used in the cooking of fish. As a result, these dishes get a fish flavor, and therefore get a name with “fish flavored”. 虽然原料中没有鱼，但其调料是民间烹制鲜鱼时所用的调料，结果便产生了鱼的香味，“鱼香”类菜品因此而得名。

双语赏析

Fish Flavored Shredded Pork is a traditional home-cooked dish which is regarded as a classic of Sichuan cuisine. It is definitely one of the most popular must-order dishes. The strange thing is that there is no fish in the raw materials for this dish. Then why has it got such a name? In fact, the name of this dish has nothing to do with the raw materials, but it has something to do with the seasonings used to cook it. Fish Flavored Shredded Pork is fried shredded pork. "Fish flavor" is a representative flavor of Sichuan cuisine. Although there is no fish in the raw materials for the dishes named in this way, the seasonings are those used in the cooking of fish. As a result, these dishes get a fish flavor, and therefore get a name with "fish flavored".

The main ingredients of this dish include pickled chili, tender ginger, garlic, sugar and vinegar, to stir-fry shredded pork tenderloin. The finished dishes are bright in color, tender in meat, salty, sweet, sour and spicy in taste, making people's mouths water. Since the day of birth, the dish has won the favor of countless people.

There is a story about the name of this dish. It is said that a long time ago a housewife in Sichuan often used a lot of onions, ginger, garlic, vinegar, soy sauce and other seasonings to remove the fishy smell because the family liked to eat fish and were particular about the color and flavor of the dishes. Once the hostess used the seasonings left over from cooking fish when cooking another dish in order not to waste the excess seasonings. When her husband came back and tasted it, he praised the dish greatly. When he asked how the dish was made, the hostess told him the fact that the seasonings for cooking fish were used, so the dish was named "Fish flavored stir-fry". Through the improvement for several years, Sichuan people has not only perfected the cooking of Fish Flavored Shredded Pork, but also invented similar dishes, such as Fish Flavored Pork Liver, Fish Flavored Eggplant and Fish Flavored Three Slices (shredded pork, tofu, green pepper). On September 10, 2018, because of its unique flavor and popularity all over the country, Fish Flavored Shredded Pork was rated as one of the top ten classic dishes in Sichuan in “Chinese Cuisine”. In December 2021, it was selected as the provincial “Tianfu Famous Dish”.

鱼香肉丝是一道传统的家常菜，堪称川菜的经典之作。它绝对是最具人气的必点菜品之一。奇怪的是，烧制这道菜的原料中并没有鱼，为何又要取这样的菜名呢？其实，这道菜的得名确实与原料没有关系，但与烹制它的调料有关。“鱼香肉丝”即炒肉丝。“鱼香”是川菜的一个代表味型。虽然原料中没有鱼，但其调料是民间烹制鲜鱼时所用的调料，结果便产生了鱼的香味，“鱼香”类菜品因此而得名。

该菜品主要的配制材料包括泡辣椒、子姜、大蒜、糖和醋，用以炒制猪里脊肉丝。成品菜颜色鲜艳，肉质细嫩，兼具咸、甜、酸、辣为一体，让人垂涎欲滴，从诞生之日起，就赢得了无数人的青睐。

说起这道菜名的由来还有一个小故事。据传很久前四川的一名家庭妇女，因为家里人喜欢吃鱼，又对菜的色泽及调味有很多讲究，因而每次在烹制鱼的时候会多放很多葱、姜、蒜、醋、酱油等去除腥味的调料。有一次女主人为了不让多余的调料浪费，在做其他菜的时候把烧鱼时剩下的配料放进了菜里。家里男主人回来品尝后对此大加赞扬，追问菜是如何做的时候，女主人才将使用烧鱼的配料炒菜的事实告知，所以这道菜被取名为“鱼香炒”。后来经过四川人若干年的改进，不仅完善了鱼香肉丝的做法，还做出了类似的菜式，如鱼香猪肝、鱼香茄子和鱼香三丝（猪肉丝、豆腐丝、青椒丝）等。2018 年 9 月 10 日，因鱼香肉丝风味独特，风靡全国，其在备受关注的“中国菜”评选中被评为四川十大经典名菜之一。2021 年 12 月，入选省级“天府名菜”。

词汇笔记

- **raw** [rɔː] *adj.* not cooked 生的，未煮过的
- **countless** [ˈkaʊntləs] *adj.* very many; too many to be counted or mentioned 无数的，数不尽的
- **particular** [pəˈtɪkjələr] *adj.* very definite about what you like and careful about what you choose; fussy 讲究的，挑剔的
- **popularity** [ˌpɒpjuˈlærəti] *n.* the state of being liked, enjoyed or supported by a large number of people 流行，普及，受欢迎

- **excess** [ɪk'ses] *adj.* in addition to an amount that is necessary, usual or legal 过多的，超额的
- **perfect** ['pɜːfɪkt] *v.* to make sth. perfect or as good as you can 完善，使完美

Hot and Sour Rice Noodles 酸辣粉

必用三句

1 Hot and Sour Rice Noodles is a traditional snack in Sichuan, Chongqing and other places. It originated from Sichuan, taking the local hand-made sweet potato flour as the ingredient. It got the name mainly because of its sour and spicy taste. 酸辣粉是四川、重庆等地的传统名小吃，起源于四川民间，取当地手工制作的红薯粉作为食材，以突出酸辣味为主而得名。

2 The flour used for making Hot and Sour Rice Noodles is made of sweet potatoes, red stalks and peas in a certain proportion, which then is made into narrow and wide noodles by traditional manual work. 酸辣粉主粉由红薯、红苕、豌豆按一定比例调和，然后由农家用传统手工漏制而成，通常有窄的、宽的两种。

3 As long as you give authentic Sichuan-style seasonings, it is easy to make a bowl of spicy and authentic Hot and Sour Rice Noodles. 只要给足正宗的川式调料，很容易能做出一碗香辣爽口的正宗酸辣粉。

双语赏析

Hot and Sour Rice Noodles is a traditional snack in Sichuan, Chongqing and other places. It originated from Sichuan, taking the local hand-made sweet potato flour as the ingredient. It got the name mainly because of its sour and spicy taste. After continuous improvement, it got popular and became a local specialty snack.

The flour used for making Hot and Sour Rice Noodles is made of sweet potatoes, red stalks and peas in a certain proportion, which then is made into narrow and wide noodles by traditional manual work. Hot and Sour Rice Noodles are chewy, spicy, sour and appetizing, deeply loved by people all over the country. Hot and Sour Rice Noodles are green food with tongue-numbing, spicy, fresh, savory, sour taste. It is oily but not greasy, known as the best noodles in the world.

There is a widely spread story about the origin of Hot and Sour Rice Noodles. During the Three Kingdoms period, after Liu Bei, Guan Yu, and Zhang Fei took Oath to become sworn brothers in the Peach Garden, the owner of Peach Garden specially cooked a dish for them. With the sweet potato flour which the local people liked as the main ingredient, the ingredients of the dish were simple while the intention was not as simple, expecting that the friendship between the three was as long as noodles. A super spicy hot pepper, pickled sauerkraut, brown sugar and coptis were used in the cooking with the aim of making the three understand that they were sworn brothers and should face ups and downs together. The famous Hot and Sour Rice Noodles evolved from this dish. After eating a bowl of Hot and Sour Rice Noodles, the friendship between the three was as long as the Peach Garden owner hoped, and it never faded after the ordeal of times. Liu Bei even established the Shu Kingdom with the help of Guan Yu and Zhang Fei. This dish gradually spread, and later generations changed the name of the dish to "Hot and Sour Rice Noodles" because of its sour and spicy taste. Today, people in Sichuan and Chongqing no longer put coptis and brown sugar in the dish, only sour and spicy flavors left. The authenticity of the dish lies in the seasonings. As long as you give authentic Sichuan-style seasonings, it is easy to make a bowl of spicy and authentic Hot and Sour Rice Noodles.

酸辣粉是四川、重庆等地的传统名小吃，起源于四川民间，取当地手工制作的红薯粉作为食材，以突出酸辣味为主而得名。后来经过不断地演变和调制而正式走上街头，成为当地的一种特色小吃。

酸辣粉主粉由红薯、红苕、豌豆按一定比例调和，然后由农家用传统手工漏制而成，通常有窄的、宽的两种。酸辣粉的粉丝劲道弹牙、口味麻辣酸爽、浓香开胃，深受全国人民喜爱。酸辣粉是纯天然绿色食品，口感是麻、辣、鲜、香、酸且油而不腻，素有“天下第一粉”之称。

说起酸辣粉的来历，广泛流传着这样的典故。三国时期，刘备、关羽、张飞在桃园三结义后，桃园的主人专门为他们做了一道菜。这道菜成分简单，但用意却不简单，主要是选取了当时比较为人喜欢的红苕粉做主料，寓意这三人的友情像这粉条一样绵长，又加了一种特别辣的小尖椒、老坛酸菜、红糖、黄连在里面，主要的意思是要让三人明白，结义为异姓兄弟后，须共进退，酸甜苦辣都不怕，著名的酸辣粉，由此演变而来。一碗“结义粉”吃下后，刘、关、张三人情谊果真如桃园主人所希望的那样绵长，几经磨砺不曾褪色，刘备更是在关羽、张飞辅助下建立了蜀国。这一碗粉渐渐流传开来，后人是因为其味酸辣入味，渐渐将菜品名称就改成了“酸辣粉”。时至今日，川渝人已不再在酸辣粉中放黄连和红糖，只留酸和辣两种口味。酸辣粉的正宗与否，灵魂在调料上。只要给足正宗的川式调料，很容易能做出一碗香辣爽口的正宗酸辣粉。

词汇笔记

- **hand-made** [hænd meɪd] *adj.* objects have been made by someone using their hands or using tools rather than by machines 手工制造
- **continuous** [kən'tɪnjuəs] *adj.* happening or existing for a period of time without interruption 连续不断的，持续的
- **proportion** [prə'pɔːʃn] *n.* the relationship of one thing to another in size, amount, etc. 比例
- **manual** ['mænjuəl] *adj.* involving using the hands or physical strength 手工的
- **oath** [əʊθ] *n.* a formal promise to do sth. or a formal statement that sth. is true 誓言，誓约
- **pickled** ['pɪkld] *adj.* (of food) preserved in vinegar 腌制的；盐渍的

Cross Bridge Rice Noodles 过桥米线

必用三句

1 This dish originated from Mengzi in southern Yunnan, and there is a beautiful legend about it. 这道菜源于滇南的蒙自，关于它还有一个美好的传说。

2 Because the virtuous wife had to pass a small bridge to deliver food for her husband, this kind of rice noodles was called "Cross Bridge Rice Noodles". 由于这位贤惠的妻子送米线时要经过小桥，这种米线就被称为"过桥米线"。又因秀才后来考中了状元，也一度被叫作"状元米线"。

3 The Cross Bridge Rice Noodles are served with individual provision, and each person respectively has a bowl of raw slices, chicken soup, vegetables, and rice noodles in front of them. 过桥米线是分食的，每人面前生片、鸡汤、蔬菜、米线各一碗。

双语赏析

When it comes to Yunnan cuisine, people will firstly think of Cross Bridge Rice Noodles. Indeed, as the most famous food in Yunnan, it is well known all over the world. This dish originated from Mengzi in southern Yunnan, and there is a beautiful legend about it. In ancient times, the South Lake in Mengzi County was beautiful. A scholar surnamed Yang built a study on a small island in South Lake in order to avoid socializing with other people. He lived alone and studied hard all day, and his wife prepared meals for him every day.

The scholar studied so hard that he often forgot to eat, making it natural to eat cold meals. Because of the irregular eating, he was losing weight day by day, which greatly distressed his wife. One day, his wife cooked a hen in a casserole together with the rice noodles and other condiments that the locals liked, and the taste was very delicious. The wife also accidentally discovered that because the surface of the soup was covered with a thick layer of chicken fat, the heat was sealed in the soup and remained warm for a long time in clay utensils with the poor heat transfer. Inspired by this interesting episode, the wife then often used this method to keep food warm. Under the careful care and encouragement of his wife, the husband finally got admitted to Zhuang Yuan (the champion) with the legend spread for a while.

Later, people imitated her cooking method, and the rice noodles are indeed delicious. Because the virtuous wife had to pass a small bridge to deliver food for her husband, this kind of rice noodles was called “Cross Bridge Rice Noodles”. And because the scholar was later admitted to Zhuang Yuan, it was also called “the Zhuang Yuan Rice Noodle” for a time.

If one who goes to Yunnan for the first time does not get advice from the locals, he is very likely to make a joke: the soup is boiling hot, but because there is a layer of chicken oil on the surface, there is no sign of heat at all, so it’s easy to burn your mouth. Therefore, you cannot drink soup directly with your mouth. When eating, you should eat quail eggs first, and then eat the raw slices after boiling them in the soup at the highest temperature. The Cross Bridge Rice Noodles are served with individual provision, and each person respectively has a bowl of raw slices, chicken soup, vegetables, and rice noodles in front of them.

说到云南美食，人们一定会在第一时间想到过桥米线。的确，作为云南最著名的一道小吃，它可谓闻名遐迩。这道菜源于滇南的蒙自，关于它还有一个美好的传说。在古代，蒙自县城的南湖风景优美。有位姓杨的秀才为了躲避迎来送往的应酬，在南湖的小岛上建了一座书斋，整天独居苦读，由妻子每日做好了饭菜给他送去。

秀才读书刻苦，经常忘记了吃饭，吃冷饭冷菜是常有的事。由于进食不规律，身体日见消瘦，妻子十分心疼。有一天，秀才妻子把家中的母鸡杀了，用砂锅炖熟后送去。并把当地人喜欢吃的米线和其他作料放入，味道很鲜美。妻子还偶然发现，汤表面覆盖着一层厚厚的鸡油，加之陶土器皿传热不佳，把热量封存在了汤内，很长时间仍然温热。妻子由此受到启发，以后常用此法保温。在妻子的细心照顾和鼓励下，丈夫终于考上了状元，一时传为美谈。

后来人们都仿效她的烹调方法，做出来的米线确实鲜美可口。由于这位贤惠的妻子送米线时要经过小桥，这种米线就被称为“过桥米线”。又因秀才后来考中了状元，也一度被叫作“状元米线”。

初去云南吃此小吃的人如不向别人请教会闹出笑话：汤是滚烫的，由于表面有一层鸡油，一点热气也没有，初食者往往误认为汤并不烫，直接用嘴去喝，这样很容易烫伤嘴。因此，不能用嘴直接去喝汤。在食用时应先食鹌鹑蛋，再食生片，趁汤是最高温的时候将生片烫熟。过桥米线是分食的，每人面前生片、鸡汤、蔬菜、米线各一碗。

词汇笔记

- **originate** [ə'rɪdʒɪneɪt] *v.* to happen or appear for the first time in a particular place or situation 起源，产生；创始，开创
- **socialize** ['səʊʃəlaɪz] *v.* to meet and spend time with people in a friendly way, in order to enjoy yourself （和他人）交往，交际
- **irregular** [ɪ'regjələr] *adj.* not happening at times that are at an equal distance from each other; not happening regularly （时间）无规律的，不定期的
- **distress** [dɪ'stres] *v.* to make sb feel very worried or unhappy 使悲伤，使忧虑
- **casserole** ['kæsərəʊl] *n.* a hot dish made with meat, vegetables, etc. that are cooked slowly in liquid in an oven 砂锅
- **quail** [kweɪl] *n.* a small brown bird, whose meat and eggs are used for food 鹌鹑

Luosifen 螺蛳粉

必用三句

1 Luosifen originated in Liuzhou, a city in Guangxi . 螺蛳粉起源于广西的柳州。

2 The authentic Liuzhou Luosifen has a strongly and strangely “stinky” smell. This “stinky” smell comes from the sour bamboo shoots in Luosifen. And the taste makes many people “shy away”. 地道的柳州螺蛳粉都会带着一股浓浓的奇葩的“臭”味，这股“臭”味来源于螺蛳粉里的酸笋，其味道让许多人“退避三舍”。

3 For Liuzhou people, Luosifen is the taste of home! 对柳州人来说，螺蛳粉是家的味道！

双语赏析

Luosifen originated in Liuzhou, a city in Guangxi. It features rice noodles soaked in a spicy broth, topped with locally grown ingredients including bamboo shoots, string beans, turnips, peanuts and tofu skin.

The reason why it is called Luosifen is that the soup is made from river snails whose Chinese pronunciation is "Luosi". Some people may not be used to the spicy and fishy taste of Luosifen, which is the biggest feature of it. The carefully brewed river snail soup has a unique flavor that is fresh but not light, numbing but not dry, and appetizing but not greasy.

Luosifen first appeared in the late 1970s. Although its history is relatively short, river snail and rice noodles have a long history in Liuzhou. The authentic Liuzhou Luosifen has a strongly and strangely "stinky" smell. This "stinky" smell comes from the sour bamboo shoots in Luosifen. And the taste makes many people "shy away", but those who appreciate it well know that it is palatable but not rotten, and that you will have a better appetite when you smell it; your mouth will water when you think about it; and even you will feel so excited when you eat it.

As the most famous snack in Liuzhou, Luosifen has never stopped developing. The taste and recipe of Luosifen are returning to tradition, and at the same time improvement and innovation of it are also ongoing, thus satisfying customers who have different requirements for the taste of it in the market. Liuzhou government has also gradually scaled and standardized the Luosifen industry, allowing Luosifen to go national and global.

The status of Luosifen as the first original snack in Liuzhou has never been seriously shaken. In 2008, Liuzhou Luosifen handmade skills were included in the Second Batch of Intangible Cultural Heritage List of Guangxi Zhuang

Autonomous Region. In 2021, Liuzhou Luosifen was included in the National Intangible Cultural Heritage List.

There is a saying: “If you don’t eat Luosifen, you are not really a native of Liuzhou”. Liuzhou wanderers who have been wandering for many years usually eat a bowl of authentic Luosifen to comfort their homesickness after returning to Liuzhou. For Liuzhou people, Luosifen is the taste of home!

螺蛳粉起源于广西的柳州。这道菜的特色是将米粉泡在辣味肉汤中，上面撒上当地生长的竹笋、酸豆角、萝卜、花生和豆腐皮等食材。

螺蛳粉之所以叫做“螺蛳粉”，是因为它的汤是用螺蛳熬成的。有人可能不习惯螺蛳粉汤辣和腥的味道，而这恰恰是螺蛳粉最大的特色。精心熬制的螺蛳汤具有清而不淡、麻而不燥、香而不腻的独特风味。

螺蛳粉最早出现于 20 世纪 70 年代末。虽然其历史较短，但嗍螺和米粉在柳州传承悠久。地道的柳州螺蛳粉都会带着一股浓浓的奇葩的“臭”味，这股“臭”味来源于螺蛳粉里的酸笋，其味道让许多人“退避三舍”，但懂得欣赏它的内涵的人，就会知道，它是香而不腐的，闻之开胃，想之流涎，吃之“打滚”。

作为柳州最负盛名的小吃，螺蛳粉一直未曾停下发展的脚步。螺蛳粉的味道和做法回归传统的同时改良创新也在持续进行，满足了市场上对于螺蛳粉口味有着不同要求的顾客。柳州市政府也已逐步把螺蛳粉产业规模化、标准化，让螺蛳粉走向全国、走向世界。

螺蛳粉作为柳州第一原创小吃的地位从未严重动摇过。2008 年，柳州螺蛳粉手工制作技艺入选广西壮族自治区第二批非物质文化遗产名录；2021 年，柳州螺蛳粉被列入国家级非物质文化遗产名单。

有句话说：“不食螺蛳粉，枉为柳州人。”在外漂泊多年的柳州游子，回到家乡后通常会吃上一碗味道正宗的螺蛳粉来告慰其多年的乡思。对柳州人来说，螺蛳粉是家的味道！

词汇笔记

- **snail** [sneɪl] *n.* a small soft creature with a hard round shell on its back, that moves very slowly and often eats garden plants 蜗牛
- **turnip** [ˈtɜːnɪp] *n.* a round white, or white and purple, root vegetable 芜菁，萝卜

- **numbing** ['nʌmɪŋ] *adj.* making you unable to feel anything 使麻木的；使失去感觉的
- **stinky** ['stɪŋki] *adj.* having an extremely bad smell 发恶臭的，十分难闻的

Guilin Rice Noodles 桂林米粉

必用三句

1 Guilin Rice Noodles are one of the traditional local flavors of Guilin and are famous for the unique flavor. 桂林米粉是桂林传统地方风味的一绝，以其独特的风味远近闻名。

2 In the streets of Guilin, wherever there is a breath of life, there will always be a burst of mellow rice noodles. 桂林的大街小巷，但凡是有生活气息的地方总会伴着阵阵米粉的醇香。

3 Guilin Rice Noodles carry the historical changes and incorporate the diligence and wisdom of Guilin people. 桂林米粉，承载着历史的变迁，融入了桂林人的勤劳与智慧。

双语赏析

Guilin is not only a tourist city, but also offers many delicacies. Just like the cultural origin of this city, Guilin is a place where diet from all over the country converges. Its cuisine is unique. Among them, Guilin Rice Noodles must be mentioned.

Guilin Rice Noodles are one of the traditional local flavors of Guilin and are famous for the unique flavor. The production process of rice noodles is derived from tradition, which is superior to tradition. It has the advantages of original rice noodles, such as fragrant and smooth rice noodles, rich brine fragrance, and rich seasonings. This is also the unique taste advantage that authentic Guilin Rice Noodles must have.

The origin of Guilin Rice Noodles still has no definite text to refer to. It can be said that it is the product of the fusion of the Central Plains diet culture and the southern diet culture after Qin Shihuang pacified the Lingnan Area, and can also be said that it is a historical story and folklore that is spread in a food in the streets that accommodates the interests of the people's life.

In the streets of Guilin, wherever there is a breath of life, there will always be a burst of mellow rice noodles. It can be said that everyone in Guilin can hardly live without rice noodles for a day. Guilin people like eating rice noodles, and rice noodles can be used as a staple food for breakfast, lunch and dinner. When a wanderer far from home comes back, he often eats a bowl of Guilin Rice Noodles to satisfy his cravings. The reason why the white and bright rice noodles can be so chewy, smooth and refreshing is because they have been repeatedly kneaded during the production process; the rice noodles themselves are light and tasteless, but they are "incentive" to the rich flavours and become very attractive. The simple appearance of rice noodles contains the philosophy of life.

On May 24, 2021, the making skills of Guilin Rice Noodles were included in the Fifth Batch of National Intangible Cultural Heritage.

Guilin Rice Noodles carry the historical changes and incorporate the diligence and wisdom of Guilin people. Before you taste it, just the smell of it is refreshing; when you try it, it is mellow and glutinous; and after you taste it, it has a long lingering finish. It becomes the nostalgia of every Guilin person through the taste receptors.

桂林不只是一座旅游城市，也是一座美食城市。正如这座城市的文化源流一样，桂林是四方饮食的融汇之地，它的美食是独具特色的，其中不得不提的便是桂林米粉。

桂林米粉是桂林传统地方风味的一绝，以其独特的风味远近闻名。米粉制作工艺源于传统，优于传统，有独创的米粉香滑、卤水香浓、佐料丰富等优势，这也是正宗桂林米粉所要具备的独特口感优势。

桂林米粉的起源至今仍没有确切的文字可考，它可以说是秦始皇平定岭南之后中原地区与南方饮食文化融合的产物，也可以说是街头巷尾流传于一道美食里的容纳了百姓生活趣味的历史故事和民间传说。

桂林的大街小巷，但凡是有生活气息的地方总会伴着阵阵米粉的醇香。可以说，桂林的男女老幼几乎不可一日无米粉。桂林人爱吃米粉，早、中、晚三餐都可以把米粉当主食，远在他乡的游子一回来，往往先要去吃上一碗桂林米粉解馋。外表洁白光亮的米粉之所以能如此韧滑爽口，是因为在制作的过程中经过反复的揉搓；米粉本身淡而无味，却因为海纳百味而变得无比诱人。外表朴素的米粉，其中却蕴藏着人生的哲学。

2021 年 5 月 24 日，桂林米粉制作技艺被列入第五批国家级非物质文化遗产。

桂林米粉，承载着历史的变迁，融入了桂林人的勤劳与智慧。初识辛香扑鼻、一品醇厚糯滑、食后回味绵长。它透过味蕾，沁人心脾，是每一个桂林人舌尖上的乡味和乡愁。

词汇笔记

- **origin** ['ɒrɪdʒɪn] *n.* the point from which sth. starts; the cause of sth. 起源，起因
- **fusion** ['fjuːʒən] *n.* the process or result of joining two or more things together to form one 融合，结合
- **wanderer** ['wɒndərər] *n.* a person who keeps travelling from place to place with no permanent home 流浪者
- **philosophy** [fə'lɒsəfi] *n.* a set of beliefs or an attitude to life that guides sb's behaviour 人生哲学，生活（工作）准则

Buttered Tea 酥油茶

必用三句

1 In Tibet, everyone can't do without Buttered Tea. Buttered Tea is an indispensable food for every Tibetan every day and a necessity for life on the Tibetan plateau. 在西藏，家家都离不开酥油茶。酥油茶是每个藏族人每日不可缺少的食品，是西藏高原生活的必需品。

2 Tibetan people regard Buttered Tea as a miracle, because it can cure altitude sickness, prevent the lips from bursting due to dry weather, and play a good role in keeping out the cold. 藏族人民视酥油茶为神之物，因其一来可以治高原反应，二来可以预防因天气干燥而嘴唇爆裂，三来可以起到很好的御寒作用。

3 People say that if you have not drunk Buttered Tea, it means that you have never been to the Tibetan Plateau. 人们说，没有喝过酥油茶，就算没有到过西藏高原。

双语赏析

In Tibet, everyone can't do without Buttered Tea. Buttered Tea is an indispensable food for every Tibetan every day and a necessity for life on the Tibetan plateau. The Tibetan people live on the Qinghai-Tibet Plateau. The alpine plateau climate and harsh living environment have created the Tibetan people's brave and resolute character, and also formed the Tibetan people's unique plateau diet culture: in the diet structure, milk and meat account for a large proportion while vegetables and fruits are scarce, so Tibetans serve the Buttered Tea with meals and drink it for every meal. Tea contains vitamins, which can reduce the damage caused by the lack of fruits and vegetables in the plateau. The Tibetan people drink ghee and tea together, providing themselves with a simple and effective disease prevention and health care method and creating a ghee tea culture.

Buttered Tea is made from ghee and strong tea. First put an appropriate amount of ghee into a special bucket, add salt, then pour in the boiled strong tea, and repeatedly stir with a wooden handle, so that the ghee and the tea juice are dissolved into one, and become milky. Buttered Tea is usually served with Zanba (a staple of Tibetan people, a mixture of fried barely and bean powder).

Tibetan people regard Buttered Tea as a miracle, because it can cure altitude sickness, prevent the lips from bursting due to dry weather, and play a good role in keeping out the cold. When it is cold, Buttered Tea can ward off cold; when eating meat, you can get rid of tiredness; when you are hungry, you can satisfy your hunger; when you are tired, you can relieve fatigue; and when you are sleepy, you can clear your mind. Milk Buttered Tea has a very high calorie, pure fragrance and delicious taste. After drinking a sip, you will feel refreshed and have a strong milk flavor. It is indeed a good thing to replenish your strength.

People say that if you have not drunk Buttered Tea, it means that you have never been to the Tibetan Plateau. There is a classic song in Tibet, *Please Have A Cup of Buttered Tea* which was composed to thank the PLA for its contribution to the Tibetan people, and also conveyed to the world the sacred status of Buttered Tea in the hearts of Tibetans.

在西藏，家家都离不开酥油茶。酥油茶是每个藏族人每日不可缺少的食品，是西藏高原生活的必需品。藏族人民生活在青藏高原上，高寒的高原气候，严酷的生存环境，造就了藏族勇敢刚毅的民族个性，也形成了藏族独具高原特色的饮食文化：食物结构中，乳肉类占很大比重，而蔬菜、水果较少，故藏族人民以茶佐食，餐餐必不可少。茶叶中含有维生素，可以减轻高原缺少果蔬带来的损害。藏族人民将酥油与茶同饮，为自己提供了一种简便有效的防病保健法，创造了酥油茶文化。

酥油茶是用酥油和浓茶加工而成。先将适量酥油放入特制的桶中，佐以食盐，再注入熬煮的浓茶汁，用木柄反复捣拌，使酥油与茶汁融为一体，呈乳状即成。酥油茶多作为主食与糌粑一起食用。

藏族人民视酥油茶为神之物，因其一来可以治高原反应，二来可以预防因天气干燥而嘴唇爆裂，三来可以起到很好的御寒作用。寒冷的时候可以驱寒，吃肉的时候可以去腻，饥饿的时候可以充饥，困乏的时候可以解乏，瞌睡的时候还可以清醒头脑。牛奶酥油茶具有极高的热量，醇香可口，喝上一口，精神顿爽，有比较浓的奶味，确是补充体力的好东西。

人们说，没有喝过酥油茶，就算没有到过西藏高原。西藏有一首经典歌曲《请你喝杯酥油茶》，此曲是为感谢解放军为西藏人民所作的贡献而作，同时也向世人传达了酥油茶在藏民心中的神圣地位。

词汇笔记

- **ghee** [giː] *n.* a type of butter used in south asian cooking 酥油
- **stir** [stɜːr] *v.* to move a liquid or substance around, using a spoon or sth. similar, in order to mix it thoroughly 搅拌，搅和（液体等物质）
- **dissolve** [dɪ'zɒlv] *v.* to mix with a liquid and become part of it （使）溶解
- **resolute** ['rezəluːt] *adj.* having or showing great determination 坚决的，果断的

Highland Barley Wine 青稞酒

必用三句

1 Highland Barley Wine is made from highland barley, a main food produced on the Qinghai-Tibet Plateau. 青稞酒是用青藏高原出产的一种主要粮食——青稞制成的。

2 For Tibetans, Highland Barley Wine is not only a festive drink, but also a symbol of joy, happiness and friendship, not a "comfort" for sorrow. 青稞酒之于藏族，既是喜庆的饮料，又是欢乐、幸福、友好的象征，绝非"消愁"之用品。

3 Tibetan people also have many rules when toasting and drinking. The first cup of Highland Barley Wine is quite particular: "Propose a toast to the sky, the earth, and the friendship". 藏族人民在敬酒喝酒时也有不少规矩。第一杯青稞酒颇有讲究，"敬天，敬地，敬友谊"。

双语赏析

Highland Barley Wine is made from highland barley, a main food produced on the Qinghai-Tibet Plateau. It is the favorite drink of people on the Qinghai-Tibet Plateau. It is indispensable for festivals, marriage, childbirth, welcoming and seeing off relatives and friends and is also one of the typical representatives of Tibetan culture.

Brewing skills of Highland Barley Wine is a traditional craft with a long history of Qinghai people. According to legend, in 641 AD, Princess Wencheng got married and brought the advanced winemaking techniques and craftsmen from the Han to Tibet to improve the original Highland Barley Wine production process and promote the development of Highland Barley Wine. After more than 1,300 years of historical changes, the Tibetan wine culture with Highland Barley Wine as the carrier is well-known at home and abroad for its unique charm, and has stood out among the hundred gardens of wine culture in China and even the world. In November 2011, Highland Barley Wine and its brewing technology were listed into China's Third Type of Intangible Cultural Heritage.

For Tibetans, Highland Barley Wine is not only a festive drink, but also a symbol of joy, happiness and friendship, not a "comfort" for sorrow. A glass of Highland Barley Wine embodies the wisdom and sweat of the people on the plateau. Highland Barley Wine has a unique style of being fragrant, mellow, sweet and refreshing, no headache and no thirst after drinking. The spirit of Highland Barley Wine has been passed down for 400 years and has been prosperous so far. It is praised as "Pearl of Plateau, Wonderful Flower of Wine Forest" by the national brewmasters.

Tibetan people also have many rules when toasting and drinking. The first cup of Highland Barley Wine is quite particular: "Propose a toast to the sky, the earth, and the friendship". First dip the ring finger into the wine, raise it over the head to toast the sky, then dip again to toast the ground, and finally to toast friendship. The host and guests drink the first cup of Highland Barley Wine in one go. This is the highest drinking ceremony for receiving guests, full of ceremonial sense.

A glass of Highland Barley Wine is full of highland sentiment. When you go to Tibet, you must taste the Highland Barley Wine, and enjoy taking up the wine and chatting with others, which will make your trip to Tibet more complete!

青稞酒是用青藏高原出产的一种主要粮食——青稞制成的。它是青藏人民最喜欢喝的酒，逢年过节、结婚、生孩子、迎送亲友，必不可少，是藏族文化的典型代表之一。

酿造青稞美酒，是青海人民历史悠久的传统工艺。相传，公元 641 年，文成公主出嫁，将汉地先进的酿酒技术和工匠带到西藏，对原有的青稞酒制作工艺进行改良，促进了青稞酒的发展。经过 1300 多年的历史变迁，以青稞酒为载体的藏族酒文化，以其特有的魅力享誉海内外，成为中国乃至世界酒文化百花园中的一枝独秀。2011 年 11 月，青稞酒及其酿造技术列入第三批国家级非物质文化遗产名录。

青稞酒之于藏族，既是喜庆的饮料，又是欢乐、幸福、友好的象征，绝非“消愁”之用品。一杯青稞酒凝聚了高原群众的智慧和汗水。青稞酒具有清香醇厚、绵甜爽净，饮后头不痛、口不渴的独特风格，青稞酒魂承传 400 年，至今兴盛不衰，被全国酿酒专家誉为“高原明珠、酒林奇葩”。

藏族人民在敬酒喝酒时也有不少规矩。第一杯青稞酒颇有讲究，“敬天，敬地，敬友谊”——先用无名指点上一滴酒，举过头顶敬天，再点上第二滴酒敬地，最后点第三滴酒敬友谊。主人与大家一起把第一杯青稞酒一饮而尽。这是接待客人的最高酒礼，充满了仪式感。

一杯青稞酒，浓浓高原情。去西藏，一定要尝尝青稞美酒，与人把酒笑谈，让你的西藏之旅更加圆满！

词汇笔记

- **barley** [ˈbɑːli] *n.* a plant grown for its grain that is used for making food, beer and whisky 大麦
- **craft** [krɑːft] *n.* an activity involving a special skill at making things with your hands 工艺，手艺
- **charm** [tʃɑːm] *n.* the power of pleasing or attracting people 魅力，魔力
- **toast** [təʊst] *v.* the act of a group of people wishing sb. happiness, success, etc. by drinking a glass of sth., especially alcohol, at the same time 为……举杯敬酒，为……干杯

Stone Pot Chicken 石锅鸡

必用三句

1 Stone Pot Chicken is a Tibetan dish. 石锅鸡是西藏菜品。

2 When it comes to Stone Pot Chicken, the most famous one is Lulang Stone Pot Chicken. 提到石锅鸡，最负盛名的莫过于鲁朗石锅鸡。

3 Today, Stone Pot Chicken has become a major business card of Lulang. The local farmers and herdsmen also benefited a lot from Stone Pot Chicken. 如今，石锅鸡已成为鲁朗的一大名片。当地的农牧民，也因为石锅鸡受益良多。

双语赏析

Stone Pot Chicken is a Tibetan dish.

The authentic Stone Pot Chicken is made from raw materials such as conic gymnadenia tuber and chicken, which are stewed in a stone pot over slow fire. Compared with the chicken soup that people often eat, Stone Pot Chicken soup is fresher and thicker. The secret of that lies in the stewed pot, Tibetan chicken and conic gymnadenia tuber, which are native products of Tibet.

When it comes to Stone Pot Chicken, the most famous one is Lulang Stone Pot Chicken. Lulang Town is the only access to the Sichuan-Tibet line. When it comes to this town which is 80 kilometers away from Bayi Town, Linzhi City, Tibet as the “Oriental Little Switzerland” in the eyes of many people, almost everyone who has ever driven into Tibet will tell you that you must try the local Stone Pot Chicken. The stone pot of Lulang Stone Pot Chicken does not come from an ordinary stone, but is cut and chiseled with a mica stone called “soapstone”, which is only produced in Motuo. At high temperatures, the trace elements in the stone pot can be decomposed into the soup, so that the original delicious dishes and fresh soup will have beneficial and priceless trace elements, enhancing anti-wrinkle, anti-aging and body-building effects. Therefore, Stone Pot Chicken has now become an instant hit, and is popular all over the country.

Today, Stone Pot Chicken has become a major business card of Lulang. The local farmers and herdsmen also benefited a lot from Stone Pot Chicken. When traveling on the Sichuan-Tibet line, many tourists tasted the delicious Stone Pot Chicken in Lulang. They were amazed and could not forget it for a long time. They even wanted to take this deliciousness home to share with their relatives and friends.

The Chinese have never bound themselves to a boring food list, but have tried every means to switch inspirations to seek tacit cooperation. Lulang Stone Pot Chicken is not only a natural delicacy, but also a symbol of a place with outstanding people. Some people will fall in love with a city because of one person, and many will fall in love with Lulang because of a taste.

石锅鸡是西藏菜品。

正宗的石锅鸡是以手掌参、土鸡等原料，经石锅慢火炖制的。相对于人们常食用的鸡汤，石锅鸡汤更鲜、更稠。其秘诀就在熬制的炖锅、藏鸡和手掌参，这些都是西藏土产。

提到石锅鸡，最负盛名的莫过于鲁朗石锅鸡。鲁朗镇，川藏线的必经之地。提到这个距离西藏林芝市八一镇 80 公里的小镇——很多人眼里的“东方小瑞士”，几乎每个曾自驾进藏的人都会告诉你：一定要尝一尝当地的石锅鸡。鲁朗石锅鸡的石锅并非一般的石头，而是用一种叫“皂石”的云母石砍凿而成，而这种石头仅产于墨脱。在高温作用下，石锅中的微量元素会分解于汤中，使本来美味的菜肴和鲜汤，又增添有益无价的微量元素，在味美鲜极，扑鼻香溢的同时，达到防癌、抗皱、延缓衰老、增强体质的养身功效。所以石锅鸡就一炮而红，红遍大江南北。

如今，石锅鸡已成为鲁朗的一大名片。当地的农牧民也因为石锅鸡受益良多。很多游客在川藏线旅行时，在鲁朗品尝到了石锅鸡的美味，赞叹不已，久久不能忘怀，甚至想把这种美味带回家与自己的亲戚朋友们分享。

中国人从来没有把自己束缚在一张乏味的食品清单上，而是想尽各种办法转换着灵感去寻求默契的配合。鲁朗石锅鸡，不仅是一道天然的美食，更是一个地方人杰地灵的象征。有人会因为一个人爱上一座城，也有很多人会因为一种味道爱上鲁朗。

词汇笔记

- **authentic** [ɔːˈθentɪk] *adj.* true and accurate 传统的，正宗的
- **mica** [ˈmaɪkə] *n.* a clear mineral that splits easily into thin flat layers and is used to make electrical equipment [矿物] 云母
- **relative** [ˈrelətɪv] *n.* a person who is in the same family as sb else 亲戚，亲属
- **inspiration** [ˌɪnspəˈreɪʃən] *n.* the process that takes place when sb sees or hears sth. that causes them to have exciting new ideas or makes them want to create sth., especially in art, music or literature 灵感；启发灵感的人（或事物）

附录　以食为媒走天下——不可不知的中华美食英文表达

1. 中国菜的分类 Classifications of Chinese Cuisine

八大菜系 Eight Famous Cuisines

鲁菜 Lu Cuisine (Shandong Cuisine)

川菜 Chuan Cuisine (Sichuan Cuisine)

粤菜 Yue Cuisine (Guangdong Cuisine)

闽菜 Min Cuisine (Fujian Cuisine)

苏菜 Su Cuisine (Jiangsu Cuisine)

浙菜 Zhe Cuisine (Zhejiang Cuisine)

湘菜 Xiang Cuisine (Hunan Cuisine)

徽菜 Hui Cuisine (Anhui Cuisine)

2. 菜品分类 Types of Courses

凉菜类 Cold Dishes

热菜类 Hot Dishes

汤羹粥煲类 Soups, Congees and Casseroles

主食和小吃 Main Food and Snacks

开胃菜 Appetizers

主菜 Main Courses; Entrées

配菜 Side Dishes

甜点 Desserts

饮品 Drinks

3. 烹饪方式 Cooking methods

煮 boil

烤 roast

煨 simmer

熏 smoke

腌 marinate

蒸 steam

炒 stir-fry

油炸 deep-fry

焖烧 braise

4. 中国菜谱 Chinese Cuisine

北京烤鸭 Beijing Roast Duck

辣子鸡丁 Saute Diced Chicken with Hot Peppers

宫保鸡丁 Kung Pao Chicken

红烧鲤鱼 Braised Common Carp

糖醋里脊 Pork Fillets with Sweet & Sour Sauce

炒木须肉 Saute Shredded Pork with Eggs & Black Fungus

回锅肉 Saute Pork in Hot Sauce; Twice-cooked Pork

糖醋排骨 Saute Chops with Sweet & Sour Sauce

醋溜白菜 Saute Cabbage with Sweet & Sour Sauce

鱼香茄子 Saute Eggplant with Fish Flavor

家常豆腐 Fride Tofu with Sliced Pork & Pepper

麻婆豆腐 Stwed Tofu with Minced Pork in Pepper Sauce; Mapo Tofu

韭菜炒蛋 Saute Leek Sprouts & Eggs

酸甜咕噜肉 Sweet & Sour Pork

红烧豆腐 Fried Tofu; Braised Tofu

白灼虾 Boiled Prawns

椒盐虾 Spicy Salt Prawns

咖喱鸡 Curry Chicken

梅菜扣肉 Preserved Vegetable & Pork; Braised Pork with Salted Vegetables (Mei Cai)

姜葱牛肉 Ginger & Green Onion Beef

虾米粉丝煲 Dried Shrimp & Noodle in Clay Pot

干烧四季豆 Braised Green Bean

烧茄子 Braised Egg Plant

蒜茸豆苗 Garlic Pea Greens

清炒时菜 Sauteed Vegetable

蒜茸西兰花 Garlic & Broccoli

火锅 Hot Pot

5. 中式早点 Chinese breakfast

饺子 Jiaozi / Dumplings

包子 Baozi

馒头 Mantou / Steamed Buns

花卷 Huajuan / Twists

烧麦 Shaomai

肉包 Steamed Meat Dumplings

豆沙包 Bean Paste Dumplings

水煎包 Lightly Fried Chinese Bread

小笼包 Steamed Small Meat Dumplings in Basket

馄饨 Wonton

大饼 Bannock

豆腐脑 Tofu Jelly

茶叶蛋 Egg Boiled with Salt & Tea

八宝饭 Steamed Glutinous Rice with Eight Treasures; Eight-treasure Rice

葱油饼 Green Onion Pie

锅贴 Pot Sticker

烧饼 Clay Oven Rolls

油条 Deep-fried Dough Sticks

韭菜盒子 Fried Leek Dumplings

蒸饺 Steamed Dumplings

水晶饺 Pyramid Dumplings

饭团 Rice and Vegetable Roll

芝麻球 Glutinous Rice Sesame Balls

蛋饼 Egg Cakes

皮蛋 Pidan; Preserved Egg

咸鸭蛋 Salted Duck Egg

麻花 Mahua; Fried Dough Twists

春卷 Spring Rolls

红豆糕 Red Bean Cake

绿豆糕 Green Bean Cake

豆浆 Soybean Milk

稀饭 Rice Porridge

白饭 Plain White Rice

地瓜粥 Sweet Potato Congee

鱼丸汤 Fish Ball Soup

贡丸汤 Meat Ball Soup

蛋花汤 Egg & Vegetable Soup

紫菜汤 Seaweed Soup

酸辣汤 Sweet & Sour Soup

6. 面 / 饭 Noodles & Rice

馄饨面 Wonton & Noodles

刀削面 Sliced Noodles; Daoxiao Noodles

麻辣面 Spicy Hot Noodles

麻酱面 Sesame Paste Noodles

海鲜面 Seafood Noodles

酸菜肉丝面 Pork & Pickled Mustard Green Noodles

米粉 Rice Noodles

炒米粉 Fried Rice Noodles

扬州炒饭 Yang Chow Fried Rice

虾仁炒饭 Shrimp Fried Rice

番茄牛肉炒饭 Tomato & Beef Fried Rice

糯米饭 Glutinous Rice

卤肉饭 Braised Pork Rice

蛋炒饭 Fried Rice with Egg

招牌炒面 House Chow Mein

番茄牛肉炒面 Tomato & Beef Chow Mein

海鲜炒面 Seafood Chow Mein

肉 / 鸡丝汤面 Noodles in Soup with Pork/Chicken

担担面 Noodles with Sesame Paste & Pea Sprouts; Dandan Noodles

龙须面 Thin Noodles

排骨面 Soup Noodles with Pork Rib

阳春面 Noodles in Superior Soup

参考文献

[1] 纪骁峰. 齐鲁胶东菜[M]. 济南：山东科学技术出版社，2003.

[2] 王仁兴. 国菜精华[M]. 北京：生活·读书·新知三联书店，2018.

[3] 孙建权，刘铁梁，王凯旋. 东北非物质文化遗产丛书：民间饮食技艺与习俗卷[M]. 沈阳：东北大学出版社，2018.

[4] 郑昌江，张惠. 东北菜[M]. 哈尔滨：黑龙江科学技术出版社，1997.

[5] 金跃军，才永发. 中华趣味饮食[M]. 北京：京华出版社，2008.

[6] 邱俊霖. 闲说鸡架[J]. 家庭百事通，2021，（17）.

[7] 饱妹. 鸡架[J]. 意林，2021，（13）.

[8] 刘竺岩. 长春街头的烤冷面[J]. 百柳，2013，（3）.

[9] 墨非. 吃遍全中国：中国各地美食全攻略[M]. 北京：中国华侨出版社，2016.

[10] 超狭. 锅包肉，东北三省的“老味道”[J]. 风流一代，2020，（28）.

[11] 吴杰，吴昊然. 家常炖烩菜[M]. 北京：中国中医药出版社，2008.

[12] 阿城. 舌尖上的东北[M]. 武汉：武汉大学出版社，2013.

[13] 王晓东，陈勇. 吃遍中国09东北菜[M]. 北京：中国民族摄影艺术出版社，2004.

[14] 张卉妍. 传说老北京[M]. 杭州：浙江工商大学出版社，2018.

[15] 佟长友. 北京风味小吃[M]. 北京：金盾出版社，1992.

[16] 戴文妍，龚建星. 美食情怀：新民晚报夜光杯文选[M]. 上海：上海科学技术出版社，2002.

[17] 姚伟钧，刘朴兵. 中国饮食史[M]. 武汉：武汉大学出版社，2019.

[18] 章采烈. 中国美食特色旅游[M]. 北京：对外经济贸易大学出版社，1997.

[19] 金洪霞，赵建民. 中国饮食文化概论[M]. 北京：中国轻工业出版社，2019.

[20] 《尚游旅图》编委会. 舌尖中国美食游[M]. 北京：星球地图出版社，2016.

[21] 姚伟钧，刘朴兵. 中国饮食史[M]. 武汉：武汉大学出版社，2019.

[22] 陈连生，肖正刚. 北京小吃[M]. 北京：中国轻工业出版社，2009.

[23] 冯怀申. 小吃大艺：记忆中的老北京小吃（珍藏版）[M]. 北京：中国纺织出版社，2018.

[24] 漾文澜．天津小吃地图[M]．北京：中国铁道出版社，2014.
[25] 李云清．天津小吃[M]．北京：中国轻工业出版社，2002，（2）.
[26] 白中阳．近代以来享誉津门的“四大小吃”[J]．寻根，2022.
[27] 巴陵．丝绸之路上的味道[M]．成都：电子科技大学出版社，2018.
[28] 《中国烹饪》编辑部．地方风味[M]．北京：中国商业出版社，1985.
[29] 《中国商品大辞典》编辑委员会．中国商品大辞典：肉禽蛋分册[M]．北京：中国商业出版社，1997.
[30] 陈芳．家庭营养早餐[M]．哈尔滨：黑龙江科学技术出版社，2016.
[31] 梁顺俭．兰州牛肉拉面宝典[M]．兰州：甘肃科学技术出版社，2012.
[32] 田兆元．美食故事[M]．上海：上海锦绣文章出版社，2014.
[33] 乔海龙，话说内蒙古：乌兰察布集宁区[M]. 呼和浩特：内蒙古人民出版社，2017.
[34] 韩锡文．话说内蒙古：海拉尔区[M]．呼和浩特：内蒙古人民出版社，2018.
[35] 林鑫，倪娜，张海婷．奶豆腐的营养、加工、贮藏及产业展望[J]．北方农业学报，2016，44（3）.
[36] 张开屏，田建军．吃出营养吃出健康——乳品的科学吃法[M]．呼和浩特：内蒙古人民出版社，2017.
[37] 《亲历者》编辑部．畅游新疆[M]．北京：中国铁道出版社，2018.
[38] 陈培毅．无肉不欢，这样吃肉才健康[M]．北京：中国轻工业出版社，2017.
[39] 陈志田．舌尖上的中国[M]．北京：北京联合出版公司，2014.
[40] 王忆晓．春食烫面韭菜盒子[J]．烹调知识，2020，（3）.
[41] 陈志田．舌尖上的中国[M]．北京：北京联合出版公司，2014.
[42] 邱念念．肉夹馍[J]．农业知识，2014，（16）.
[43] 张同武．“肉夹馍”与“三明治”[J]．美文，2022，（3）.
[44] 张同武．泡馍江湖[J]．美文，2019，（13）.
[45] 陈世元，老妖．丝绸之路陕西美食[J]．旅游，2016，（6）.
[46] 秦瑞言．西安古城名小吃——牛羊肉泡馍[J]．趣味（作文与阅读），2018，（5）.
[47] 银川市新闻传媒集团．寻味宁夏[M]．银川：宁夏人民出版社，2018.
[48] 戴文海．宁夏美食之旅[M]．青岛：青岛出版社，2013.
[49] 《走遍中国》编辑部．走遍中国：甘肃宁夏[M]．北京：中国旅游出版社，2016.
[50] 庄山．最是那一抹乡愁[M]．西安：三秦出版社，2017.

[51] 彭忠富．碗筷留香[M]．石家庄：花山文艺出版社，2018.
[52] 董宪民．陕西旅游系列丛书：食（2）[M]．西安：陕西旅游出版社，2012.
[53] 邓明．良风美俗：城关民俗散记[M]．兰州：甘肃文化出版社，2017.
[54] 米海萍，贺喜焱．中国民俗知识：青海民俗[M]．兰州：甘肃人民出版社，2008.
[55] 《驴行天下丛书》编委会．驴行天下：青海[M]．北京：科学技术文献出版社，2007.
[56] 姚伟钧，刘朴兵．中国饮食文化史•黄河中游地区卷[M]．北京：中国轻工业出版社，2013.
[57] 申红兴，李毅．青海省文化产业发展研究[M]．北京：经济日报出版社，2017.
[58] 何苗苗，尼佬，盛洋等．Lonely Planet旅行指南系列：青海[M]．北京：中国地图出版社，2016.
[59] 赵建民，曲均记．中国鲁菜文脉[M]．北京：中国轻工业出版社，2016.
[60] 杜鹏程．精品京味鲁菜[M]．北京：中国纺织出版社，2019.
[61] 新东方烹饪教育组．鲁菜[M]．合肥：安徽科学技术出版社，2018.
[62] 屈浩．屈浩说菜 九转大肠[J]．餐饮世界，2020，（4）.
[63] 赵建民，曲均记．中国鲁菜文脉[M]．北京：中国轻工业出版社，2016.
[64] 张宝庭．养生鲁菜[M]．北京：中国纺织出版社，2019.
[65] 吴昊天，吴杰．新编精品鲁菜[M]．北京：金盾出版社，2010.
[66] 赵建民，曲均记．中国鲁菜文脉[M]．北京：中国轻工业出版社，2016.
[67] 姚常珠．关于德州扒鸡文化的传承和保护研究[J]．中国集体经济，2020.
[68] 徐曼菲．德州扒鸡简史[J]．今商圈，2020，（3）.
[69] 山东省德州地区史志编纂委员会．德州地区志[M]．济南：齐鲁书社，1992.
[70] 张稚庐．济南菜之“奇葩”[J]．走向世界，2013，（12）.
[71] 钟倩，王啸．把泉水的生活过成诗[J]．走向世界，2017，（26）.
[72] 孙一慰．济南的糖醋鲤鱼[J]．餐饮世界，2005，（4s）.
[73] 高文麒．文化中国系列：山西三晋文化 [M]．北京：经济科学出版社，2013.
[74] 林留清怡．寻味中国[M]．胡韵涵，译．重庆：重庆大学出版社，2014.
[75] 李廷芝．中国烹饪辞典（新版）[M]．太原：山西科学技术出版社，2019.
[76] 骑驴观景走四方．晋城过油肉[J]．饮食科学，2017，（11）.
[77] 《中华传统食品大全》编辑委员会山西分编委会．山西传统食品[M]．北京：中国

轻工业出版社，1993.
[78] “中国地理百科”丛书编委会．武汉三镇[M]．北京/西安：世界图书出版公司，2017.
[79] 金新．老祖宗说饮食[M]．杭州：浙江古籍出版社，2016.
[80] 秦少油．亲爱的湘菜[M]．北京：电子工业出版社，2015.
[81] 《趣味导游知识》编辑部．趣味导游美食知识[M]．北京：旅游教育出版社，2015.
[82] 赵成松．湘菜[M]．成都：成都时代出版社，2009.
[83] 王仁兴．国菜精华[M]．北京：生活·读书·新知三联书店，2018.
[84] 吕峰．梦里天堂[M]．太原：北岳文艺出版社，2017.
[85] 徐郑冰，沈娟．字绘上海[M]．武汉：湖北美术出版社，2017.
[86] 袁甲．舟山老味道[M]．宁波：宁波出版社，2018.
[87] 坨坨妈．坨坨妈·小吃诱惑[M]．杭州：浙江科学技术出版社，2014.
[88] 张学伟．百病食疗大全（超值全彩白金版）[M]．北京：中医古籍出版社，2015.
[89] 镇江民间文化艺术馆．影响中国的镇江传说[M]．镇江：江苏大学出版社，2016.
[90] 张洪山．风味小吃制作[M]．呼和浩特：内蒙古人民出版社，2014.
[91] 周建新．中国节日志•春节（江西卷）[M]．北京：光明日报出版社，2017.
[92] 宁波市文化广电新闻出版局．甬上风华•宁波市非物质文化遗产大观（奉化卷）[M]．宁波：宁波出版社，2012.
[93] 《浙里繁花》编写组，浙里繁花：浙江非遗印象[M]．杭州：浙江教育出版社，2016.
[94] 黄水品．金华火腿[M]．杭州：浙江科学技术出版社，2017.
[95] 李建国．中国大锅菜•南方卷[M]．北京：中国铁道出版社，2018.
[96] 戴爱群，张婕娜．口福：今生必食的100道中国菜[M]．2版．北京：生活·读书·新知三联书店，2019.
[97] 潘君明．苏州民间传说丛书 苏州经典美食传说[M]．苏州：古吴轩出版社，2018.
[98] 孟祥健．新手下厨[M]．青岛：青岛出版社，2015.
[99] 晓瑀．岁月的光泽[M]．青岛：青岛出版社，2019.
[100] 张立辉，李平．舌尖上的中国美食大全集[M]．北京：中国画报出版社，2012.
[101] 朱秀芳，曹贝妮等．中西名菜厨艺[M]．上海：上海科学技术出版社，2019.
[102] 刘自华．中华味道[M]．北京：中国书籍出版社，2019.

[103] 马达．什么值得吃，什么值得做[M]．北京：中信出版社，2019.
[104] 周松芳．广东味道[M]．广州：花城出版社，2015.
[105] 周松芳．岭南饮食文化[M]．广州：广东人民出版社，2019.
[106] 冼剑民，周智武．中国饮食文化史（东南地区卷）[M]．北京：中国轻工业出版社，2013.
[107] 广东省职业技术教研室．中国粤菜故事[M]．广州：广东科技出版社，2020.
[108] 好豆网．民间经典广东菜[M]．北京：东方出版社，2012.
[109] 彭一万．闽南饮食[M]．厦门：鹭江出版社，2009.
[110] 林贞标．玩味潮汕[M]．广州：中山大学出版社，2016.
[111] 宋德剑，罗鑫．客家饮食[M]．广州：暨南大学出版社，2015.
[112] 黎章春．客家味道 客家饮食文化研究[M]．哈尔滨：黑龙江人民出版社，2016.
[113] 梧桐．最客家SO土楼[M]．厦门：厦门大学出版社，2012.
[114] 吴伟峰．广西饮食文化[M]．南宁：广西民族出版社，2021.
[115] 黄琼，蓝竹梅．广西特色饮食文化[M]．北京：对外经济贸易大学出版社，2019.
[116] 倪铫阳．柳州螺蛳粉[M]．南宁：广西人民出版社，2016.
[117] 李志刚．桂林米粉[M]．北京：经济科学出版社，2014.
[118] 桂林市文化新闻出版广电局．桂林非物质文化遗产概览[M]．桂林：广西师范大学出版社，2018.
[119] 朱方桐．桂林饮食文化[M]．桂林：广西师范大学出版社，2015.
[120] 《走遍中国》编辑部．海南[M]．北京：中国旅游出版社，2010.
[121] 郑娜娜，骆仪，田婷婷，等．海南[M]．北京：中国地图出版社，2014.
[122] 纪俊超，李秀英．中国导游十万个为什么：海南[M]．北京：中国旅游出版社，2006.
[123] 欧阳应霁．香港味道2：街头巷尾民间滋味[M]．北京：生活·读书·新知三联书店，2018.
[124] 潘英俊．粤厨宝典：砧板篇（升级版）[M]．广州：广东科技出版社，2017.
[125] 魏国安．这里是香港：香港人的地道香港味[M]．北京：旅游教育出版社，2012.
[126] 陈训廷．惠州风物撷胜[M]．广州：广东人民出版社，2016.
[127] 尚厨美食研究中心．新编大众家常菜典[M]．成都：四川科学技术出版社，2017.
[128] 林斯瑜．梅州客家饮食文化研究[M]．广州：暨南大学出版社，2020.

[129] 李子明. 寻味福建[M]. 北京：北京出版社，2016.

[130] 徐先玲，李相状. 中国饮食文化[M]. 北京：中国戏剧出版社，2005.

[131] 吴谋高. 黔东南州特产志[M]. 昆明：云南科技出版社，2016.

[132] 王琰，康曦，霍俊其. 晚清重臣丁宝桢与宫保鸡丁[J]. 民间传奇故事（A卷），2010，（1）.

[133] 江礼旸. 为“宫保鸡丁”正名[J]. 食品与生活，2002，（6）.

[134] 熊涵. 酸汤鱼的前世今生[J]. 大众科学，2021，（1）.

[135] 周礼. 贵州美味酸汤鱼[J]. 烹调知识，2017，（10）.

[136] 越山青. 从酸汤鱼说起贵州人吃盐的历史[J]. 中外文摘，2021，（8）.

[137] 石叶馨，张洋. 麻辣烫的火红时代[J]. 中国烹饪，2021，（4）.

[138] 孙双双. 麻辣烫：惊艳冬奥的传统美食[J]. 中国食品工业，2022，（4）.

[139] 王婧铭，汪海峰. 麻辣烫可以健康吃[J]. 康复，2020，（11）.

[140] 王蕾. 麻婆豆腐[J]. 医食参考，2018，（1）.

[141] 刘飞龙. 麻婆豆腐[J]. 烹调知识，2017，（12）.

[142] 彭逸晨. 麻婆豆腐的由来[J]. 烹调知识，2018，（6）.

[143] 刘燕. 成都“三大炮”[J]. 乡镇论坛，2020，（3）.

[144] 九吃. 三大炮[J]. 饮食保健，2019，（5）.

[145] 梁雨. 三大炮[J]. 中华养生保健，2016，（1）.

[146] 贺秋. 老少皆爱的回锅肉[J]. 餐饮世界，2021，（10）.

[147] 钱国宏. 川菜之王“回锅肉”[J]. 烹调知识，2018，（10）.

[148] 李琼霞. 最是平常回锅肉[J]. 食品与健康，2020，（10）.

[149] 石光华. 我的川菜味道[M]. 成都：四川文艺出版社，2017.

[150] 老波头. 食话实说2——川菜平反论[M]. 上海：上海文化出版社，2017.

[151] 潘七七. 带着味蕾去远方[M]. 上海：文汇出版社，2017.

[152] 高维微，李野. 酸辣粉“嗦”出的成渝味[J]. 今日重庆，2020，（10）.

[153] 郝晓燕. 从街边小吃到网红速食酸辣粉品牌化成大势所趋[J]. 中国食品，2019，（6）.

[154] 高兴明. 解放碑的酸辣粉[J]. 重庆与世界，2015，（8）.

[155] 陈强. 过桥米线[M]. 昆明：云南人民出版社，2007.

[156] 关明. 云南过桥米线机密[M]. 昆明：云南科学技术出版社，2008.

[157] 功夫包子. 过桥米线无可奉告[M]. 南京：江苏凤凰文艺出版社，2021.
[158] 方鹏程. 爱茶[M]. 北京：北京时代华文书局，2017.
[159] 袁晓文（益希汪秋）. 雪域之光——藏族（上）[M]. 上海：上海锦绣文章出版社；上海：上海文化出版社，2017.
[160] 本书编委会. 西藏四季旅行[M]. 北京：中国铁道出版社，2017.
[161] 琼达. 西藏民俗旅游文化[M]. 北京：中国社会出版社，2016.
[162] 方铁，冯敏. 中国饮食文化史（西南地区卷）[M]. 北京：中国轻工业出版社，2013.
[163] 苏三. 云上的日子——西藏手绘旅行[M]. 杭州：浙江科学技术出版社，2015.
[164] 李韬. 舌尖上的中国乡土小吃[M]. 北京：旅游教育出版社，2013.
[165] 磊子. 一脑门儿杂念[M]. 济南：山东大学出版社，2012.

随手笔记

随手笔记